D1616971

GENDER IN PRACTICE

GENDER IN PRACTICE

A STUDY OF
LAWYERS' LIVES

John Hagan
Fiona Kay

New York   Oxford
OXFORD UNIVERSITY PRESS
1995

Oxford University Press

Oxford   New York
Athens   Auckland   Bangkok   Bombay
Calcutta   Cape Town   Dar es Salaam   Delhi
Florence   Hong Kong   Istanbul   Karachi
Kuala Lumpur   Madras   Madrid   Melbourne
Mexico City   Nairobi   Paris   Singapore
Taipei   Tokyo   Toronto

and associated companies in
Berlin   Ibadan

Copyright © 1995 by Oxford University Press, Inc.

Published by Oxford University Press, Inc.,
200 Madison Avenue, New York, New York 10016

Oxford is a registered trademark of Oxford University Press

Library of Congress Cataloging-in-Publication Data
Hagan, John, 1946–
Gender in practice : a study of lawyers' lives / John Hagan and Fiona Kay.
p.   cm.
Includes bibliographical references and index.
ISBN 0-19-509282-1
1. Women lawyers—Canada.   2. Women lawyers—United States.   I. Kay, Fiona.   II. Title.
KE332.W6H34   1995
349.71'082—dc20
[347.10082]   94-27128

246897531

Printed in the United States of America
on acid-free paper

For the
Principles in Practice
of
The Honourable
Justice Bertha Wilson

Preface and Acknowledgements

The entry of large numbers of women into law and the growth and concentration of firms are developments that demand the attention of the legal profession as well as academics. This is reflected in the appointment by bar associations and other professional bodies of task forces and commissions to analyze and propose changes in the organization and regulation of legal practice. A series of issues addressed in this book — including barriers to and ceilings on women's promotions and earnings, conflicts between careers and family, and disappointments with and departures from legal practice — are increasingly and intensively debated by members of the profession.

Some in the profession have adopted what we describe as a human capital perspective on these issues, assuming that women are by choice less committed than men to advancing their careers. Others have endorsed what we identify as a gender stratification perspective, suggesting that what men often perceive as choices are more accurately understood as constraints that make women's persistent efforts to develop careers in law all the more notable. There is no perfect correlation between age and gender and these views of legal practice, but fault lines are nonetheless clear, with a result that law is today not simply a changing profession, but a contested profession as well.

This book represents our efforts to better understand some of these issues in legal practice. It hopefully makes constructive suggestions about how human capital as well as gender stratification theories might better inform us about possibilities for change in the profession. If our approach to some of these issues is in the end successfully pragmatic, it is no doubt because of the unique and constructive counsel we received along the way in developing our research.

This counsel derived from our participation in two unique professional undertakings. Hagan served as a member and Kay as a consultant for the Canadian Bar Association's Task Force on Gender Equality in the Legal Profession and its 1993 Report, *Touchstones for Change: Equality, Diversity and Accountability.* The Task Force was chaired by the Honourable Justice Bertha Wilson, to whom this volume is dedicated, and also included Patricia Blocksom, Sophie Bourque, Daphne Dumont, Sharon McIvor, Alec Robertson and Her Honour Corrine Sparks. With the inspired leadership of Justice Wilson, the Task Force provided a unique learning experience, and its members were an invaluable sounding board for many of the ideas explored in this book.

In addition, Kay served as the author and Hagan as a consultant for a 1991 report on *Transitions in the Ontario Legal Profession* for the Women in the Legal Profession Committee of the Law Society of Upper Canada. This Committee was Chaired by Fran Kiteley and included as members Thomas Bastedo, Denise E. Bellamy, Colin Campbell, Lee Ferrier, Ann-Marie Stewart, Shelley R. Birenbaum, Mary A. Eberts and Mary Jane Mossman. This distinguished group better informed us about many of the issues addressed in this volume, and the Law Society allowed data gathered for the Committee from across the Province of Ontario to be reanalyzed for the present study.

Other individuals and organizations further contributed to our work. Richard Tinsley, Secretary of the Law Society, James Spence, Treasurer of the Law Society and Chair of the Research and Planning Committee, and Alan Treleaven, Director of Education at the Law Society, provided generous support and assistance. So too did Denise Ashby, Meg Angevine, Andrew Brockett, Linda Johnston and Gemma Zecchini.

The Social Sciences and Humanities Research Council of Canada provided funding for two waves of data collection in the development of the Toronto panel study of lawyers that is a focal point of this study. Patricia Parker contributed her unique talents in administering the Toronto data collection. The Social Sciences and Humanities Research Council also provided Kay with a doctoral fellowship. Hagan was appointed a Killam Fellow for two years by the Canada Council. Melina Buckley, of the Canadian Bar Association, was extremely helpful in facilitating many aspects of our work. Jeff Leon and Eleanore Cronk were sources of important insights as well as constructive scepticism. Dagmara Suszek provided invaluable assistance in the preparation of the manuscript.

However, our greatest debt is no doubt to our respondents for answering our questions. As the pages of this book reveal, many of these hard working lawyers took considerable time to comment at length on issues we raised. These lawyer respondents are articulate and often eloquent spokespersons for their beliefs. Of course, lawyers are trained to be so. However, along side the reality that these talents have become costly commodities, the pages of this book also attest to a willingness of many lawyers to literally as well as figuratively give freely of their time in thinking not only critically but also constructively about their profession. We hereby acknowledge our indebtedness to the lawyers who made this research possible, and at the same time apologize for errors and omissions that may accompany our efforts to fully capture their thoughts and experiences within the pages of this book.

Toronto, Canada
February 1995

John Hagan
Fiona Kay

Contents

GENDER IN PRACTICE

1

A Changing Profession

The days of the middle-aged male (three-piece suit, cigar-smoking, home in Rosedale, with wife and three kids) as the image of a lawyer are going. I am single, female, live alone, socialize in bars, go to rock shows, and people I meet are surprised that I am a lawyer. I reply that there are lots of lawyers like me, that I'm not unusual.

A Private Profession Goes Public

There may be no setting more significant than the legal profession for observing the advances and setbacks that women today are experiencing in a changing world that structures work and family roles. Lawyers are often powerful players in the organization of social, economic, and political life, and women, often acting as lawyers, are now participants in these arenas of public and private influence. Yet there is serious doubt whether this participation is translating into opportunities for women to contribute all they can in and through the legal profession. The pace of gender-related changes in the profession is so fast, and the opportunities to gain knowledge and insight into this profession are so recent, that it is difficult for members of the profession or scholars who study it to gain perspective on the unfolding events.

As recently as the 1960s and early 1970s there were too few women in the legal profession to allow much attention to issues of gender. One result is a gap in our knowledge, so that even landmark studies of the legal profession published within the past decade have given little or no attention to the presence of women lawyers (e.g., Heinz and Laumann, 1982; Nelson, 1988; Galanter and Palay, 1991). This is so even though Abel (1988a:202) observes that the change in women's representation in law over the last two decades is "nothing short of revolutionary," while Epstein (1981:95) notes that for women these decades have marked "the beginning of a new era of access to jobs within the profession . . . far wider than could have been imagined a generation before."

This is certainly not the first time a gap has become apparent in our knowledge of the legal profession. The landmark studies just cited represent unique advances in our knowledge of a profession that for much of its history has been largely sealed off. This impenetrability has made it difficult to learn much about the professional and personal lives of men as well as women lawyers.

Thus for many years the legal profession was known for its guardedness, and sometimes outright secrecy. This almost exclusively male elite preserve not only excluded women but most of the rest of society as well from knowledge of its workings. Large and influential firms in particular viewed their activities with a sense of propriety that restricted possibilities for public awareness as well as access. Publicity was disdained and regarded as indiscreet, something akin to advertising, which was, of course, unethical.

Even fictional treatments in novels, television, and movies were largely confined to the Perry Masons of criminal law and to the occasional attentive secretary like Della Street, until the late 1970s and early 1980s, when films like *The Paper Chase*, *Legal Eagles*, and *The Verdict*, and television series such as *The Associates* and then *L.A. Law*, followed by *Street Legal* and *Civil Wars*, brought the wider practice of law to public attention (Macaulay, 1987). Gradually, lawyers, including some women lawyers, were perceived as being as telegenic as doctors. During this period doors opened to the suites and other legal settings occupied by lawyers, and opportunities for scholarly as well as fictional treatments of the profession became more common. The profession that was revealed was highly stratified, intensely competitive, and undergoing extraordinary change. Of course, one of the most extraordinary changes involved the entry of women.

Studying a Profession in Transition

This book explores the lives of women and men lawyers in a changing profession. It is built around two studies, which we introduce briefly here and in greater detail in the second half of the chapter. The first is an ongoing study of the lives of more than 800 lawyers first surveyed in the city of Toronto in 1985, and recontacted and resurveyed in 1991. This "panel" study was designed to include an approximately equal number of men and women lawyers evenly distributed across large and small firms and nonfirm settings. The second study also equally represented men and women and was undertaken in 1990 through a survey of more than 1,100 lawyers across the larger province of Ontario, including more than 100 lawyers, disproportionately women, who had left the practice of law. The goal of both studies was to explore professional and personal experiences that occur in the lives of lawyers. The first study is unique in that it tracks changes across the lives of lawyers with successive surveys timed five years apart in a panel design, while the second study is also unique in its attention to women who have left legal practice.

In focusing on a specific city, Toronto, and the surrounding province, this book joins a tradition of research on lawyers that has emphasized particular settings. The research includes several studies in New York City (Carlin, 1966; Smigel, 1969), Chicago (Lortie, 1959; Carlin, 1962; Heinz and Laumann, 1982; Nelson, 1988), Boston (Spangler, 1986), and Detroit (Ladinsky, 1963), as well as a small pioneering survey in Toronto (Arthurs et al., 1971). There are also national studies of lawyers in the United States (Halliday, 1986; Curran, 1985; Erlanger, 1980) and Canada (Stager and Arthurs, 1990). The combined breadth and depth of these studies, along with increasing research on lawyers in Europe and other parts of the world, is beginning to provide a comparative base of knowledge about this important profession (see Abel, 1989).

Several features combine to characterize the changing structure of legal practice. These include the growth of the profession, the centralization and concentration of lawyers in its increasingly large firms, and the entry of women into the ranks of the profession — even the large firms that so long and stubbornly resisted their participation. As we note in greater detail later, these changes have occurred over much of this century, but especially the past few decades, when the expansion of the legal profession has seemed to some to be out of control (see Abel, 1986). Those who have commented on this growth are divided in their assessments about its effects on the lives of lawyers, their clients, and the general public. It is notable that these comments often neglect the role of gender relations in the profession.

For example, observers express concern about the earnings of lawyers and about a perceived prospect of diminished compensation (see, e.g., Stager and Foot, 1988). Others are concerned about increasing competition and dissatisfaction with practice that may be associated with increasing numbers of lawyers in the profession. Still others fear that an increasing supply of lawyers is feeding a growing propensity for legal conflict that some believe is producing a "litigation explosion" (but see Galanter, 1983). In all of this, little attention or appreciation is given to the potential benefits of a growing diversity in the profession, or to the possibility that more lawyers are providing broader and fuller access to legal services. In particular, little attention is given to how the increasing numbers of women in the profession may be changing the contours of all these concerns, or to how women are affecting or are affected by the profession they have entered.

We will address many aspects of these issues in this book. However, we first establish the basic dimensions of change involved. We begin by considering the early entry of women into the legal profession in the United States and Canada and the parallel expansion of the profession in both countries. The expansion of lawyering in these countries involves many points of similarity as well as some differences, providing interesting possibilities for comparison.

A Century of Reluctance and Growth

Medicine opened its doors to women before law did, but through the first half of this century, both occupations were primarily concerned with establishing their professional identities by restricting their memberships, both to women and others (Larson, 1977; Abel, 1986). Medicine probably opened its doors to women earlier than law because this occupational role was closer to stereotyped conceptions of women as maternal and nurturing, while legal work was regarded as more adversarial. At the core of these conceptions was the notion that women and men naturally occupied separate spheres, so that even before the legal profession became more restrictive in allowing individuals into its membership, women were joined with convicted felons as two groups generally excluded from legal practice (Rhode, 1984). Women found earlier acceptance in education, nursing, and clerical jobs.

The reluctance to accept women into the legal profession was apparent from its beginnings in the United States and Canada. The first American female attorney was addressed in person and in early court records as "Gentleman Margaret Brent" (Morello, 1986). In 1869, Arabella Mansfield was the first woman to be admitted to a U.S. state bar, in Iowa. However, only a few years later an 1873 U.S. Supreme Court decision confirmed that Myra Bradwell could not be admitted to the Chicago Bar, and in 1894 the Supreme Court confirmed a decision that denied Belva Lockwood the right to practice law in Virginia, because she was not a "male person." Three Supreme Court Justices concurred in the earlier *Bradwell* decision that

[t]he family organization, which is founded in the divine ordinance, as well as in the nature of things, indicates the domestic sphere as that which properly belongs to the domain and functions of womanhood. The harmony, not to say identity, of interests and views which belongs, or should belong, to the family institution is repugnant to the idea of a woman adopting a distinct career from that of her husband. (Cited in Rhode, 1988:1168)

Through this decision, the Supreme Court invested a separation of the spheres of domestic and waged work with a combination of spiritual and constitutional authority. This separate spheres doctrine would prove hard to dispel, even harder than was implied by the early and difficult battles over admission to the profession.

In Ontario, it took Clara Brett Martin six years to overcome opposition to her admission to the Law Society of Upper Canada, the first such admission to the bar in the British Commonwealth (Backhouse, 1985). She began her fight in 1891 when she was denied admission to study law by the Law Society of Upper Canada, on the grounds that the authorizing statute applied exclusively to males. Martin persuaded the Ontario legislature to pass an Act to Provide for the Admission of Women to the Study and Practice of Law in 1892, but still the Law Society denied her admission. The attorney general of the province intervened, and after finally being admitted for study and completing her articling period and required examinations, it was necessary for the legislature to pass another Act to Amend the Act to Provide for the Admission of Women to the Study and Practice of Law in 1895. It was only after still further intervention by the attorney general that Martin was finally admitted as a barrister in 1897 (*Evening Star*, February 3, 1897).

These struggles before the turn of the century in the United States and Canada suggest that the plight of women in both countries was much the same. However, it is significant to note that this apparent similarity occurs against a backdrop of other frequently studied differences between these countries. For example, even though the two countries are economically entwined and share elements of English legal culture, it is often argued that Canadians are less conflictual and confrontational than their southern neighbors in their social and political practices (e.g., Lipset, 1968; 1986; Clark, 1942; 1976). Of course, it also bears note that if Canada for structural or cultural reasons was indeed less conflictual and confrontational at the turn of this century, it was not apparent in the record of Clara Brett Martin's admission to the legal profession.

It remains an open question whether interpenetration of the economies of the United States and Canada might now be producing a convergence in national trends in lawyering and other areas (see Davis, 1971; Horowitz, 1973; Hagan, 1991), including the entry of women into the profession. There is no doubt that some forces, including shifts in business cycles, are experienced in close proximity by these countries. Yet it is unclear whether Canada and the United States are becoming more alike as a result, or whether they might experience some changes in common, such as the entry of women into legal practice, while retaining a larger overall pattern of difference. There is the further question of whether it makes sense to compare these nations at all, or whether more specific comparisons are necessary focusing, for example, on specific parts of these countries, such as French and English Canada.

For these reasons, it may be important to consider patterns of growth in lawyering not only in Canada and the United States, but also for Ontario and Quebec more specifically. We begin by considering the early overall growth of the legal profession in the United States and Canada and then return to separate consideration of men and women and their experiences in Ontario and Quebec.

Census data on the per capita growth of the legal profession reveal that throughout the first half of this century the ratio of lawyers to population was substantially higher in the United States than in English or French Canada. This national difference persisted in the face of dramatic growth in the number of lawyers and the general population in both countries. In the first half of this century there was an approximate doubling of lawyers and the general population in Canada as well as the United States. Because lawyers and the general population in these countries grew in tandem over this period, the ratio of lawyers to population remained until 1961 at about 0.7 per 1,000 persons in Canada, and at about 1.25 per 1,000 in the United States. With only one minor deviation in 1921, in every decade from 1911 to 1961 the number of lawyers per 1,000 population was more than one and a half times larger in the United States than in Canada.

However, while the ratio of lawyers to population remained nearly constant in both of these countries during the first half of this century, the ratio of men to women lawyers was already declining. When these ratios are calculated with census data, they initially seem to exaggerate the rate of change, because the early addition of even a few women lawyers quickly reduced the size of the ratios. Nonetheless, although law historically has been a male-dominated profession, small but steady gains occurred for women in both countries through most of this century, with the most pronounced gains in the past two decades, especially since 1971. These gains obviously did not come easily.

As Mossman (1990) notes, the Law Society of Upper Canada hardly opened the floodgates when it grudgingly admitted Clara Brett Martin to membership in 1897: only one woman was admitted as a lawyer by the Law Society in each of the years 1902, 1907, 1908, and 1913. Although the number of women entering the profession in Ontario was still not large by the end of World War I, the number at least was beginning to grow. By 1923, 27 of the 35 women who had entered the profession had been admitted after 1918. Of the 100 admitted by 1939, more than half had entered the profession in the 1920s and 1930s. The pace was perceptibly increasing.

Brief descriptions of some of the notable women (cited in *Crossing the Bar*, 1993) who entered the profession in the 1920s and 1930s give a sense of the slowly changing times:

•Helen Kinnear was called to the bar in 1920 and became the first woman to appear before the supreme courts of Ontario and Canada. She was also the first woman appointed king's counsel in the British Empire and as a judge of the county bench in Ontario.

• Margaret Hyndman was called to the bar six years later, in 1926, and became the second woman named king's counsel. She actively campaigned for women's rights and helped establish the Women's College Hospital in Toronto.

• Vera Parsons graduated in 1924 and became the first woman criminal lawyer in Ontario and the third woman king's counsel. Vera Parsons was among the first women lawyers to visibly confront challenges of multiple discrimination, having been physically disabled as a child by polio. She was the first Ontario woman to appear before a judge and jury.

• Edra Sanders graduated in 1930 and joined her father in the family firm that became Sanders & Sanders. She assumed many leadership positions in the community of St. Thomas, Ontario, and was the first woman appointed to the senate of the University of Western Ontario.

These women are representative of the 1920s and 1930s and the challenges women confronted and overcame in joining the legal profession and public life. Still, the barriers remained, and representation was token.

The numbers of women entering the profession increased slightly in the forties and fifties. There were 73 women lawyers in Ontario in 1941 and 107 in 1951. World War II took men away from law schools and firms and women were encouraged to fill office needs, although they rarely appeared in court (*Crossing the Bar*, 1993). Women were still excluded from most professional organizations and clubs in Ontario, and they formed their own Kappa Beta Pi sorority and the Women's Law Association of Ontario. In 1961 there were still only 162 women lawyers in Ontario. By this time in the United States, women earned about one half of all college degrees and one-third of all graduate school degrees, but they accounted for about only 7 percent of doctors, 4 percent of full professors, 3 percent of all lawyers and architects, and 1 percent of all engineers (Rhode, 1988:1173). The experiences of Sandra Day O'Connor and Bertha Wilson, later to become the first women Supreme Court Justices in the Unites States and Canada respectively, were representative of women entering law at mid-century: both were obliged to accept background office positions in firms. These real-life experiences are a striking contrast to the portrayal, in the 1949 film *Adam's Rib*, of a spirited courtroom battle between a wife and husband who were also lawyers, played by Katherine Hepburn and Spencer Tracy.

The 1960s and 1970s brought the beginning of major changes for both women and men (Halliday, 1986). This was signaled by an especially sharp shift upwards in the 1970s in the growth curves for both U.S. and Canadian lawyers. Although there are signs that this upturn began slightly earlier in the United States, the number of lawyers in both countries more than tripled over the following quarter century. In relative terms, in the single decade between 1971 and 1981 in Canada, the number of lawyers per 1,000 population nearly doubled, from 0.76 to 1.41, and continued to increase to 1.69 in 1986. By 1986 there were 2.76 lawyers per 1,000 population in the United States. The figures adjusted to population in Ontario and Quebec are similar to those for Canada. So, in spite of the growth in the ratio of lawyers to population during this period in both countries, there remained more than one and a half times more lawyers per 1,000 population in the United States than in Canada.

Women accounted for a large part of the growth in the legal profession of both countries during this period. The number of women increased from 3 to 14 percent of U.S. lawyers (Rhode, 1988:1178), and from about 3 to over 15 percent of Canadian lawyers (Hagan, 1991). This mirrored more general changes in the labor forces of both countries. Nearly 40 percent of women were in the labor force by the early 1960s, and their involvement increased steadily over the next quarter century. This increase was in part a response to the growth of postsecondary education generally and legal education specifically.

The Law Society of Upper Canada finally relinquished its professional hold over legal education in Ontario in the 1950s, and the Osgoode Hall Law School, previously operated by the Law Society, moved to York University. The University of Toronto and a number of other universities in the province of Ontario also established law faculties. Women increased from about 4 percent of the students entering law schools in the 1950s to about 50 percent by the early 1990s.

Many reasons can be given for this change, including demographic, social, and ideological forces. Life expectancies were increasing and women were therefore living greater parts of their lives without children in the home. Marriages were becoming less permanent and women became more independent. The expansion of education, the civil rights movement, and the feminist movement encouraged new attitudes and ambitions. The legal profession was more clearly a part of the changing social surroundings than a leading force in all of this.

Although in 1911 there were only 7 women lawyers in all of Canada, by 1986 there were nearly 10,000. The rate of change initially was faster in the United States. At four decade intervals, beginning in 1941, the ratios of men to women lawyers in Canada were respectively 66:1, 45:1, 38:1, and 20:1. In the United States they were 41:1; 28:1, 28:1, and 20:1. In 1981 in both countries the ratio was about 6:1, and in 1986 these ratios were below 4:1. The latest figures from the 1991 census put the ratio in the United States at about 3:1 and in Canada at about 2.4:1. So, although the change in the Canadian ratios lagged the American for a number of decades, Canada has more recently outpaced the United States in increasing the relative representation of women in the profession. At the current rate of change, women should constitute more than a third and may approach one half of the legal profession in both countries by the turn of the century (Morello, 1986). Women currently form about half of the younger and larger cohorts of the profession.

Brief note also should be taken of an interesting gender difference in Canada between Ontario and Quebec. The ratios of men to women lawyers in these provinces indicate that historically the legal profession was much more male dominated in Quebec than in English Canada or the United States; however, these ratios of men to women converged and crossed in 1971, when the ratios in Ontario and Quebec were nearly identical, at about 19:1. In 1981 and 1986 the ratios were smaller in Quebec: 4.45:1 and 2.93:1, compared to 6.89:1 and 4.01:1 in Ontario. In 1991 the ratio of men to women lawyers in Quebec was 1.94:1, and 2.63:1 in Ontario. This difference may follow partly from the movement of francophone males into the business sector of Quebec society in the 1970s and 1980s, and an emergence of a large francophone business class in Quebec. This may have expanded the number of vacancies for women in a profession where demand already was exceeding supply. Changes engendered by the Quiet Revolution in Quebec may also have encouraged more women to enter the legal profession. However, there are indications that this difference between French and English Canada also is mirrored in comparisons of France and England (Menkel-Meadow, 1989a). Meanwhile, the situations in Ontario's English Canada and the United States now appear rather similar with regard to gender.

Overall, our data indicate differences as well as similarities in the United States and Canadian experiences. There continue to be substantially fewer lawyers in Canada than in the United States, and until recently changes have come more slowly in Canada. However, the overall growth of the profession and the increased representation of women are remarkable trends in both countries. Apparently, structural and cultural differences between the United States and Canada have established parameters within which parallel processes of social change have operated. We turn next, then, to the introduction of two theories that attempt to explain contemporary patterns and developments in the practice of law.

Two Theories of the Profession

Although there is little disagreement that the legacy of the legal profession includes a history of gender discrimination, there is disagreement about how the profession currently operates. This disagreement is expressed in the development of two theories of legal practice. These theories have scholarly origins, but they also have lay variants and followings in the profession itself. The first, human capital theory, derives from the field of economics and finds some of its most ardent followers among the "human capitalists" who manage law firms. The second, gender stratification theory, derives from the field of sociology and finds its most ardent followers among feminist legal scholars and lawyers who advocate changes in the profession. These theories are a focal point of discussion and analysis in this book.

Human capital theory explains patterns and developments within the legal profession as products of the combined operation of efficiency and choice. By making efficient choices to invest in human resources, individuals and firms develop their human capital. There are a number of dimensions along which this basic assumption is elaborated, some of which are explored in following chapters, and not all of which impinge directly on issues of gender. However, surely the most provocative of these developments is a version of what we will call the "chosen spheres" argument. This argument resurrects the emphasis on the separation of work and family that was expressed, for example, by the U.S. Supreme Court in the *Bradwell* decision. While that decision leaned heavily on spiritual and constitutional sources, the dimension of human capital theory that we consider here uses biological differences to build an explanation of why women are often less successful than men in law.

This argument is expressed most prominently in work of the Nobel prize-winning economist, Gary Becker (1991). Becker asserts that there are intrinsic biological differences that give comparative advantages to women in the home and to men elsewhere. These intrinsic differences, which Becker acknowledges may not be great initially, are magnified through subsequent investments of human capital by women and men in the separate spheres of home and work. He reasons that "a small initial difference can be transformed into large observed differences by the reinforcing effects of specialized investments" (1991:63). The assumption is that individuals make different, highly specialized investments that are often shaped by biological and socialized differences of gender.

It is significant to note that Becker also introduces a second, quite different dimension to human capital theory, in what we will call a "restricted spheres" argument. Here Becker acknowledges that gender discrimination could produce differences in outcomes through male exploitation of the comparative specializations of women in the home and men in other work. This possibility is not emphasized in Becker's human capital theory, which instead argues that this process is more often choice- and efficiency-driven. That is, specializations in home and work more often are regarded as freely and rationally chosen in Becker's human capital theory, while issues like constraint, discrimination, and exploitation are left for separate consideration. For Becker, "exploitation is largely a separate issue from efficiency in the division of labor by gender" (1991:4). However, by opening the door to a restricted spheres argument, Becker's theory does acknowledge that exploitation as well as efficiency may be at work in determining occupational outcomes.

Meanwhile, the inferences drawn from the chosen spheres argument are explicit: individuals will experience greater success in legal practice, as in other occupations, as an efficient reward for their investment of greater effort and therefore better-developed human capital; that is, greater success is awarded to more highly committed individuals who have chosen to give priority to their occupational careers (Becker, 1985; 1991; Mincer, 1985). The implication of this theory is that if women made similar choices and efforts as men, they would achieve success that is comparable to that of men. Of course, the assumption of the chosen spheres version of human capital theory is that this does not happen. This version of the theory tends to focus on women who have children, because it regards having a child as a choice to invest in family and child care, and such choices are assumed to reduce career commitment and effort necessary for occupational advancement.

In contrast, gender stratification theory argues that differences in the occupational success of women and men in law, as elsewhere, are the combined product of inefficiency and constraint. In this way, gender stratification theory develops, as a central theme, the deemphasized restricted spheres dimension of Becker's human capital theory; it claims that the profession inefficiently penalizes the comparable efforts of committed women who, often in spite of constraining demands of family and inadequate rewards in occupational advancement, invest heavily in their careers (e.g., England, 1982; Tienda et al., 1987; Bielby and Bielby, 1988). According to this theory, women who are similar to men in their career commitment are not rewarded at levels similar to men. The theory is sensitive to the experiences of women who have children and are expected to devote more time than men to family, because these investments, it claims, often are made without reducing career commitment and investments on the job and without corresponding rewards in career advancement. Gender stratification theory sees hierarchical work structures as inflexible and unyielding sources of disparities in the opportunities and rewards open to women; the structures are seen as discriminatory and are understood to perpetuate the subordination of women.

The chosen spheres version of human capital theory is clearly opposed to gender stratification theory on key points, and these contradictions will be explored in this book. However, the restricted spheres version of Becker's theory also opens a door to the insights of gender stratification theory, and there are important contexts in which each of these theories usefully supplements the other. For example, in the following chapter some ideas are drawn from human capital theory to develop a perspective on why law firms are formed in the first place and on how firms grow. Human capital theory also serves as a helpful guide to how those who manage most law firms, the human capitalists, think about what they are doing. Indeed, it is probably impossible to understand how modern law firms operate without incorporating aspects of this theoretical account. Nonetheless, we will argue, with evidence from our research, that human capital theory also often distorts issues of gender and the advancement of women. That is, we will argue that some basic assumptions of the theory are wrong. Before we begin to develop these points in following chapters, we need to describe in greater detail the context in which the research reported in this book unfolds.

The Upper Canadian Setting

Our research is undertaken in what is known historically as Upper Canada, in the city of Toronto and the surrounding province of Ontario. In this section we provide a general description of the City and the region, with only a few observations about experiences of women within this setting. Our purpose is to describe the more general social and legal context of the study. In the section that follows we introduce our research design and its comparative focus on the experiences of women and men in law.

One in every three Canadians lives in Ontario, and more than one in three Ontarians live in Toronto. Because of its location, at the center of Canada and adjacent to large population centers of the United States, Toronto and Ontario are at the heart of Canada and have played a leading role in the economic and social history of this nation.

Ontario's economy and growth is concentrated in its cities, especially in the five cities that cluster around the western end of Lake Ontario in the area called the Golden Horseshoe, which includes Oshawa, Toronto, Burlington, Hamilton, and St. Catherines. The remaining sizable cities are Ottawa to the northeast and London, Kitchener, and Windsor to the southwest.

The 1970s and 1980s were for the most part a boom period in the economy of the Toronto area. While Montreal during the first half of this century was the financial center of Canada, the latter half of the century brought greater financial activity to Toronto and its neighboring cities. Much of this growth was fed by immigration, with more than a third of all Canada's immigrants choosing to live in Toronto in recent years, making it a truly multicultural city. The larger Toronto metropolitan area grew from about one million people in 1950, to over two million in 1970, to a population close to four million in 1990.

Toronto's skyline is a metaphor for its growth. It includes the world's tallest freestanding structure, the CN Tower, the futuristic SkyDome stadium, an architecturally celebrated city hall, and a stunning array of bank towers that flank Bay Street, Toronto's symbol of corporate power and affluence. It is a city that alternates between its aspirations to be "world-class" and its fears of urban malaise and misfortune symbolized in a preoccupation with becoming "Manhattanized."

Toronto is, not coincidentally, Canada's leading financial center and its legal center, as well. All of Canada's major banks and many of its major corporations, insurance companies, and brokerage houses have head offices in Toronto. The Toronto Stock Exchange is the largest in the country, and second only in its volume to the New York Stock Exchange on this continent. Ontario accounts for half the manufacturing productivity of Canada, and Toronto employs close to half of the manufacturing workers in the province. By any measure, Canada's wealth is highly concentrated in Ontario, and more specifically in Toronto.

For these reasons, it is not surprising that the legal profession of Canada is concentrated disproportionately in Ontario, especially in Toronto. While about 8 percent of America's lawyers work in New York City (Epstein, 1981:17), approximately one quarter of Canada's lawyers are in Toronto (Arthurs et al., 1971:500). It long has been argued that Canada is a more elite-based society than the United States (e.g., Porter, 1965; Lipset, 1968) and that lawyers in Canada are more highly represented among economic (Clement, 1975) and political (Prestus, 1973) elites than lawyers in other western nations. This makes Upper Canada an interesting setting in which to study the profession of law.

Still, in other ways indicated in the previous section, Upper Canada's lawyers are experiencing many of the same changes that are occurring elsewhere. This is especially apparent in the centralization and concentration of lawyers in large firms in Toronto. As of the late 1980s, more than two thousand of the eight thousand lawyers in Toronto were in firms of twenty lawyers and larger (Hagan et al., 1991:247), and by 1990 there were nineteen Toronto firms with a hundred or more lawyers (Daniels, 1993). As Galanter (1983:21) observes, "The attraction of this style of lawyering is not confined to the United States. In recent years, the American big firm became a model for firms in Canada, Australia, and England." There is a further and related process involving the transnational interpenetration of markets and firms. Galanter (1983:155) remarks of American firms that "twenty years ago the occasional Washington or foreign branch office seemed anomalous." This has changed and coincidentally, between 1985 and 1990, fourteen Canadian firms opened eighteen foreign offices (Daniels, 1992:11). Toronto is clearly a part of the changing global economy and the transnational growth of law firms.

As such, it should be noted that Toronto and the province more generally also shared in the North American recessions of the early and late 1980s, with the latter continuing into the 1990s. These recessions brought unemployment to historically high levels of 11 percent in Toronto and the surrounding province. Welfare caseloads increased markedly, and food banks served hundreds of thousands of people during these recessionary periods.

It is widely believed that these recessions were felt within the legal profession as well. The explosive periods of growth before and between the recessions at the beginning and end of the decade saw, for example, merchant bankers, stockbrokers, and lawyers playing central roles in major mergers and acquisitions. These transactions often involved large amounts of time and many lawyers, and when the deals began to decline, these lawyers had to find alternative work. Some full-service firms could reassign lawyers from the shrinking corporate area to insolvency and litigation activities, which traditionally increase in recessionary periods. However, even this transition may have involved longer hours of work, at reduced profit margins, and with a generally much lower profile. One newspaper account summed up the more difficult situation at the end of the decade by tersely observing, "Firms are competing . . . fiercely for the available work. Fees have been cut, and firms are raiding each other for clients" (*Globe and Mail*, October 23, 1990).

It will be important in the analyses presented in following chapters to take this economic context into account. Both the panel and cross-sectional surveys cover boom-and-bust periods of legal practice in Upper Canada. Such periods will occur in the experiences of any sample that includes subjects of different ages and different periods. Nonetheless, there is an opportunity here to see how growth and contraction are experienced by different kinds of individuals and in different sectors during a unique period when the legal profession was undergoing other rapid and important changes.

The Lawyer Surveys

By the 1990s the legal profession was becoming more self-conscious of its growth and change, especially of the increasing representation of women within the profession. The numbers had increased far beyond the token stage, and new issues involved the degree to which women were advancing in the profession and having an impact on it. A number of state bar associations in the United States commissioned inquiries that surveyed the treatment of women in the justice system and also gave attention to the advancement of women as lawyers. Several Canadian law societies and the Canadian Bar Association also established task forces and undertook surveys of their members, producing valuable descriptive data about the distribution and experiences of women in the profession (see Buckley, 1993).

However, it is one thing to document the increasing representation and obstacles to the advancement of women in law, and quite another to develop and assess explanations of the problems and processes of change in this profession. The next stage of research in this area is by necessity more analytic. Because there are now many women in the profession with varying degrees and kinds of experiences, it is possible to begin analyzing the progress women are making, with a wide range of their experiences taken into account and compared to men. As we note next with examples, analyses of new kinds of survey data on lawyers allow us to assess explanations of the career aspirations and achievements of women in law. For example, we can assess the assumption that women differ from men in their commitment to the practice of law over their careers, especially if they have children.

As we noted earlier, a gender stratification theory of occupations challenges the chosen sphere aspects of human capital theory. Human capital theory, especially when applied by the human capitalists of the profession who manage law firms, assumes that men build and sustain higher levels of commitment to work across their careers than women do. It is noted that some women leave the profession to have children, interrupting the trajectories of their careers, and that many of these women never return to legal practice. Human capital theory generalizes from such cases to make the claim that women are less "invested" in their work, that is, that they invest less effort in developing their human capital through their professional careers (see Becker, 1991).

In contrast, gender stratification theory suggests that women characteristically exhibit high levels of work commitment, in spite of the fact that employers often provide little accommodation for periods of child bearing. It asserts that based on their differences from men, especially in terms of involvement in childbearing, women find themselves in separate strata of the profession, which are treated disadvantageously, and that these circumstances sometimes lead to the complete departure of women from the profession. The separate strata theme amplifies the restricted spheres argument of human capital theory and rejects its alternative chosen spheres assumptions; it is suggested that women leave law more by constraint than choice and that this does not reflect an abandonment of commitment.

To explore and test differences within and among these theories, it is necessary to collect special kinds of data on lawyers, data that have rarely been available or extensively analyzed. The data must provide detailed information about the work and parenting experiences of women and men that can be used to analyze changes in work commitment and other career developments. To be most revealing, they should be collected over time so that causal sequences of events and outcomes can be recorded and analyzed. To do so requires that the same respondents be surveyed at more than one point in time, with detailed information collected about continuing and changing experiences as they occur for individuals over their careers. Tracking large numbers of subjects over time and resurveying them is an expensive and time-consuming undertaking, known as panel research, which is often contrasted with cross-sectional surveys that consider a range of experiences among a sample of subjects at one point in time only. Both kinds of surveys have their purposes, and both are a part of our research design.

The surveys were undertaken in Toronto and in the surrounding province and were designed to complement one another. The Toronto panel study of men and women lawyers was organized in a mail-back fashion, with a first wave of surveys completed in 1985. The sample was originally stratified by gender and type of practice to include equally men and women in larger firms (twenty-six or more lawyers) and smaller firms (up to twenty-five lawyers) as well as nonfirm settings. We were particularly concerned to include sufficient numbers of women in a variety of legal settings to allow statistical comparisons involving gender. We mailed survey questionnaires to 1,609 respondents in the first wave of the Toronto study, and, with two reminders, 1,051 questionnaires (65.3 percent) were returned.

However, as useful as these data were by themselves, for reasons already indicated in a general way and now made specific to this survey, the first-wave data could only tell part of the story that interested us. The majority of the women included in the initial wave of this survey were in their first years of practice, with little opportunity for their experiences and commitments to undergo much change. Furthermore, even though we collected extensive information on their careers to the date of the first survey, it was not the same as having more complete information on the many aspects of personal and professional lives that change and that can be assessed through repeated contacts over a period of time. For example, it is one thing to know objective features of first and current positions in the profession, but it is quite another to have information on how the respondent subjectively feels about his or her commitment to such positions, as reported in sequence while these positions are held.

Furthermore, longitudinal or panel data collected over time can also provide a better basis for assessing the role of causal forces, such as having children, that shape careers; for example, when data are collected over time it is possible to establish sequences of events and subjective feelings, such as the timing of births, leaves, and transitions to partnership, and to establish with greater certainty the order of causation among these events and putatively related attitudes, such as commitment to work.

It is also possible to obtain greater control over the influence of extraneous variables with longitudinal data. For example, one can examine changes in work commitment within individuals, many of whose other characteristics, such as background and area of practice, will not have changed over time; such persons can act as their own "controls," in the sense that extraneous sources of background variation (e.g., personality and ability) are removed that might account for differences in their commitments. Changes within, as well as between, individuals' careers can be analyzed with longitudinal data, increasing the possibilities of establishing patterns of causation. This is important because, if, for example, it can be established that similarities in work commitment between men and women who continue to work full-time in their careers are not altered in a negative way by intervening births of children, it would provide compelling evidence against the chosen spheres version of human capital theory and in favor of restricted spheres and separate strata theories of the involvement of women in the profession.

For these kinds of reasons, we organized a second-wave survey of our Toronto respondents five years after our first contact with them. This effectively changed a cross-sectional study into a longitudinal panel design. Of the 1,051 Toronto lawyers surveyed in the first wave of the study in 1985, 815 were resurveyed in the second wave in 1991. If retired and deceased lawyers are excluded, the response rate to the second survey was almost 80 percent (79.3 percent). This relatively high rate of retention in our panel study allows a good representation of the continuing lawyer population of Toronto. This point is established in greater detail in the discussion of sampling in the Appendix to this volume.

However, these longitudinal data could not answer all our questions. For one thing, they could not tell us about the experiences of lawyers who entered the profession after the initial wave of the Toronto sample in 1985, or about lawyers who worked in smaller cities and towns outside Toronto. Attitudes can change quickly, and this may be especially true in a city like Toronto. We were also anxious to learn more about lawyers who had left the practice of law. With these concerns in mind, a second cross-sectional survey was undertaken in 1990. As we noted above, by 1990 Toronto and the surrounding province were in a period of economic recession.

This second survey considers entrants to the practice of law from 1975 to 1990 across the entire province of Ontario. This sample is random within strata equally representing men and women, but it also includes all possible respondents who were designated in Law Society records as "temporarily absent" or "suspended" from practice at the time of the survey. Absent or suspended respondents are important because they have departed from the practice of law on either a temporary or a more permanent basis. We wanted to learn about the disappointments as well as opportunities involved in these departures from the profession. Inclusion of these respondents allows us to consider exits from as well as entries into the practice of law, thereby broadening our consideration of these major life course transitions in this profession. Surveys were sent in 1990 to 2,358 otherwise randomly chosen Ontario lawyers, and with a follow-up mailing, 1,143 instruments (67.7 percent) were returned.

Both the Toronto panel and the Ontario survey contain a wealth of information about lawyers' lives. They include detailed job histories, from entry to (in some cases) exits from the profession; extensive information about past and current positions in the profession in terms of power, authority, and autonomy; measures of work commitment, feelings of depression and job satisfaction; indicators of professional contacts and networks; and relatively complete information on income, marriage, parenthood, and leaves. Particular attention is given to the timing of personal life events and movements in the profession, especially the attainment of partnerships and departures from the profession. Additional attention is given to the changing organization of the profession over time, for example, in terms of the growth of the overall profession and changes in its partnership structure, and especially in relation to the issue of a "glass ceiling" in legal careers. This makes it possible to link career transitions and trajectories of individuals to changes simultaneously occurring in the profession and surrounding economy.

A considerable amount of qualitative data was also collected over the period of our research. We conducted fifty interviews in 1985 with what is best described as a "snowball sample" of respondents. Our purpose was not to generate a random sample but rather to gather further evidence and insight into the patterns observed in our quantitative data. Respondents in our surveys also were invited to comment on questions we asked them, and many did so at some length. Some of this material was instrumental in guiding our analysis, for example, in suggesting new and more revealing ways to assess gender differences in job satisfaction, as we do in chapter 7. More generally, the comments from the surveys and interviews provided a rich source of insights into the careers of women and men lawyers, and they are woven extensively into analyses reported in the chapters that follow. Three or sometimes four quotes from separate respondents often are introduced to establish that a point of view or experience described is not idiosyncratic or random but rather repeated in the comments and interviews. This may sometimes seem repetitive, but the point is to document that patterns are involved.

The Context of Change

We began this chapter by noting that until recently, relatively little was known about the inner workings of the legal profession. This was a result of outright secrecy in some sectors of legal practice and reticence about publicity in others. But the situation is changing rapidly. This is important, because the legal profession is powerful and is experiencing rapid changes that reflect important social trends in the surrounding national and world economy. The profession has experienced enormous growth, with increasingly large firms leading the way in centralizing and concentrating the resources of the profession, and incorporating large numbers of women in the process.

We certainly are not the first to note interconnections between law and the larger society. For example, C. Wright Mills (1966) portrayed lawyers as both proactive and reactive participants in the economy. He noted the external proactive roles lawyers often play in shaping "the legal framework of the new economy" (the phrase is from Mills and cited in Fligstein, 1992), and he observed that lawyers increasingly are found in highly stratified work environments that reactively mirror the economic arrangements they often help to form for client corporations. Mills (1966:122) concluded that "in fulfilling his function the successful lawyer has created his office in the image of the corporations he has come to serve and defend." When Mills wrote this passage, his use of masculine pronouns would have been unquestioned.

Today women are a much more prominent part of the legal profession, but Mills's comments are otherwise timely. The "successful lawyer" that Mills describes is the "human capitalist" introduced in this chapter, a representative of a theory that will occupy much attention in this book. We are particularly interested in the treatment of women lawyers by the human capitalists and by human capital theory. We introduced in this chapter the sources of data we have collected in Toronto and the province of Ontario to assess this theory and the elaborations and challenges often posed to it by gender stratification theory. These theories attempt to account for contemporary patterns and developments involving women and men lawyers that are far more complex than in earlier periods of this century when women were excluded from the profession or were admitted in token numbers. Where earlier accounts could simply point to the relative scarcity of women lawyers, today there are many women in practice, and a more sophisticated analysis is required to reveal how the involvement of women is socially and often disadvantageously organized within the profession.

This book contributes to such an analysis by first considering the changing structure of the profession and the emergence of ceiling effects on the upward mobility of women lawyers. The chapters that follow begin the process of disaggregating this picture, so that we can explore how individual women enter and move through and sometimes out of the profession. We start by considering how women find their first positions in the profession on graduation from law school. Following chapters analyze the process that leads to partnership decisions and the early departures and transitions of women and men from and through the early years of practice, with particular attention to the different responsibilities women and men bear in balancing work on the job with work in the family. Perhaps the most complicated analysis in this book considers changes in earnings of lawyers over time in practice, and how gender differences in income involve issues of perceived productivity and work commitment. Another chapter addresses concerns about the stresses and strains that men as well as women experience in the practice of law.

This book is designed to set the foundation for a final discussion of the use of law and other remedies to address issues of gender discrimination in the legal profession. Our discussion considers the extent to which antidiscrimination laws protect women in the profession and examines the factors that make the use of such laws infrequent, but nonetheless significant. In the end we will consider the possibility that greater responsibilities must be shifted from affected individuals to affecting organizations, including firms and governing bodies, such as bar associations and law societies. However, to make this argument we must first establish the dimensions of the problems that women encounter in the contemporary practice of law.

2

Ceiling Effects in Practice

The large firms, and the legal profession in general, remain very hierarchical and in order to advance, junior lawyers have to learn and play by the 'rules.' The problem for women is that the rules are not yet established. However, one thing is certain, young women can't expect to succeed by following the same rules as are appropriate and time-tested for male lawyers. In the sense that their path to success in the profession is more difficult to plan and predict, female lawyers do not yet enjoy equal opportunities and may suffer from a form of discrimination which is not overt but is built into the system.

First Questions

Two questions focus much of the current interest in the entry and advancement of women in the legal profession. The first asks how and why law firms in recent decades at last opened their doors to entering women. The second asks whether this participation of women is accompanied by a changing structure of practice that places a ceiling on the advancement of women in the profession. We argue in this chapter that answers to these two questions are linked in that the entry of large numbers of women into the profession has helped facilitate a change in the structure of legal practice that in relative terms provides "less room at the top." We will demonstrate that a glass ceiling, much discussed among women at higher levels of the occupational structure, has emerged generally during these decades of the growing involvement of women in law. We make these points by first discussing the expanded participation of women in legal practice.

Unbarring the Firms

There is an important commonality in the changing structure of legal practice across Western industrial societies that is perhaps most clearly and consistently reflected in the growth discussed in chapter 1 in the numbers of
practicing lawyers and in the increasing representation of women in law.
Across settings, then, there is the interesting initial question of what has
caused this expansion in the profession and its gender composition.

Some economists (e.g., Pashigian, 1978) have pointed to cyclical
changes in the demand for legal services that can produce wavelike patterns
of growth. Other social scientists (Abel, 1979; Auerbach, 1976; Larson,
1977) focus on variations, especially earlier in this century, in efforts of bar
associations to monopolistically control the supply of new lawyers.

However, accounts of the more recent and rapid growth of the profession give particular attention to the entry of women, because in the 1970s
and 1980s the increased numbers of women law students accounted for much
of the profession's expansion. Abel (1989:100) reports that in the United
States "[m]ale entry to the profession . . . declined after 1973, and all further
expansion represents new women lawyers." Between the early 1960s and
early 1980s in Canada, the number of female students increased by twenty-
four times (Arthurs et al., 1988).

We noted in the previous chapter that the recent influx of women into
the profession has been attributed to the women's movement, changes in
birth control, increasing access to higher education, and variations in the
availability of nontraditional jobs to women (Abel, 1988a:35; Menkel-
Meadow, 1989b:305). During the same period, the profession relinquished
most of its control over the supply of lawyers, so that, for example, the Law
Society of Upper Canada shifted its attention to the regulation of the profession, and legal education became a function of law schools associated with
universities. The universities became the dominant institutions, displacing
or reducing the direct involvement of the profession. The changing roles of
the universities and of women reduced social barriers to law and made it
possible for women to enter the profession in rising numbers (Abel, 1988a:35).

Yet the profession, especially through its expanding firms, also played
a new and major role in this transformation. We have seen that for most of
the first three quarters of this century the entry of women into law was slow.
Women first entered the profession primarily through government and family firms (Chester, 1985). It was not until the 1970s that larger firms began
to open their doors to women in increasing numbers, as these firms themselves were growing. To understand this important shift in the profession,
we give considerable attention in this chapter to the nature of these firms
and to the organization of their work.

The Concentration of Capital in Firms

Despite its professional status, legal practice is similar to other occupations in that it involves relations between labor and capital. These relations often involve lawyers employed by other lawyers in firms that have ownership claims to the resulting work. This is so despite the fact that the content of law is a cultural system that involves the manipulation of legal symbols rather than machines, tools, or other physical materials and objects (see Bourdieu, 1977:188).

That is, the product of legal work is a cultural commodity distributed through a professional service industry (cf. Balbus, 1977; Rueschemeyer, 1973; Stinchcombe, 1979). This commodity is marketed through contractual relations between producers (i.e., lawyers) and consumers (i.e., clients). The information flows involved in these symbolic transactions form the cultural base of the profession, and the transmission of knowledge about the manipulation and exchange of these symbols is what is involved in teaching law students and newly employed lawyers "to think and act like lawyers" (Zemans and Rosenblum, 1981; Macaulay, 1982).

The conceptual language introduced in the preceding paragraph helps to make clear that the practice of law is a business, albeit a commercial enterprise that is grounded in cultural symbols. The participants in our study certainly were aware of this. One of our respondents remarked, "It is time to stop calling it the practice of law and start calling it the business of law"; another explained, "It is not an academic exercise nor is the profession composed of 'gentlemen professionals' — they are individual work units with all the good and bad characteristics of the entrepreneur"; a third observed, "I think the biggest change in the past five years has been the increasing emphasis on law as a business. I was prepared for the pressures of client expectations and the difficulties of the work but the emphasis on the 'numbers' is harder to deal with."

Contractual relations in the business of law have shifted historically from a mode of legal production organized largely around solo practitioners to a mode of production more often organized around law firms with partners and tiered levels of lawyer employees. This makes the practice of law not only a business, but also an occupation with its own internal hierarchical structure, which we operationalize in the form of a typology presented later in this chapter.

Our knowledge of the transition from self-employment and small-firm organization to larger firms is limited by the uncertain quality of historical data on the decline of solo practice and the growth of firms. However, Curran (1985) estimates that in the United States the proportion of lawyers who practice law alone fell from 64 percent in 1960, to 52 percent in 1970, to 49 percent in 1980. Similarly, Abel (1989) estimates that while 64 percent of all lawyers practiced by themselves in 1948, only 37 percent did so by 1970, and 33 percent by 1980. Only 16 percent of Chicago lawyers practiced by themselves in 1975 (Heinz and Laumann, 1982), while about 12 percent did so in Toronto in 1985 (Hagan et al., 1988).

Seen another way, there were only 38 U.S. law firms with more than 50 lawyers in the 1950s (Smigel, 1969), while there were 508 firms this size by the mid-1980s (Curran, 1986). Galanter (1983:153) describes this as a trend toward "mega-lawyering," and it is now common to note that the dominance of larger firms has segmented lawyers into what Heinz and Laumann (1982; see also Nelson, 1983) call the two hemispheres of the profession. In one of these hemispheres major corporations are usually represented by large firms, while in the other small businesses and individuals are usually represented by small firms or by lawyers practicing alone.

Lawyers in small firms are affected as much as or more than lawyers in large firms by the growth of the profession. Comments from a partner in a small firm in our sample provided an insightful explanation of how the great increase in new law graduates has facilitated the concentration and centralization of legal talent in large firms.

> It's actually in their [the large firm's] interest to increase the number of lawyers in the profession, to just let it increase . . . , because it will not affect their client base and it will create a situation where they will have a great deal of control over the people whom they choose to work for them. . . . In the late sixties, when the balance was not the way it is today, when arguably there might not even have been enough lawyers to service the market, the older people in the larger firms were very much at the mercy of the younger people in their own firms. If you had a large firm and four or five of your corporate people announced that unless things changed they were leaving, you had a very serious problem. You didn't have the people to re-place them. That will not happen today because, as I said, the number of people who would line up to take these positions would be enor-mous. And if you're an older person, the last thing in the world you want is to work twelve or fifteen hours a day, or whatever insane regime you would have to endure, to cope with all the work. . . . It also creates a situation where they (the large firms) can pay what they want to pay to attract the better people. The smaller firms, es-pecially the one- and two-man firms, certainly cannot compete fi-nancially. So they'll get people at what they can afford to pay, but they won't be the top people. So if you continually employ the best, then you just further increase the qualitative differences. You even-tually reduce it to a half-dozen (large firms) fighting among them-selves.

So as law firms expand they can centralize and concentrate the human and cultural capital of the profession. The term *human capital* is often used by economists to refer to the kinds of technical skills that are acquired through education and experience and that are applied in many kinds of work settings (see Becker, 1964; Mincer, 1970), including law firms (see Gilson and Mnookin, 1985; Galanter and Palay, 1991). However, because legal education and experience are grounded so heavily in cultural symbols, this kind of human capital also contains elements of what anthropologists and sociologists call cultural capital. Nontechnical social and symbolic assets constitute further forms of cultural capital (see Bourdieu, 1977; DiMaggio and Mohr, 1985) that in legal practice include client relations and professional reputations (Hagan et al., 1991). Partners accumulate disproportionate shares of cultural capital, and this capital is increasingly centralized and concentrated in the partnerships of large firms.

Law firms grow by aggregating lawyers and rationalizing the use of labor and capital. Thus Galanter and Palay (1991) observe that successful firms centralize and concentrate four kinds of assets: education, experience, reputation, and clients. As we have suggested, education and experience can be thought of as producing a mixture of human and cultural capital (see Robinson and Garnier, 1985:254n), while professional reputation and client relations are predominantly cultural in content. A key to the formation and growth of these firms is that cultural capital, in the form of reputation and clients, often grows faster than human capital, the availability of educated and experienced lawyers to serve the clients that reputation can bring.

In good economic times, this is why law firms emerge and expand. That is, individual lawyers and firms often develop excess cultural capital, especially reputational and relational capital in the form of clients, which leads to engaging the labor of other lawyers as nonpartner associates to make use of this reputation and to service these clients. Of course, it is also imperative that reputation and clients be protected, so lawyers with excess cultural capital do not simply employ other lawyers on a case-by-case basis. As Galanter and Palay (1991) explain, the sharing of capital assets involves the organization of trust relations (see also Macaulay, 1963) through the formation of firms. But before we discuss how this is done, it is important to underline how vulnerable the concentration of cultural capital in firms can be, and why firms are therefore organized to protect this capital.

Professional reputations and client relations are fragile cultural commodities. Bourdieu (1977:182) notes that, much as in families, professions like law and medicine share a "hypersensitivity to the slightest slur or innuendo" and that such institutions develop a "multiplicity of strategies designed to belie or avert them." He explains this "by the fact that symbolic capital is less easily measured and counted than land or livestock and that the group, ultimately the only source of credit for it, will readily withdraw that credit and direct its suspicions at the strongest members, as if in matters of honour, as in land, one man's greater wealth made the others that much poorer" (132). A result is that the cultural form of legal capital, especially its reputational and relational forms, generates a hyper- (but nonetheless rational) sensitivity to potential devaluation. Lawyers and firms with this capital reasonably worry about its loss. The cultural capital of lawyers and their firms is vulnerable in ways that other forms of capital are not.

Gilson and Mnookin (1985) point to three sources of vulnerability that lawyers and firms face in engaging the labor of other lawyers: put succinctly, the propensity of these laboring lawyers to shirk responsibilities, grab assets, and/or leave. Firms are organized into partner-associate tiers that help to guard against these risks. These tiers of authority use subordinating and monitoring mechanisms identified in the typology we develop below to protect the cultural capital of the firm and its partners, while of course simultaneously extracting a profit from the labor of the employed lawyers.

We can now address the issue of why in recent decades law firms have grown so fast and, in turn, how this is connected to the large-scale entry of women into the profession and to their career prospects. The core of this argument is that each time a former "associate" lawyer is made a partner in a firm, as must occur at least sometimes to maintain an incentive structure to recruit into this professional labor market, new employees must be added in an exponential fashion to maintain the profit base. In good and perhaps also bad economic times, the effect is to generate what Galanter and Palay call a partner-associate pyramid. As we argue below, in good times this pyramid effect may occur through growth at all levels except the very top, while in bad times the pyramid effect may be achieved by selective attrition.

Assuming a sufficient pool of capital, the broader the base of this pyramid the better. Thus Stewart (1983:376) writes, "the key to profitability in such firms is the partner/associate ratio and 'pyramid' staffing of client matters. There must be more associates than partners — the bigger the disparity the better — since the firms make money from associates by billing their clients for their work at rates which more than compensate for associate salaries and overhead." The desirability of pyramiding is recognized in large firms. Abel (1989:124) reports that "[i]n the United States, the ratio of associates to partners rises from 0.25 for firms with 2 to 5 lawyers to 1.04 for firms with more than 50. In the 50 largest U.S. firms, the ratio rose from 1.1 in 1975 to 1.6 in 1979; that year it was 2.36 in the 10 largest New York City firms."

However, the growth dynamic that has characterized large law firms in recent decades, at least until the recession of the eighties and early nineties, has a further cultural dimension. We have already noted the special sensitivity of cultural capital to insults and innuendos. Conversely, firms are also sensitive to the lure of image enhancement. A common response to this sensitivity in the 1970s and 1980s was to demonstrate vitality through growth, which involved increased competition, diversification, merger activity, lateral movement, and intensified recruitment efforts; that is, to increasing concentrations of centralized cultural capital. The structure of this growth led to many new activities, including the provision of fuller services to corporate clients, such as merger, acquisition, and bankruptcy work that prominent firms would not have undertaken fifteen years earlier. The structure of this growth also involved new forms of competition, including corporate clients choosing lawyers and firms for particular matters rather than for full representation.

Professional periodicals in the United States and Canada, like the *National Law Journal*, the *American Lawyer* and the *Canadian Lawyer*, regularly recorded stories of new associate and summer student recruitment programs and related merger and acquisition activities that resulted from the pace of this growth dynamic. Against this backdrop were less frequent stories of firms that failed, that grew too fast, diversified too much, or extended too far or too quickly. In the early to mid-1980s and again later in the same decade the growth dynamic of the legal profession was tempered further by cyclical recessions that plagued the larger economy. So again there was the shadow of vulnerability. Within this context, and more generally, there was a constant concern with monitoring growth, assuring that new associates and partners were responsible, trustworthy, working hard, and ultimately focusing on whether prospective partners could generate sufficient new cultural capital to sustain growth.

We can now look back and place this discussion in the context of the growth of the profession that we documented in chapter 1. The key point is that beginning in the 1960s, the production of new lawyers did not keep pace with the expanding cultural capital of firms. This was so despite the fact that between 1960 and 1980 the numbers of lawyers more than doubled in both the United States and Canada.

The fact that up to 1960 the lawyer population grew at about the same rate as the general population, and then more than doubled in relation to population over the next several decades, testifies to the growth dynamic of this profession during this period. This growth is apparent in the corporate, government, and law firm sectors of the profession. Government expansion presumably reflected increased regulatory and administrative responsibilities, but the private sector firms also helped to lead this growth. Furthermore, and as anticipated above, the growth was on a scale that could not have occurred without a new willingness of firms to hire women. We now move to a consideration of the form this expansion took and the place of women lawyers within it.

Professional Growth and the Entry of Women

Two major explanatory frameworks, postindustrial theory and Marxian theory, classically are opposed to each other in efforts to predict the changing shape of Western capitalist economies in this century. By implication, both of these theories also have something to say about the changing shape of the legal profession.

Marxian theory (e.g., Wright and Singelmann, 1982) predicts that the structural transformation of the economy will result, presumably in law and elsewhere, in a declining ratio of capital to labor; that is, the (cultural) capital of the profession held by partners in firms will form a shrinking proportion of the profession, while the labor is performed by a proportionally increasing pool of largely nonautonomous employees — a "deprofessionalized proletariat" or new class of "mental workers" that we later discuss in greater detail in the context of our typology.

Postindustrial theory, as well, predicts a decline in the ownership sector, but it more distinctively predicts that notable growth will occur in the middle levels of the economy and, as a consequence, in the middle ranks of the legal profession as well. The argument is that the information and technology demands that drive the formation of a "new class" in the postindustrial economy require employees that have new and more rewarding levels of autonomy (see Glazer, 1979). So where Marxian theory predicts an expanding professional class lacking in autonomy, a kind of burgeoning professional proletariat, postindustrial theory predicts the expansion of a more autonomous, or at least semiautonomous class occupying a position between managers and nonautonomous employees, with the latter class expected to decline.

There is, however, a further possibility: that all or most levels of employed lawyers would in relative terms grow, while the employer (i.e., partnership) group declines through a centralization and concentration of partnerships, thus reducing the relative size of the partnership pool within the legal profession. A focus on cultural capital makes this outcome seem more likely by emphasizing the sensitivity of firms to the perceived need to grow (to the extent broader economic circumstances allow) and to provide some mobility for new recruits in the process. Ironically, then, a more eclectic perspective implies more intense periods of centralization and concentration of legal capital (i.e., in response to anxieties about perceived position as well as profitability) than does a Marxian framework, while allowing for limited upward mobility as well. The catch is that upward movement is effectively limited, because the relative size of the pool of centralized and concentrated partnerships is shrinking.

But what of women? What happens when economic circumstances decline? And are these two concerns connected?

Recall that the accumulation of cultural capital in firms requires a combination of growth and control. Both are required to facilitate the accumulation of cultural capital, which may be more precarious than other forms of capital, and which is therefore perceived as highly vulnerable. Growth of the law firm sector therefore requires an educated and motivated, but compliant pool of labor. Now consider MacKinnon's (1989:80) observation that in theory as well as in practice "so long as women are excluded from socially powerful activity, . . . [they] will be valued only for the ways they can be used." Our point is that women in particular may have been "used," albeit probably unconsciously, to play a vital demographic role in the centralization and concentration of the cultural capital that is transforming the legal profession. In making this suggestion we in effect are proposing an account of the emergence of what is popularly known as the glass ceiling in the organization of law firms.

This ceiling may have formed in the following way. For the past several decades women may have represented a convenient maximization of several important possibilities. First, as we have seen, the numbers of women lawyers have grown steadily in tandem with demand. Second, there are some indications that women law students and graduates are even slightly better educated and motivated than men (Epstein, 1981). Third, women may have been perceived as more compliant than men — that is, in the terms used earlier, women may have been seen as less likely than men to "shirk" responsibilities and/or "grab" assets.

As we note in some detail in later chapters, women do leave practice at higher rates than men, often in response to combined pressures of work and family. However, these departures usually are not harmful to firms in ways suggested by the expression "shirk, grab, and/or leave," and these departures may even be advantageous in limiting demands for promotion to partnership and increased earnings. This brings us to the crux of the matter, for women may more generally have been perceived to be more compliant, a compliance that could be translated into lower levels of compensation and mobility (Hagan, 1990) that culminate in a ceiling effect. A woman lawyer in our sample described a source of this kind of ceiling effect when she observed, "I have been left with the feeling that there are still many firms who exploit their juniors. . . . They pay them poorly and then replace them a year or two down the line when they have acquired a degree of competence and a voice to demand more pay. Constant turning over of juniors at low pay, with no attempt at educating them can be a trying influence on a young lawyer." Another young woman in our sample summarized her perception of her senior partners by observing that "they expect women to work harder and better than men for less money."

The above kinds of perceptions and practices may have provided firms a hedge on spiraling demands for rewards in a period of growth, rewards that were further jeopardized by feared and actual shifts in economic circumstances during the recession of the eighties and early nineties. Popular discussions of "the mommy track," and the common assumption that women are socialized to be less aggressive and less likely to protest than men, as well as to be less willing to uproot themselves and otherwise sacrifice their families, may all have contributed to stereotyped perceptions of women and to their differential treatment during this period of rapid change. It is important to note that the perspective we propose predicts that the concentration of legal capital that we have described should exert its predicted effects on both women and men. However, it is also predicted that these effects will be felt more strongly among women.

The possibility that the concentration and centralization of legal capital exerts its effects more strongly on women than men is, of course, consistent with concerns widely expressed about the glass ceiling for women in many sectors of society, and in the legal profession in particular. Thus Carrie Menkel-Meadow (1989a; 1989b) has noted that simple increases in the number of women lawyers is only one aspect of the transformation of this profession, and that even at this fundamental level important questions remain to be answered. Catherine MacKinnon (1986) effectively articulates one such question when she asks if only exceptional women will rise in the hierarchy of the legal profession, or if "average women" will do as well as "average men." "A few token success stories among women are not enough," remarked one respondent in our Toronto sample. Another made the same point by observing with reference to two extraordinary Toronto lawyers that "[r]eal equality is not in the achievements of the Mary Eberts and Rosie Abellas of this world. Real equality . . . is when mediocre women achieve at the same level as mediocre men." More specifically, Menkel-Meadow (1989b:208) observes that it is important to uncover "the places and rates of female attrition, failure or discouragement." We do this in detail in following chapters, but first in this chapter we offer an overall picture of changes in the structure of the profession that will help to assess the accuracy of the predictions our perspective has offered of the fates of men and women in contemporary legal practice. The first step in developing this picture of the changing structure of the legal profession involves the presentation of a typology that articulates the hierarchical structure of lawyering.

A Hierarchical Typology of Lawyers

The kind of census data on lawyers that we summarized in chapter 1 only begins to suggest the changing structure of this profession by indicating overall patterns of growth. Also central is the element of hierarchy. The profession itself partially obscures the presence of its hierarchical structure by formally defining its membership in terms of law school graduation, bar admission, and the payment of professional fees. However, there are acute power differences, some obvious and others more subtle, associated with positions in the profession. A comment by a large-firm partner from our study expresses a fatalistic sense of ambivalence about this hierarchical dimension of firm practices.

> Hierarchy in law firms comes from two sources, one that's appropriate, and one that's totally inappropriate, but nonetheless present. The appropriate one is economics. It's just not economic, for a firm or for a client, for a very senior person to be researching law or to be drafting a very simple document that a student can be doing. . . . The hourly rates mean that everyone's going to be unhappy if senior people do that, and I think that's appropriate. The other thing is there's a strong power hierarchy, at least in the big firms I know about, and I think in any firm bigger than three people who are equal partners. And that reflects itself in a desire not just to delegate work because it makes sense, but to delegate it as a show of strength, because in a large way there isn't so much to differentiate people: four corner offices per floor, and that tells you who's different, but the other thing that tells you who's different is the ability of people to command the firm's human resources, and as you move up the ladder you have more control, . . . because whatever comes in you shuffle off to other people, and it's appropriate you should, too. You tend to be dealing, as you do in any large organization, with decisions, and the actual work gets done by other people, so you're dealing more with refined things, and a series of them; you become more removed, for better or worse. . . . My opportunity to get control over my own life has improved as I've moved along here, and I expect that it will continue to do so.

Our initial empirical task in this chapter is to capture this element of hierarchy by using the first Toronto lawyer survey introduced in chapter 1 to operationalize a typology that focuses on inequalities in positions of power occupied by lawyers.

Several dimensions of occupational power are incorporated in our typology. These dimensions include considerations of corporate linkages, ownership and partnership, organizational size, authority, involvement in decision making, autonomy, and hierarchical position. Fortunately, these are all dimensions of power relevant to individual lawyers that can be probed in survey questions without seriously raising concerns about confidentiality and secrecy. Individually and collectively, answers to questions about these dimensions reveal much about the social structure of power relations that organize everyday legal life. The dimensions are adapted from analyses undertaken by Wright et al. (1982) of the larger occupational structure, and in this sense they have relevance across a range of jobs as well as within the legal profession.

The typology of positions that results from our consideration of the several dimensions of power is displayed in the first column of table 2.1. The remaining column headings indicate the dimensions used to sort individual lawyers into this typology of positions. (The actual survey items used to place respondents into these categories are described in Hagan et al., 1988.)

Two of the most important dimensions in our typology are *ownership* and *number of employees*. Although these terms may not commonly be used in discussions of the legal profession, we use them purposefully here to underline again the important point that law is a business as well as a profession. The literature on lawyers commonly draws a distinction between two kinds of ownership positions in the legal profession: solo practitioners and partners. Because solo practitioners often if not usually employ at least one other person, for example, a secretary, both solo practitioners and partners are treated as employers in our typology. We then further distinguish among employers in terms of the number of persons employed at their place of work.

Four additional measures are used to further distinguish positions of power in our typology of lawyers. *Hierarchical position* is a measure that sorts lawyers in terms of the number of levels of persons below the respondent in the organization. About a third of the Toronto sample (34.9 percent) had two or more levels of persons below them, while another 60 percent had one level of persons below them, and only about 6 percent had nobody below them in the organizational hierarchy.

Table 2.1
Hierarchical Typology of the Legal Profession

Legal Description	Link to Dominant Corporation	Ownership Relation	Number of Employees	Authority	Decision Making	Autonomy	Hierarchical Position
Managing Partner in Large, Elite Firm	Through firm	Employer	≥30	Sanctioning or task authority	1 or more area of decision making	N.A.	2 or more levels below respondent
Managing Partner in Medium to Large Firm	N.A.	Employer	≥10	Sanctioning or task authority	1 or more area of decision making	N.A.	2 or more levels below respondent
Supervising Partner in Medium to Large Firm	N.A.	Employer	≥10	No managing or task authority[a]	Provides advice	N.A.	N.A.
Partner in Small Firm	N.A.	Employer	2–9	N.A.	N.A.	N.A.	N.A.
Solo Practitioner	N.A.	Employer	0–1	N.A.	N.A.	N.A.	N.A.
Associate, Corporate, or Government Managing or Supervising Lawyer	N.A.	Employee	N.A.	Sanctioning or task authority or nominal supervisor	N.A.	N.A.	1 level below respondent
Semiautonomous Associate, Corporate, or Government Lawyer	N.A.	Employee	N.A.	Nonsupervisor[b]	N.A.	Designs some or all aspects of work	No level below respondent
Nonautonomous Associate, Corporate, or Government Lawyer	N.A.	Employee	N.A.	Nonsupervisor	N.A.	Designs few or no aspects of work	No level below respondent

[a] Respondents without task and sanctioning authority *or* without decision-making responsibility are classified as nonmanaging partners.

[b] "Nonmanagerial decision-makers": people who make decisions but have *no* subordinates and are classified as "nonmanagement" in terms of levels of supervision were merged with semiautonomous employees (if they are autonomous) or workers (if they are nonautonomous) throughout.

37

Authority is a four-level measure of whether a lawyer has in relation to others (1) sanctioning authority (can impose sanctions on subordinates, such as assigning raises and promotions), (2) task authority (gives directions to subordinates), (3) nominal supervision (supervises without sanctioning or task authority), or (4) no supervisory responsibility (supervises nobody other than clerical subordinates). About a third of the Toronto sample had sanctioning or task authority (36 percent), while nearly two-thirds had no specific supervisory authority other than in relation to clerical employees (63 percent).

Decision making is a measure that distinguishes lawyers in terms of amount of participation in organizational decisions. Just over 70 percent of the Toronto sample participated in at least one area of decision making, while another 17 percent provided advice only, and about 12 percent were uninvolved.

Autonomy ranks lawyers according to the amount of independence they exercise in designing aspects of their work. About 88 percent of the Toronto sample designed at least some aspects of their work, but the remaining 12 percent of this sample designed few or no aspects of their work, and were in this sense nonautonomous.

This collection of measures is particularly helpful in distinguishing among lawyers in the middle and lower levels of professional practice. An important purpose of our typology is to differentiate among a range of positions at these levels that is noticed but only articulated in a general way by lawyers, as reflected in the following comment by a respondent: "When you're younger you're more at the beck and call of the more senior members of the firm. . . . As I get more senior I can work on those parts of the case that I feel need my attention or would interest me, and I can ask one of the juniors to do what you might say is the more tedious work. . . . The more junior people in the corporate department, they read the agreement to make sure the commas are in the right place, the periods are in the right places, etc." Our typology adds precision to the more general distinctions implied by such comments.

A final distinction among employers of lawyers is drawn in terms of representation in, or *corporate linkages* into, the directorships and executive positions of dominant corporations. This distinction derives from the work of Clement (1975; see also Niosi, 1978), who defines an "elite law firm" as one in which one or more partners serve as directors or executives of a dominant corporation, that is, a corporation with over $250 million in assets and $50 million in annual income. The *Financial Post "500"* and *Directory of Directors* were used to identify these corporations and representation from Toronto law firms.

We can now begin to use these dimensions of power to distinguish among employers of lawyers. First, lawyers who are designated by our typology as *managing partners in large elite firms* are partners who directly participate in at least one area of firm decision making and who have two or more levels of subordinates over whom they have sanctioning or task authority, in an elite firm with thirty or more employees. In the vernacular of the profession, these are senior or managing partners of large elite firms. However, note that the profession itself has no operational criteria to identify specifically persons occupying such positions.

Next in our typology are *managing partners in medium to large firms*, who are distinguished by some of the same criteria (ownership, authority, decision making, and hierarchical position) as members of the former group, but who differ in that no member of their firm sits on the board or is the executive of a dominant corporation and the firm may have as few as ten employees (including partners). The latter number is somewhat arbitrary but is suggested in the work of Wright et al. (1982:717).

We refer to *non*managing partners of medium and large firms as *supervising partners*. These are partners with no sanctioning or task authority and no direct participation in decision making, working in firms with more than ten employees.

Partners in small firms are the next group in our typology. Their firms have two to nine employees. *Solo practitioners* are identified as having zero or one employee.

The remaining lawyers in our typology are employees. *Managing and supervising lawyers* are employees who are associates in firms, or lawyers in government or corporate settings, who have at least nominal supervisory responsibilities and at least one level of employees below them.

The last levels of our typology consist of semiautonomous and nonautonomous lawyers. *Semiautonomous lawyers* have no managerial or supervisory responsibilities and no one below them organizationally other than secretaries, but they do design some important aspects of their work. *Nonautonomous lawyers* design only a few or no important aspects of their work. This last grouping may correspond to what some have called a "deprofessionalized working class," "mental workers," or a "professional proletariat" (Derber, 1982; Spangler, 1986).

While lawyers do not talk in explicit terms of the kinds of positions we have identified in our typology, there is, as noted earlier, an awareness of differences of power among lawyers that is often discussed in terms of seniority and areas of practice. For example, it frequently is noted that the early years of corporate and commercial practice in firms can involve work that is often highly routinized and nonautonomous, so that even young lawyers doing corporate and commercial work often fall into the categories of semiautonomous and nonautonomous lawyers. With allowance for overstatement, one respondent in our Toronto sample commented that "[b]eing a junior lawyer in a Toronto firm is probably the last of the 'slave shops.'" Another respondent remarked of his activity during this period that "most of the work was on files, not for clients. I call it assembly-line law, and I did it for four years. It was stressful and unsatisfying." A third respondent observed that during this time "practicing law was like working as a glorified factory worker. The tasks were repetitive and involved little imagination, although a good deal of mental stamina."

An idea of the form this work can take is provided in the comment of a managing partner working in the securities area of a large firm:

> I guess the lower you are the more your priorities are determined by other people . . . . It's probably that, certainly in my practice anyway, there's a meeting function, there's an answering the telephone function, and there's a paperwork function. And sort of dealing with the clients tends to go more to the senior people, in terms of structuring or more sophisticated things; the dealing with them at a level of collecting information and things falls to more junior people; the meeting function gets split up in the way I described, but the actual generation of paper tends to go to junior people, and even with word processors and routine and everything, it's a major time-consuming task and so if you come around here at night, that is mostly what the junior people do. So, at the end of meetings apart from other things I do, I could in theory go home, then come back and do that work and my involvement would be a review of that. It might take me 1/2 hour to review something it takes them 10 hours to produce. And I guess that's the difference.

Such comments communicate a sense that the time and drudgery involved in the work of younger nonautonomous lawyers is noticed, but also expected. A corporate and commercial partner in a large firm observes,

> There is a progression . . . that goes through, I think for the first couple of years, being a lackey, because really all you can do is work, work . . . . I look at our juniors and see the kind of hours they put in and I find it amazing that they do it and put up with it . . . . It is a tremendous sacrifice in terms of their health, in terms of outside interests and family life. It really does get decimated, and . . . certainly in the rest of the firm, . . . [there] is unquestioned acceptance of the premise that they should be doing this . . . . It would be thought of as a bad thing if more people were going home at five o'clock. And it would be a bad thing because there is no conceivable way you can do enough work . . . with an eight-hour day . . . . It would not produce the kind of economic returns people expect.

Table 2.2
Percentage of Lawyers by Typology Category, Toronto, 1985

Category	Best Estimate	Minimum	Maximum
Managing Partners in Large, Elite Firms	4.5%	2.7%	12.0%
Managing Partners in Medium to Large Firms	12.4	11.4	13.8
Nonmanaging Partners in Medium to Large Firms	11.9	11.8	21.9
Partners in Small Firms	15.7	5.9	19.0
Solo Practitioners	9.1	5.0	N.A.
Managing/Supervising Lawyers	12.1	11.0	36.4
Semiautonomous Lawyers	25.6	9.1	31.8
Nonautonomous Lawyers	8.7	2.9	26.2

Notes: $N = 995$.

Ranges were based on the following criteria:

Managing Partners in Large, Elite Firms: minimum = employer + more than 30 employees + elite firm + task and sanctioning authority + participates directly in policy making + no level above respondent + 2 or more levels below respondent; maximum = employer + more than 30 employees + task or sanctioning authority + 2 or more levels below respondent decision-maker.

Managing Partners in Medium to Large Firms: minimum = employer + 10 or more employees + task and sanctioning authority + 2 or more levels below respondent + participates directly in policy making; maximum = employer + 10 or more employees + task and sanctioning authority + 2 or more levels below respondents.

Nonmanaging Partners in Medium to Large Firms: minimum = employer + 10 or more employees + 2 or more lawyers (including self) + 1 or more levels below respondent; maximum = employer + 2 or more employees.

Partners in Small Firms: minimum = employer + 2 or more employees; maximum = employer + 1 or more employees.

Solo Practitioner: minimum = sole practitioner + 0 employees; maximum = N.A.

Managing/Supervising Lawyers: minimum = employee + decision-maker + task and sanctioning authority + 2 or more levels of authority; maximum = employee + non-decision-maker + 2 or more levels of authority.

Semiautonomous Lawyers: minimum = employee + high autonomy + minimum criteria for managers; maximum = employee + limited autonomy + minimum criteria for managers.

Nonautonomous Lawyers: minimum = employee + no autonomy + minimum criteria for managers and semiautonomous employees; maximum = employee + some autonomy + minimum criteria for managers and semiautonomous employees.

These comments suggest that our typology has face validity in distinguishing between hierarchical levels that distinguish the kinds of work lawyers do. There is no perfect way of operationalizing such distinctions, but as we demonstrate next, it is nonetheless possible, using such a typology, to provide estimates that constitute reasonable approximations of the hierarchical structure of the profession, and, in turn, of how it is changing.

We do this by first using our typology in table 2.2 to describe the structure of the legal profession in Toronto in 1985, using the Toronto panel sample weighted to represent the lawyer population of this city. This table varies the operational definitions of the categories in our typology to provide maximum, minimum, and "best" estimates of the different groupings and to allow more detailed consideration of arbitrary or arguable aspects of the typology categories. For example, one of the most interesting findings in table 2.2 is that the largest category is composed of about a quarter of our sample, who by our best estimate are semiautonomous employees (25.6 percent). However, if our definition of supervising lawyers is restricted to require task and sanctioning authority, then the maximum estimate of the semiautonomous group of lawyers increases to 31.8 percent. When added to our best estimate of the nonautonomous grouping, at 8.7 percent, the result is a combination of categories with limited autonomy that makes up more than 40 percent of the sample. Alternatively, if the operational definition of semiautonomous lawyers is constrained to include only lawyers who have high levels of autonomy, the size of the nonautonomous grouping is increased to over a quarter (26.2 percent) of the sample. In any case, our combined best estimates of semiautonomous and nonautonomous lawyers include over a third (34.3 percent) of the sample, a finding that indicates the legal profession has a large group of lawyers whose independence is restricted and who in this sense are a subordinated group.

Further evidence of the highly stratified structure of the legal profession is the size of the employer groupings. Our best estimate is that 4.5 percent of the sample are managing partners of large, elite firms. If elite firm membership is removed from our operationalization, that is, if we define this grouping as simply managing partners of large firms, this estimate increases to 12 percent. The latter figure is comparable in size to the groupings of managing and supervising partners in medium to large firms. So between a quarter and a third of our 1985 Toronto sample is made up of partners in firms with more than ten persons. Another 15.7 percent are partners in small firms, while solo practitioners make up 9.1 percent of the sample.

In sum, our typology reveals that nearly half the lawyers in the 1985 Toronto sample are employees. Together, managing/supervising, semiautonomous, and nonautonomous lawyers are 46.4 percent of the sample. Since the managing/supervising lawyers make up only 12.1 percent of this figure, a great many lawyer employees assume roles that are subordinate and restricted in autonomy, even if they may still be relatively well paid. Overall, the typology displays a profession that is highly stratified, with managing partners in large, elite firms at one extreme, and semi- and nonautonomous lawyers at the other. We now can use this typology to assess our predictions that in relative terms the partnership pool of the profession is shrinking, while all other categories of employed lawyers are growing — to the disadvantage of many men, and the greater disadvantage of women.

The Changing Structure of Legal Practice, 1977–1988

Specific kinds of data are required to explore the predictions we have made about the changing structure of the legal profession. To begin, considerable detail is required of the kind included in our typology to locate individuals correctly in terms of the positions they occupy in the structure of the profession, and further information is required on how individuals are distributed across these positions at different points in time. Data for this kind of analysis of the legal profession are difficult to assemble.

This is not surprising, since it is also true in the study of occupational stratification more generally. However, we have described in detail elsewhere (Hagan et al., 1991) the application of a strategy developed in the literature on occupational stratification to combine data sets to analyze changes in occupational structure over time (see Wright and Singlemann, 1982). We can summarize this work to give a general picture of the changing structure of the Toronto legal profession over a ten-year period; we then follow this with a shorter five-year asessment based on a comparison of the primary data from our surveys of Toronto lawyers. Although restricted to a half rather than a full decade, the latter comparison should be more precise than our earlier analysis, and it includes the beginning of the recession of the eighties and early nineties. To the extent the two accounts converge, we can be confident in our conclusions.

First, we bring together data from the initial wave of the 1985 Toronto lawyer survey with data gathered from 1977 and 1988 records of the Law Society of Upper Canada. Together, these data allow us to estimate aggregate changes over more than a decade in the structure of legal practice for men and women in Toronto.

We do this with the assistance of our typology, which separates lawyers into managing partners, supervising partners, partners in small firms, solo practitioners, managing/supervising lawyers, semiautonomous lawyers, and nonautonomous lawyers. Because of limitations in the Law Society data, the criteria for managing partners must initially be relaxed to represent this group more broadly as including firms with ten or more employees. Later, the restriction of managing partners to larger, elite firms is reintroduced to make further comparisons. For the moment, then, managing partners are employers (i.e., they are partners), in a medium-to-large firm (i.e., ten or more employees), where they exercise sanctioning authority (e.g., deciding promotions, raises, etc.) or task authority (e.g., giving directions), participate directly in decision making, and have two or more levels of subordinates below them.

The linkage of information from the different data sets involves imputing the lawyer categories from the 1985 Toronto survey results into the 1977 and 1988 Law Society records based on cruder types of employment and experience groupings that can be identified in all three sources. The assumptions and transformations involved are documented in considerable detail elsewhere (Hagan et al., 1991:247-51). The results are summarized on the left side of table 2.3.

The results in this part of table 2.3 support our speculation about the centralization and concentration of cultural capital by indicating that in relative terms the structure of the profession has expanded at the lower and middle levels, while it has contracted at the top. For example, the proportion of male lawyers in the lower semiautonomous and nonautonomous groupings increased from about 23 to 33 percent, while the proportion of female lawyers in these groupings increased from about 47 percent to over 58 percent. There was also growth for men and women in managerial supervisory positions: from about 9 to 13 percent for men, and from about 13 to 18 percent for women.

However, the patterns of redistribution differ for men and women. The decline in female partnerships is most marked in small firms, from about 14 to 6 percent, while the proportionate declines of male lawyers are quite uniform across partnerships and solo practice, with reductions of around 3 to 4 percent. Both men and women experienced relative reductions in all kinds of partnerships, including managing partners, supervising partners, partners in small firms, and solo practitioners.

Overall, of course, a much smaller proportion of women than men are partners. For example, in 1988 nearly 17 percent of men, compared to less than 6 percent of women, were managing partners, and altogether about 54 percent of the men were partners, compared to about 24 percent of the women. In 1977 the respective figures were about 69 percent for men and 40 percent for women. Both genders lost in terms of partnership shares over the decade, but in relative terms women lost more.

It might reasonably be argued that these aggregate changes within genders in partnership shares reflect changes in the experience composition of men and women lawyers in the profession, for we have seen that many young lawyers entered legal practice over this period. We will not elaborate here a shift-share analysis we undertook to address this kind of issue (but see Hagan et al., 1991:251-53). However, we can note that this analysis does not alter the general picture. This is because by 1977 women had already entered the profession in large numbers and (as we saw in chapter 1) with few predecessors, so that by 1988 their aggregate age actually in-

Table 2.3
Changes in the Structure of the Legal Profession for Women and Men, Toronto, 1977–1988, 1985–1990

| | 1977–1988 Estimates | | | | 1985–1990 Estimates | | | |
| | Men Lawyers | | Women Lawyers | | Men Lawyers | | Women Lawyers | |
Positions	1977 N = 3,796	1988 N = 6,537	1977 N = 251	1988 N = 1,842	1985 N = 583	1990 N = 574	1985 N = 185	1990 N = 265
Managing Partners [a]	20.5	16.9	6.4	5.5	14.1(3.6)	8.3(7.1)	6.0(2.5)	3.3(2.8)
Supervising Partners	15.5	12.2	6.0	4.9	11.3	11.2	5.0	5.2
Partners in Small Firms	18.2	15.2	13.9	5.6	13.2	3.4	7.2	1.9
Solo Practitioners	14.5	10.1	13.9	8.1	8.6	18.7	7.9	8.1
Managing/Supervising Lawyers	8.9	13.0	12.8	17.6	12.5	10.2	11.9	9.7
Semiautonomous Lawyers	17.7	24.9	31.5	39.9	29.3	32.2	34.9	42.7
Nonautonomous Lawyers	5.7	7.7	15.5	18.3	9.1	14.8	17.2	19.0
Part-time or Unemployed Lawyers					1.8	1.1	9.9	10.1

[a] Figures for managing partners in large, elite firms in parentheses.

45

creased. So women should actually have *increased* their partnership shares between 1977 and 1988. Yet both men and women encountered a ceiling on mobility during this period, and women were affected by this ceiling more than men. To ensure that our findings were not an artifact of changes in the government/corporate sector of the profession, we replicated our analyses with the latter sectors deleted, with little change in results.

The Changing Structure of Legal Practice, 1985–1990

We can now confirm and extend the preceding analysis by combining re-sults from the first-wave 1985 Toronto survey with results from the 1990 Ontario survey. In doing so, we will also check on problems of representa-tiveness that may have emerged as a result of attrition of respondents be-tween the 1985 and 1991 waves of the Toronto survey. (This issue is dis-cussed further in the Appendix.) Our primary purpose remains that of docu-menting the changing structure of legal practice, this time from 1985 to 1990, using primary survey data rather than Law Society record estimates for the two time points.

To first assure the representativeness of our two-wave Toronto sur-vey, we compared the distribution of Toronto lawyers across positions in 1985, as indicated by the wave 1 and wave 2 samples surveyed in 1985 and 1991 in Toronto. The purpose of this comparison was to determine if the limited attrition of lawyer respondents in the second wave of the survey had in notable ways systematically impaired the representativeness of the To-ronto panel design. It will be important to know in later chapters if such an attrition bias occurred. However, the distributions of respondents by cat-egories were quite similar across waves, suggesting that selective attrition did not reduce the representativeness of the panel sample. Other compari-sons also indicated little or no reason to think that selective attrition was a problem across waves. For example, 81.1 percent of the weighted sample was male in 1985, compared to 79.2 percent in 1991, a difference that could easily result from expected gender differences in mortality.

More interesting substantive comparisons can be made between the Toronto panel begun in 1985 and the Ontario survey undertaken in 1990, in terms of the changing structure of the profession that we considered in the preceding section. In that analysis we joined the 1985 Toronto survey with Law Society data to estimate decade-long shifts in the profession, which we concluded involved a contraction in the employer sector and an expansion in the employee sector of the profession. With adjustments, we can use the Toronto and Ontario surveys to further explore this shift in the distribution of lawyers across the profession.

One obvious adjustment is that the 1990 Ontario survey had to be divided into those lawyers working inside and outside Toronto. In addition, because the Ontario survey included only entrants into the profession for the previous fifteen years (1975–1990), it was necessary to restrict the 1985 Toronto survey to a comparable fifteen-year period (1970–1985). The wave 1 Toronto survey is restricted in this way and divided by gender in the right-hand side of table 2.3, along with the part of the Ontario survey that includes those lawyers working in Toronto and also divided by gender (overall comparisons undivided by gender are presented in the Appendix). Adjusted in these ways, results of the two surveys presented in the right side of table 2.3 provide an overall picture of the Toronto legal profession in 1985 and 1990; that is, before and during the recent economic recession.

The comparison presented shows again a growth in the lower levels of the profession that include nonautonomous and semiautonomous lawyers, which are the largest segments of the profession. As well, the important role of gender can be further observed. Thus the largest grouping of lawyers in this as in the other tables includes the semiautonomous lawyers, with the representation of women in this position increasing from about 35 to 43 percent, while men's representation increased only from about 29 to 32 percent. Meanwhile, both men and women experienced relative declines in positions as managing partners and small-firm partners, with women almost disappearing from among the latter. Alternatively, almost all of the growth in solo practice occurred among men, with nearly 19 percent of men in solo practice in 1990. And, when managing partnership is restricted to large, elite firms, almost the entire gain is among men (from 3.6 to 7.1 percent) rather than women (from 2.5 to 2.8 percent). Both men and women increased their representation in nonautonomous positions.

Overall, this set of comparisons confirms the shift noted in the preceding section from employer to employee positions in the profession: from 53.7 percent of Toronto lawyers being employees in 1985, to 61.7 percent in 1990. Beyond this, the most striking findings involve the gains for men as managing partners in large, elite firms but not for women; the shrinking proportion of both men and women lawyers in positions as other kinds of managing partners and partners in small firms; the increase in the proportion of men who are now solo practitioners; the increase in the proportion of men and women who are nonautonomous lawyers; and the increasing proportion of women in positions as semiautonomous lawyers. All of these changes reflect shifts in the structure of the profession. Particularly striking are the increases in the proportions of lawyers in nonautonomous and semiautonomous positions. In 1990 in Toronto, about 47 percent of men lawyers are in these positions, compared to about 62 percent of women. Again, men and women are affected by these changes, but women are affected more.

A Ceiling in Legal Practice

Professions traditionally have prided themselves on the autonomous careers they provide their members. Yet we have found that the proportions of lawyers who today achieve autonomy is declining, and that the majority of contemporary men and women lawyers do not have extensive autonomy in determining their work environments. Men and women are developing careers in a legal profession whose parameters are changing in ways that traditional conceptions of professional autonomy would not predict.

One of the most notable of these changes involves the process by which cultural capital is being centralized and concentrated in the partnerships of firms. This process of change has resulted in women being unable proportionately to increase their share of powerful partnership positions in the profession, while their representation in nonmanagerial positions has increased. This is not simply a product of the larger number of younger lawyers in practice but rather reflects a change in the structure of the profession itself. This pattern is consistent with the popular notion of a glass ceiling on upward mobility at high levels of the occupational structure for women. While in absolute terms the actual numbers of men and women lawyers at the top of the profession is increasing, in relative terms women lawyers are not expanding their share of the powerful partnership positions that dominate this profession. This ceiling affects some men as well, but it is more pronounced for women.

It is important in all of this to keep in mind how demanding the nonautonomous and semiautonomous roles of lawyers struggling at the lower levels of the legal profession can be, in spite of the ample salaries. The comments from an interview with a woman lawyer in our research provides some insight into the strains of maintaining a personal life in the face of unyielding demands at the lower levels of practice.

> My first two years I really screwed up, no question about it whatsoever. My spouse left me, last October, as a result of the amount that I was working; he said he couldn't handle that anymore. He left, I sort of looked around at that point and said, you know, 'What am I doing?' I had gained, from the time that I had started practicing, thirty pounds, and that was from sitting at my desk eating chocolates, cookies, you know, and whatever fast munchy food, and not looking after myself. Not exercising. . . . So, when my spouse left, sort of like closing the gate after the horse is gone, but I started reevaluating it

and, you know, there has to be some room for balance and if I have to give this much time to my career, then maybe I shouldn't be doing it. Maybe I'm not cut out for this. So, in the past ten months, I guess, I've made a concerted effort to get a better balance. I've gone to the fitness club, I've lost the thirty pounds. . . . Now I try to exercise regularly, although I keep getting these colds, so I go weeks without doing it. And I've tried to take one day of the weekend off, for sure. [So you work one day of the weekend?] Yes. [Here or home?] Here, usually. . . . It's really hard. [Do you work evenings?] Yes. [Late?] Yes. [And you obviously get in early.] I'm not a morning person, I try to get here by 8:30, but I don't always make it. Some mornings I'm here by 7:30. . . . The work just keeps coming. And notwithstanding the fact that I do have a partner, sort of more or less my mentor, the person I junior for, kind of looking after me, I got caught in a kind of Catch-22 because he's an absolute workaholic, so he just sends out copious amounts of work, and at the same time, although we have a junioring system, you can't be, you don't want to cut yourself off from the rest of the firm, because that one person is not going to be, when the vote comes to be a partner, isn't going to be enough to swing it, so you've got to do work for other people so they get to know you and get to know the quality of the work that you can do.

One might discount the significance of accounts like this by regarding them as unfortunate but atypical, or as a regrettable but transitory phase of private practice in firms. As if to make our point by counterexample, a male respondent in our study advised,

There is money to be made in law in Toronto. However, it is being made by the survivors of over five years at bar with (a) employment and advancement in a big firm, or (b) a private practice in which the costs have been kept under tight control, and (c) an ability not to feel compelled to buy personal big-ticket items shortly after graduation, plus (d) a working spouse. For us survivors, practice in Toronto is a hell of a lot of fun!

For some lawyers this is true, but for others the ordeal lingers, or changes in only marginal ways, or results in leaving private practice or practice entirely. The proportion of lawyers in the profession in employee roles is increasing, while proportionately fewer lawyers are rising to partnership positions, and women are more affected by these trends than men.

This chapter has provided a series of empirical snapshots taken at several points of time over approximately the last decade. They reveal a profession that is, to use the currently popular term, restructuring. Many men as well as women are affected, but women are affected more, as they try to break through the glass ceiling to join the shrinking partnership class.

How does this happen in the careers of individual women, compared to men? In the following chapters, we consider how women find legal jobs and begin to practice, how they sometimes become partners and in other instances change legal sectors or leave practice entirely, the ways in which they balance their work lives with families, how they fare compared to men in earnings, and the pleasures and perils they find in practice. In short, we will examine a number of dimensions and stages in the lives of lawyers who are moving through a profession that is itself in a process of change.

3

Beginning to Practice

Though I am very satisfied with my job, I might have waited and looked for other positions with other firms before taking my present position, had the job market not been so tight. But my name and family background probably helped me. My father was well known in the investment business, and I come from a very WASP Toronto family. On the other hand my marks and ability are very good, so I believe the employers wanted me more for my ability than family connections.

Auspicious Beginnings

First jobs are often memorable, and finding them sometimes more so, at least for the individuals involved. This may be especially so for law graduates, for whom entry into the profession can be an auspicious beginning, full of possibility and promise. Yet we know little about the process of seeking first jobs, and the risks as well as opportunities provided by the jobs found. It is commonly assumed that first jobs are important, in part because they can establish career paths, for example, of earnings and influence. Beyond this, the process of job finding remains somewhat mysterious, subject to frequent but largely uninformed speculation by job seekers and holders alike. However, there is some comparative and empirical material to draw on, which we review before turning to findings from our own research in Toronto.

Legal Practices of Apprenticeship

Forms of apprenticeship are a common, though perhaps declining, require-
ment of beginning legal practice in many countries. Abel (1989:90) suggests
that there may be a loose inverse relationship between formal education and
apprenticeship, in which the former gradually replaces the latter. An example of this might be the case of the United States, where apprenticeship in
law virtually disappeared with the rise of formal university training at the
turn of the twentieth century. However, Abel notes that even in the United
States associate positions with large firms and clerkships with judges, as
well as many first jobs in legal aid or government settings, have taken on
some features of apprenticeship. Formal apprenticeships continue in such
countries as Great Britain, Germany, France, Belgium, Italy, and, most importantly for our purposes, in Canada.

So that while Canadian universities also have assumed the primary
responsibility for educating lawyers, law societies nonetheless have retained
control over entry to the profession through a process of "articling" throughout
the country. Arthurs, Weisman, and Zemans (1986) suggest that the continuing Canadian attachment to apprenticeship through articling reflects a
distinctive long-term commitment by the profession to the socialization of
its new members. They write that ". . . the primary function of both articling
and bar admission courses . . . has been less to educate than to socialize
students, to symbolically continue the nineteenth-century system of professional formation" (498). This is especially apparent in the large firms, where
a professional sense of purpose and position is quickly transmitted to new
initiates, and where "idiosyncratic personal behavior, political views, or life-
styles are tolerated only to a limited degree" (499).

Yet the process of articling is rather loosely structured, despite efforts by the law societies to establish standards and expectations for articling principals and their students. These standards and expectations oblige
principals to teach students how to practice, to observe standards of professional conduct, to manage the business affairs of the law office, and to deal
with other institutions and actors in the legal system. However, the reality is
that the articling process is not directly monitored, and the relationship between principal and student becomes individualized in relation to specific
practice needs. Legal research and drafting are often the most advanced
forms this work takes, and more often the work of articling involves more
prosaic forms of logistical support, with little opportunity for interviewing,
advocacy or negotiation that form more central parts of the contemporary
practice of law.

Students seek articling positions with firms through an interviewing process that is much like other forms of job finding. This leaves room for personal and proactive contacts, as well as more formally structured methods of job finding. In Ontario, students who wish to be certified to practice complete an articling period and then undertake a bar admission course and final bar admission examination, given by the Law Society of Upper Canada.

Arthurs et al. point out that while education is secondary to socialization as a purpose of legal apprenticeship, it is also the case that this process is further oriented toward finding more permanent positions that will continue beyond articling. Large firms in particular use articling as a mechanism to "try out" students who they might want to "hire back" as new associates following their completion of the bar admission course and call to the bar. Smaller firms are more likely to use articling students as a means of easing their workload, with students less frequently hired back into more permanent positions. Students more eagerly seek large-firm placements, then, not only for their prestige and professional quality, but also for the prospects of continuing employment they provide.

While students clearly compete for placements, firms also compete for the best students. Especially during the expansionary period of the 1980s, large firms aggressively recruited top students with pregraduation summer employment and compensation programs that continued through the bar admission course and examination period. Arthurs et al. (1986:499) argue that these competitive pressures helped to make the process of articling less particularistic than in the past, especially in large firm settings. They suggest that

> [w]hile historically these firms may have tended to recruit new members primarily on the basis of the "old school tie," there is now a much greater emphasis on academic credentials. This reflects, in part, the need for able students and juniors to handle sophisticated legal work; in part, the diminishing acceptability in Canada of discrimination in any form of employment; and in part, the growing economic power of various minority groups, whose legal business is more likely to gravitate to law firms that are seen to be willing to hire their best young members, than to those firms that discriminate against them.

In making these points, Arthurs et al. are not suggesting that legal practice is an undifferentiated or distinctively meritocratic profession. For example, they also note that historically entry to the profession has been disproportionately reserved for persons from professional families and other privileged socioeconomic groups and that there is an overrepresentation of white Anglo-Saxon males compared to minorities and women in the upper reaches of private and public practice. Minorities other than women are so poorly represented in our study that their fates could not be analyzed beyond making this basic point. However, the point that Arthurs et al. make is that these sources of stratification have operated most prominently through the educational process that leads up to admission into legal education, and through the processes of promotion and advancement that structure middle and later stages of legal careers.

In between, selection into articling positions and first jobs may be more meritocratic, at least for majority-group women and men entering the field today. That is, entry into legal careers may begin for these men and women on a relatively even playing field, and then become more uneven with the passage of time. As Abel (1989:118) notes, "Subsequent decisions are less visible and centralized, allowing greater opportunity for discrimination." Oddly, research on the legal profession and other occupations has not spent much time considering the possibility that employment discrimination varies across groups and stages and with time in careers. As we will suggest later, this possibility has potentially important implications for the experiences of individuals as well as for our understanding of occupational stratification more generally. Meanwhile, note that relative equality at the articling and first-job stages of professional practice would also fit with the need described in the previous chapter for large firms of the profession during the expansionary phase of the 1980s to employ large numbers of compliant new lawyers into lower-paying positions with uncertain mobility prospects. To put the matter in the vernacular of human capital theory, if the growing demand for new entry-level lawyers was to be met in an efficient fashion, the selection of new members into the profession would need to be relatively open and meritocratic. The needs of the profession would be best met by recruiting the best new human capital available.

Studies of Entry into the Legal Profession

Research documenting entry into the legal profession has primarily examined the extent to which the allocation of articling positions and first jobs has, as Arthurs et al. (1986) suggest, overcome its earlier prejudicial and particularistic tendencies, particularly in regard to its treatment of women. This research literature is not extensive, but it does provide consideration of England and the United States as well as Canada.

An English study reported in the early 1980s by Podmore and Spencer (1982) begins by describing a three-tier structure of legal practice in England that at the time consisted of a top, virtually all-male, professional tier, a virtually all-male middle tier made up of managing clerks and legal executives, and a nearly exclusively female lower tier of secretaries, typists, and receptionists. They suggest on this basis that the English legal profession is an excellent example of a sex-typed "male" profession, with normative expectations that keep it so.

Of course, the sex-typing of legal practice and its representation in the tiered structure of this profession is a feature of lawyering that is more broadly noted in the United States, Canada, and elsewhere (see Epstein, 1981). This point is illustrated by a respondent in our research, who commented:

> When I was in private practice, sexual harassment was a major issue. Some was overt, but most was of the undermining type, for example, being called "sweetie" or "dear" in front of clients, attention brought to one's dress, lack of general respect as an equal. At my firm, a partner once fired a receptionist because he thought she wasn't pretty enough and then boasted about it. When I reviewed my personnel file prior to leaving, I read the hiring partner's notes on my original résumé — "easy on the eyes." I guess that was the basis upon which I was hired as the second female lawyer in the firm!

Another woman lawyer commented, "[A]rticling was a horrible experience. . . . I was sexually harassed, verbally abused, and generally miserable." A third respondent who reported having filed a successful complaint during her search for an articling position warned that "usually the discrimination is more subtle because lawyers often are savvy enough to disguise it. Garden-variety remarks include, 'she's nice, just not cutthroat enough.'" Another woman lawyer recalled, "Although I sincerely believe that the profession generally is trying to beat discrimination, it is out there and alive and well. I particularly noticed this when applying for jobs. There were a few jobs that I was well qualified for but did not get, I believe, because I was not male. . . . There are still many firms out there that will only hire lawyers that are male . . . , regardless of qualifications."

For their English study, Podmore and Spencer interviewed twenty-eight barristers and forty-eight solicitors, mostly in private practice, about their experiences in entering this sex-typed legal profession. At the time of this study in England, entry into the profession required a period of apprenticeship through articles with a solicitor or pupillage with a barrister. This study found, as have other studies that address this issue, that many women encounter lines of inquiry and attitudes of hostility that make interviewing for positions of apprenticeship a harrowing experience. For example, respondents report:

> The main concern of those that interviewed you was that, apart from being a woman, I was married, and they felt that being married it was virtually inevitable that I would have children. . . .

> On a couple of occasions . . . it was stated quite clearly that they didn't want another woman, because you'd probably no sooner get settled than you'd get married and want children, and what was the point?

> As soon as you sign Miss or Mrs. at the bottom of the letter [of application] . . . you're at a disadvantage straightaway.

Women in this study also reported that they received little general training during their articles and that they felt this tended to channel them toward "desk-bound" areas of practice such as conveyancing (particularly property transactions), wills and probate, and matrimonial (divorce) work. These views parallel reports in our surveys that "women lawyers tend to get slotted into family law and into other areas where there are fewer partnership and income opportunities."

However, Podmore and Spencer found a quite different picture when they considered the transition to first jobs following articles and pupillage. The results indicate that of twenty-three barristers in private practice, twenty-one obtained a tenancy in the same chambers where they apprenticed, while the two who were not retained in positions found tenancies elsewhere in a short time. Similarly, Podmore and Spencer (1982) report that "[S]olicitors in general had few problems at this stage because a place is usually made in practice (or other work organization) for the newly qualified solicitor who has demonstrated his or her efficiency as an articled clerk" (348).

A final point that emerges in this English study involves the special characteristics of first jobs and the role we have suggested this may play in opening the profession to women at the entry level. In earlier chapters we noted that during the expansionary 1980s women may have been willingly accepted into lower-level entry positions because they were highly qualified, eager to work, and, in human capital vernacular, relatively unlikely to shirk responsibilities or grab assets, while displaying compliance in relation to demands for mobility and compensation. Women in the study by Podmore and Spencer (1982:353) echoed these impressions. For example, respondents reported that:

> I think they like having women work for them, because they think they will probably work harder (which they tend to do) and work for less money (which they also tend to do) and wouldn't be so keen on picking up a partnership, which is true as well.

> I think the disadvantage comes now, at the stage that I've reached, where you're talking about partnership . . . if you were a man you'd automatically be offered some sort of future within a firm, and I don't think it is so automatic with a woman. (353)

Similarly, a senior woman lawyer in our sample commented, "[W]hile women now have equal access in terms of entry into the profession, my experience is that they end up in job ghettoes where they earn less than their counterparts."

Again, the above comments are important in highlighting the possibility that discriminatory practices can vary by stage of career. Meanwhile, more recent American support for the English experience with first jobs, as reported by Podmore and Spencer, is found in a study undertaken in 1986 of 892 Stanford law graduates (Stanford Law Project, 1988). In the absence of a formal apprenticeship process in the United States, this study begins its analysis of careers in practice with first jobs. This analysis reports similarities by gender in the early job-finding experiences of men and women, with the result that "no significant differences were found in the expected or actual location of the first job after law school, or in the substantive practice area desired or realized." In general, this study reports relative equality in the process of finding first employment.

Several studies of articling and first employment are available for Canada, where we have noted that articling is required in all provinces. The first Canadian study of women in legal practice was published by Harvey in 1970, and therefore predates the large-scale entry of women into the profession. This may partly explain why although 106 respondents in this study reported they felt the existence of discrimination, 166 respondents either did not respond or stated that discrimination did not occur, indicating that it existed "only in the minds of women who were going to inordinate lengths to find or imagine it" (Harvey, 1970:11). Nonetheless, Harvey indicates that among the most common complaints were reports related to finding a first job.

Another study by Dranoff (1972) from about the same period focused on women lawyers in Toronto, finding that 74 percent of the respondents perceived discrimination while searching for articling positions, compared to 60 percent who perceived discrimination in seeking positions after the bar admission exam. In the same year, a study by Smith, Stephenson, and Quijano (1972) reported the difficulties of women in finding articling positions in British Columbia. They found women to have a significant disadvantage in their search for articles, and that more women than men settled for positions that were not of their first choice. They observe that "It is not a matter of men succeeding and women not, or *vice versa*. It is a matter of more men having more to choose from, and sooner, than most women. Not surprisingly, more men are able to place in firms that are their first choice" (162). Their conclusion is "Discrimination does exist."

The largest and most systematic study of articling and the job search in Canada was undertaken by Marie Huxter (1981) during the late 1970s in Ontario. Nearly three thousand graduates of six Ontario law schools took part in a survey focused on the search for articling positions and first jobs. The results of this study replicate some of the findings from British Columbia. For example, 71 percent of the men compared to 62 percent of the women were successful in finding articling positions with the kind or size of firm preferred, and thirty days after the bar admission course 43 percent of the men compared to 31 percent of the women had found employment. As in earlier studies, more than a third of the women also reported being asked objectionable questions. As in British Columbia, Huxter (1981:212) concludes that "discrimination exists."

Huxter also goes on to inquire what kinds of factors students thought helped or hindered seeking articling positions or first jobs. The factor thought helpful by the most respondents, both male and female, was family, social, business, or other kinds of contacts. Several of the interview comments about the role of contacts are revealing. For example, one of Huxter's (1981:196) respondents reports, "My father is a prominent Canadian political figure — which I suspect helped me get job offers in the Toronto area. On the basis of the existing job market, those being asked to stay with firms have been able to bring business with them or have personal contacts. The competence seems to be presumed if you are in a reputable firm — it is who you know that determines whether or not you stay." Another respondent in Huxter's Ontario survey (1981:200) commented on the perceived role of lack of contacts: "Lack of family or social contacts in the legal profession probably hindered me judging by the fact that schoolmates/friends with comparable qualifications obtained articling positions with far less effort because of connections and/or their political affiliations — I am thinking of three specific cases." So both the presence and absence of contacts were judged to play a role in successful articling and job finding by respondents in this research.

Meanwhile, gender was also thought to be a problem in finding positions by women, but not by men, with 44 percent of the women seeing sex as a problematic factor in obtaining articling and employment positions. Men ranked lack of contacts as their biggest hindrance in finding positions, while women ranked gender first, marital status second, and contacts third. Huxter does not speculate further about the implications of the pattern of these findings, but it is of interest to inquire how or whether these issues might be interconnected.

Our respondents also commented on the role of contacts in the job-finding process. One respondent noted, "[M]y work environment was government, and I saw many people appointed because of connections and contacts with the minister or deputy minister." Another woman lawyer in the sample linked the issue of contacts with gender by observing that "the profession is still rife with 'old school ties' and sexist crap — it's inherent in its very structure." A third respondent recalled, "I hardly got any interviews, an experience I shared with my non-connected friends. When I did get a job, in October, it was through a man I had become friends with who was getting his divorce through that firm." However, perhaps the most striking observation was from a woman who after much difficulty in the job search concluded,

> From the outset, I realize that the law school gold medal winners have no trouble finding employment, and rightly so. However, beyond this, when I entered the market, the people who did not languish unemployed were those who, in descending order, in my view and from personal experience: had connections who got them jobs that were never even advertised; people with money who could, when things looked bad, go and do an LL.M. and stop worrying about it until things improved; men with decent grades, average-performing men; WASP women.

This woman entered the profession in the early 1980s.

Overall, the research literature we have reviewed suggests that at least during the 1970s, when women first entered law in increasing numbers, gender played a significant role in the search for articling positions. However, these findings are not unequivocal in that while most of these studies report disparities at the articling stage, some report relative equality in finding first jobs. The most recent of these studies by Huxter (1981) in Ontario suggests that success in finding both kinds of positions is also influenced by grades achieved in law school, which is at least in part consistent with Arthurs et al.'s (1986) thesis and the human capital expectation that recruitment into these entry-level positions in the legal profession may have become more meritocratic and less particularistic over time. The implication is that more recent trends may be toward equality in the initial stages of hiring, with discrimination becoming more salient at later stages in the stratification of the profession. Overlaying all of this is the intriguing issue of how personal contacts may be beneficial in finding entry points into the profession, and how this may differentially affect men and women lawyers in the early stages of practice. We turn next to an analysis of such issues in data we collected on the job search from our Toronto panel study.

Finding a Place to Practice

In spite of the valuable research reported above regarding the articling and job search among lawyers, we still know relatively little about how practicing lawyers actually find their jobs. A classic sociological study of *Getting a Job* by Marc Granovetter (1974) operationalized this question by explicitly asking respondents how they found their jobs, with their answers sorted into three categories: through personal contacts, direct application, and formal means. The category of formal means is illustrated by the use of listings of openings or advertisements. "Direct application" includes going to a specific employer or writing a formal or personal intermediary. "Personal contacts" involve learning of the job directly through informal methods of referral or through a less direct series of informal contacts.

Although Granovetter (1974:11) argues that the three methods are distinct from one another in principle, and that pure cases involving these search techniques outnumber others, he also acknowledges that the differences between methods can become blurred in specific instances. Further, arguments can be made for combining into a single category the method of direct application with either personal contacts or formal means. We followed Granovetter in treating these three methods as distinct in our analyses of the job search among Toronto lawyers, but we also adopted a more specific measure of the use of personal contacts.

This more specific measure is drawn from work done by Mostacci-Calzazera (1982) and asks whether there was "anyone you know who helped you in any way to get your job?" This question, as well as the one about methods, was asked for the Toronto respondents' search for initial articling and later positions. We focus in this chapter on this search for initial articling positions and first jobs, as reported in the 1985 Toronto survey.

We began by cross-tabulating answers to the questions about the method used in finding an articling position and about whether help was received in doing so. While the great majority of the respondents reported that they found their initial articling positions by direct application (36.5 percent) and by formal (21.4 percent) and other impersonal methods (12.6 percent), nearly a third of the respondents (29.5 percent) also indicated that they used personal contacts to find positions. Similarly, about a quarter of the respondents (24.3 percent) reported that they received help in finding an articling position. As expected, the cross-tabulation of these answers indicated that the overwhelming majority of those respondents who said they used personal contacts in finding positions also reported receiving help (80.3 percent), while some of those who directly applied (14.5 percent) or used formal means also reported receiving help (5.2 percent).

Regardless of how the question is asked, then, about a quarter to a third of all students found articling positions through personal help or contacts. Studies of a number of different blue- and white-collar occupations have routinely found that more than half of sampled respondents use personal contacts to find employment (Granovetter, 1974:5-6). So, as human capital theory and its emphasis on efficiency and merit would suggest, law firms may be relatively impersonal in their selection of new employees compared to other areas of employment. Still, a substantial proportion of articling students receive help from a personal contact in finding a position. It is of interest to know more about how this happens and with what consequences.

One immediate concern is whether men might receive more help in finding articling positions than women. However, a cross-tabulation of gender with help received by our Toronto respondents indicates that the difference is statistically insignificant, with women (26.1 percent) actually slightly more likely to report receiving help than men (24.1 percent). Nonetheless, in the analysis that follows we will see that there are some subtle differences by gender in the sources and consequences of the help received in job seeking.

For example, we expected that a prominent source of personal contacts useful in job seeking might derive from private schooling experiences. As Granovetter (1973:1371) observes, "In many cases, the contact [is] someone only marginally included in the current network of contacts, such as an old college friend . . . with whom sporadic contact [has] been maintained." Although law school contacts might be a common source of assistance, as we consider later, private school friends and contacts represent a more unique form of social and cultural capital. These friends can provide connections to other individuals who are embedded in high-status networks (see Bourdieu, 1984:122) with a potential not only for sponsorship but also access to valuable information in job seeking (see Granovetter, 1974:76-80; 1992:251).

Such ties are often mentioned in discussions of the legal profession (see Arthurs et al., 1986:499), and so we asked our respondents whether they had attended private schools at any stage of their education. Men (22.2 percent) were significantly more likely than women (14.6 percent) to have done so. Furthermore, we found that having gone to private school was significantly more likely to result in receiving help in job finding for men, with 37.6 percent of the privately schooled men receiving help, compared to 20.2 percent of the publicly schooled men. The pattern was in the same direction for women, but weaker, with the respective proportions receiving help being

32 and 25 percent. This comparison suggests that men may be better positioned than women to capitalize on private school ties as a resource in their initial job searches. So the use of private school ties may at least in part be channeled by gender, providing some support for a gender stratification perspective on job finding.

Finding Positions in Large Firms

To determine further how help in job seeking might be translated into positions at articling and in first employment, we focus below on success in attaining an articling and first-employment position in a large firm. We focus on large-firm positions because of their significance in the typology of practice positions introduced in the previous chapter, and because as noted above and now in table 3.1, both men and women lawyers most often want to practice in large firms.

Table 3.1 reports information on the settings desired and attained by the lawyers in our Toronto sample. The left-hand columns in the first row of this table reveal that more than a third of all men (35.5 percent) and a quarter of all women lawyers (26.1 percent) initially want to practice in firms of more than 20 lawyers. So that even though men may be substantially more likely to want to practice in these settings than women, and while women (12.2 percent) are more likely than men (3.8 percent) to want to practice in government settings, large firms are still the preferred first-practice settings for the largest number of both women and men lawyers. Similarly, the right side of table 3.1 reveals that while neither as many men nor women attain large-firm employment as seek it, the difference in placements by gender (25.2 percent and 21.2 percent, respectively) is not large. Meanwhile, female lawyers (22 percent) are much more likely than male lawyers (9.9 percent) to find first positions in government.

The dynamics of the profession that lead more women than men toward nonfirm settings are quite apparent in comments of our respondents. One woman lawyer remarked, "[F]ull-time practice with a good firm is very difficult to reconcile with family commitments. The time commitment is massive, which is fine if you have a calling for it, but I would have found it tedious and overwhelming." Another woman lawyer who chose government work observed, "As a new mother I see working for the government as one of the few options I have in the profession. There are few concessions made for women in private practice. I need maternity leave and some flexibility in hours after I return to work. Also I don't want to work sixty-plus hours a week on a regular basis. Government provides these options, and I enjoy the nature of the work very much." These observations make clear that the decisions of many women to work in nonfirm settings are not as freely made as

Table 3.1
First-Practice Settings Desired and Attained by Women and Men Lawyers, Toronto

First Practice Setting	Setting Desired				Setting Attained			
	Men	Women	Total	N	Men	Women	Total	N
Firm with 20+ Lawyers	35.5%	26.1%	33.7%	259	25.2%	21.2%	24.4%	187
Firm with 10–20 Lawyers	16.7	17.3	16.8	129	7.2	6.7	7.1	54
Firm with 3–9 Lawyers	22.4	18.9	21.7	166	26.0	21.0	25.0	192
With Solo Practitioner	4.4	2.9	4.1	32	10.9	5.0	9.7	74
Alone	4.3	3.2	4.1	31	6.2	9.2	6.8	52
New Firm with New Lawyers	3.3	2.1	3.0	23	2.2	2.4	2.2	56
Corporation	4.1	6.6	4.6	36	7.1	7.9	7.3	17
Academic	1.1	1.9	1.3	10	0.4	0.6	0.4	3
Government	3.8	12.2	5.6	43	9.9	22.0	12.4	95
Other	4.3	8.0	5.1	39	5.0	3.9	4.8	37
	$\chi^2 = 23.808$		$p = .005$		$\chi^2 = 22.471$		$p = .008$	

human capital theory implies. Rather, these "choices" are shaped by the nature and conditions of firm work environments, as gender stratification theory suggests.

Furthermore, many women who choose nonfirm settings express reservations about doing so. For example, one respondent noted, "I have a very satisfying practice as acting crown prosecutor for youth courts and as official guardian agent." However, she also observed "while I do not have the overhead or stress of an office, neither do I have the sense that my colleagues, solicitors in particular, accept me as a 'real' lawyer." Another woman in a nonfirm setting similarly noted that "there is this 'Toronto attitude' that unless a person 'went through the hoops' of articling or associateship with a major downtown firm, then the person is useless." This respondent concluded that "the profession needs more 'people persons' than a bunch of gnomes churning out legal memos that clients can't understand."

This discontent with some of the basic premises of the profession must be kept in mind when considering the wants and expectations individuals have in entering the profession. As Schultz (1988:1756) notes in a more general legal context, "[C]ourts have assumed that women's aspirations and identities as workers are shaped exclusively in private realms that are independent of and prior to the work world. By assuming that women form stable job aspirations before they begin working, courts have missed the ways in which employers contribute to creating women workers." In particular, it is important to keep in mind a kind of discounting of work preferences that may go on among women entering the profession of law. It is perhaps only in this context that it makes sense to say in relation to table 3.1 above that, by the mid-1980s in Toronto, women were not significantly different from men in their success in finding the early forms of articling and employment positions they initially indicated they preferred. This apparent pattern is further reflected in a cross-classification of gender with success in attaining a practice setting preferred: 45.5 percent of the men compared to 48.1 percent of the women attained the setting they indicated they wanted. When we asked about area of practice wanted and attained, the difference was reversed (44 percent compared to 36 percent), but still not statistically significant.

It may be more revealing to consider table 3.2 where receiving help in job seeking is cross-classified with attaining an articling position and first job in a large firm. This table is interesting in that while it reveals no significant difference by gender in the role of help in attaining an articling position in a large firm, gender does produce a significant difference in help in finding a first job in such firms. Note how this happens. About a third of the men and women who do or do not receive help in finding articling positions

Table 3.2
Help in Finding Articling and First Positions in Large Firms among Women and Men Lawyers, Toronto

	Men	N	Women	N	Total	N
Articling Position						
Received No Help	35.8%	462	33.6%	118	35.4%	588
Received Help	38.1	147	35.5	42	37.5	189
	$\chi^2=.250$	$p=.610$	$\chi^2=.049$	$p=.825$	$\chi^2=.281$	$p=.596$
First Position						
Received No Help	22.6%	462	23.1%	118	22.4%	588
Received Help	33.5	147	15.7	42	29.5	189
	$\chi^2=6.787$	$p=.009$	$\chi^2=1.057$	$p=.009$	$\chi^2=3.807$	$p=.051$

are able to locate in large firms for their articles. Yet, when it comes to jobs following articling, although a third of men who received help finding articling positions are still located in large firms (33.5 percent), the success of people in all other categories is lower. Specifically, only 15.7 percent of women who received help at the articling stage find first jobs in large firms. This may signal one source of gender stratification of lawyers that begins to build after entry into the profession and that involves social networks. This possibility is consistent with our thesis that entry and advancement may be rather separate matters.

A Fuller View of the Large-Firm Job Search

To establish and explore more thoroughly the role of contacts in the early attainment of positions in large firms, it is necessary to consider simultaneously the role of personal contacts along with all the other factors (e.g., law school grades) that are also thought to influence getting these positions. The following part of this chapter summarizes a logistic regression analysis that allows us to consider the joint influence of a number of different variables on the large-firm job search (a brief discussion of logistic regression is presented in the Appendix to this book).

The influences of seven variables on attaining large-firm positions are summarized in the results of the logistic analysis presented in table 3.3. Since we already have noted that men and women are about equally successful in attaining positions in these firms, with more subtle differences emerging in comparisons of what influences outcomes by gender, we analyzed the large-firm outcomes separately for men and women. The variables included in this analysis are private schooling (at the secondary or postsecondary level), elite law school degree (from the University of Toronto or Osgoode Hall law schools), grades in law school (self-reported in the A, B, and C range), help in finding the position (as discussed earlier), being of white anglo-saxon background (self-reported WASP background), and coming from a household whose head owned a business that employed others or was in a professional or managerial position (as reported by respondents). With the exception of grades, these variables measure *ascribed* characteristics of individuals that are commonly considered in stratification theories, including gender stratification theory. Law school grades are a classic kind of human capital measure of personal resources developed through education. Grades therefore are assumed to be *achieved* outcomes that should, from a human capital perspective, consistently and efficiently sort new members of the profession into entry-level positions.

The results in table 3.3 reveal that grades in law school have the strongest and most consistent statistically significant effects on attaining articling positions and first jobs in large firms. It is of further interest that these effects of marks are greater for women than men at both the articling and first-job stage. So while the effect of grades can be taken as an indication of the kind of emphasis on merit that human capital theory and Arthurs et al. (1986) expect in early, large-law-firm recruitment, it may also be the case that this meritocratic criterion is applied more stringently in the selection of women than men. This is a kind of pattern that we will have reason to consider further in later chapters.

In addition, the findings in table 3.3 suggest that both at articling and first job having a WASP background is of significant benefit to men, but not women; private schooling has a significant effect in obtaining first jobs for men and women. As in the earlier tabular analysis, here we find that help in finding a job only has a significant effect in attaining large-firm employment among men, and at the stage of first job rather than at articling. Further, it should be noted that this effect, although significant, is not nearly as strong as that of grades. Nonetheless, it remains of interest that contacts help male lawyers as they begin to move into the early stages of large-firm practice.

The finding of a difference in the role of contacts for men and women and between articling and the first job draws attention to the significance of this early transition in the careers of young lawyers. At least half the respondents in our Toronto panel worked in their first job in a different place from where they articled. Most of these respondents did not indicate pre-

Table 3.3
Determinants of Articling and First Positions in Large Firms among Women and Men Lawyers, Toronto (Standard error in parentheses)

Independent Variable	Articling Positions				First Positions			
	Men (N = 608)		Women (N = 160)		Men (N = 608)		Women (N = 160)	
	Logistic Coefficient	Antilog	Logistic Coefficient	Antilog	Logistic Coefficient	Antilog	Logistic Coefficient	Antilog
Private Schooling	0.364(0.210)*	1.253	0.869(0.476)*	2.407	0.622(0.227)**	1.863	0.861(0.526)*	2.365
Elite Law School	0.225(0.190)	1.253	0.383(0.364)	1.467	-0.054(0.211)	0.948	0.359(0.429)	1.432
Grades	0.602(0.164)***	1.826	1.018(0.377)**	2.768	0.964(0.188)***	2.621	1.418(0.447)***	4.129
Help Finding Job	0.036(0.208)	1.036	0.059(0.397)	1.061	0.451(0.224)*	1.570	-0.523(0.502)	0.593
WASP	0.491(0.201)**	1.634	0.408(0.400)	1.504	0.547(0.221)**	1.728	0.080(0.480)	1.083
Parent Owns Business	-0.347(0.212)	0.707	0.245(0.453)	1.278	-0.050(0.237)	0.951	-0.052(0.546)	0.949
Parent Professional or Managerial	-0.043(0.212)	0.958	0.157(0.413)	1.170	-0.030(0.243)	0.971	0.225(0.477)	1.252
Constant	-2.055(0.409)***		-3.352(0.918)***		-3.476(0.481)***		-4.625(1.115)***	

$* p < 0.05$; $** p < 0.01$; $*** p < 0.001$, one-tailed.

67

cisely in our survey why this change occurred, and indeed they themselves may not always be certain if this change was or was not of their own choosing. Nonetheless, it is interesting to note variation by gender in our Toronto sample among those who did cite a reason for this change.

To explore this issue, we cross-classified gender with the reasons cited for changing employment after articling. About a third of both men and women simply indicated that they were not hired back into a permanent position. However, while 15 percent of the men indicated that they changed employment because of a better offer, only 3.5 percent of the women cited this reason. Alternatively, 9.8 percent of the women cited dissatisfaction as the reason for change, compared with only 3 percent of the men. These data can be taken as no more than suggestive; nonetheless, they do provide a further indication that early in these young lawyers' careers, as entry into full-time employment is occurring, there are signs of differences by gender that point to disparities in job satisfaction and to longer-term variations in career trajectories. These leads imply issues of gender stratification that we will pursue in chapters to follow.

The First Steps of Practice

Relatively little research has focused on lawyers who are just beginning to practice. Findings reported in this chapter suggest that there are subtleties in this process of entry to the profession that deserve careful consideration. However, one aspect of this process is not subtle at all, and it involves the kinds of questions that women are sometimes asked in the process of interviewing for articling positions. Huxter (1981:189–90) cites some revealing examples of what these questions can be like:

> When did I plan to have a family? How many? Did I plan to make law a career? How did I intend to care for my children? Did I think I had room in my life for a family and a law practice?

> One male interviewer asked whether I wouldn't prefer to stay home and "be happy." I was continually asked whether I intended to make law a career — they expect me to abandon law after seven years of university and a year of articling. Would they? Hardly!

> I was asked if I intended to make a career out of practicing law or planned to marry and have babies. I was asked if I had a boyfriend or fiancé. I was asked if I got along well working with men.

> Questions as to the use of birth control and or plans to have children. Questions as to whether my spouse "approved of" or would "let me" work. Objectionable because when I asked, the interviewer admitted

he would not ask male candidates the same question. Questions as to whether I was 'a women's libber.' Besides showing a hostility of sorts on the part of the interviewer, I consider this akin to asking questions of political adherence.

Although words do not always connect in a one-to-one fashion with deeds in the study of human behavior, such questions raise doubts as to whether hiring decisions for articles or first jobs are made without gender bias in the legal profession. Furthermore, research by Huxter (1981) and others indicates that at least during the 1970s women received discriminatory treatment in these hiring decisions. One respondent in our own research observed, that

> [A]lthough I have been looking since last spring, I have still not found employment. I have had interviews and made the "short list" frequently. Each time I was interviewed by the private bar I was asked questions about my marriage plans and my reproductive plans. I have been "warned" that the firm will give no pregnancy leave. I have been asked about my religious and political preferences as well as my ethnic background. I was told in one instance that the senior partners had decided against me, sight unseen, because I was a woman and would just get pregnant and leave.

At the same time, the articling process is extremely competitive. Thus, Huxter also points out that law school grades are a significant factor in hiring. During the expansion of the 1980s large law firms increasingly competed for the top students of graduating law school classes, more than half of whom were women. Arthurs, Weisman, and Zemans (1986) note that the competition among these firms to recruit top students effectively might have acted to reduce the likelihood of discrimination in the early recruitment stages of legal practice. In the previous chapter, we emphasized the advantages to firms of recruiting the best and brightest of young women graduates to spend the early years of their careers in firm settings. From a human capital perspective, open and meritocratic recruitment is efficient at the entry level. We suggested that problems of discrimination were more likely to emerge with progression into the years when partnership and remuneration decisions become more salient. So there may also be powerful structural factors that inhibit the impulse to discriminate by gender in early articling and first-job decisions.

However, there is also a subtlety to the findings of this chapter that suggests less meritocratic influences. For example, we found that personal contacts and help in finding a job are factors in a quarter to a third of all articling decisions, so that these decisions cannot be entirely meritocratic. These contacts disproportionately derive from private school connections of male lawyers seeking jobs. Male lawyers are more likely to have attended private school and are able to sustain and capitalize on these contacts in finding first jobs in large firms, which are preferred by both men and women lawyers who are beginning to practice. These findings lend some support to a gender stratification perspective. Nonetheless, law school grades are more consistent and stronger than personal contacts or other background factors as a predictor of success in seeking articling positions and first jobs, and men are not significantly more successful than women in obtaining areas or settings that they initially indicate they prefer for entry into practice. Such findings are consistent with the observation of one of our respondents that the "old school-tie bit and mutual support system of former years is now under great strain." Still, there is some evidence that women are judged more heavily than men on their grades, while men benefit more from having a WASP background as well as from helpful contacts. These findings are not all of one piece. They contain a subtlety that perhaps should not be surprising.

The early stages of lawyers' careers may have come to represent a caricature of what stratification researchers call "contest mobility," a stage in which firms, in particular, may often be content to see entrants to the profession engage in relatively unfettered competition of the kind human capital theory embraces as rational and efficient. One respondent summarizes such an orientation in hiring articling students during the recessionary period of the early 1980s: "I was called [to the bar] in 1981, at a very bad time for new lawyers. There were few jobs in Toronto with lots of competition. The policy at that time was to hire as many new articling students as the firm could afford and let them fight it out." Of course, the existence of such a policy would not mean that the profession is without prejudice or bias that is linked to gender. The kinds of questions asked in articling interviews are testimony to the strength of such biases, and to the occurrence of gender harassment if not discrimination. However, at the point of entry into practice, firms in particular may also be well served to receive the best new lawyers they can find, regardless of background or orientation. This was particularly true during the competitively expansionary 1980s, and probably remains true during the competitive retrenchment of the early 1990s.

Again, this obviously does not mean that gender bias no longer exists or that networks, contacts, and the opportunities they represent are as open to women as they are to men in this profession. The subtle traces of differences we have observed in this chapter make this seem unlikely. Combined with the kinds of comments often heard in articling interviews, the picture instead is of a profession that has admitted women into its midst, but with the prospect of problems to reemerge at later stages. A respondent observes, "I had thought that being female would make no difference to my professional career. At first, I didn't notice any problem, but as I get more senior I constantly feel that I am not treated seriously by male peers, I am paid less in the partnership, my concerns are dismissed as emotional, etc." These are the kinds of concerns we consider in the chapters that follow on patterns of partnership and earnings.

4

Becoming Partners

In my large firm, once known as a good place for women, I have witnessed a weeding out of women in senior positions. Management has put on pressure to redline partnership distributions of women who are not 'movers and shakers' and keep senior associates out of partnership on the same basis.

The Promise of Partnership

Becoming a partner in a law firm is often the most important event in the professional life of a privately practicing lawyer. For a significant number of lawyers, partnership marks a successful passage into a set of professional relationships that enhances lifetime earnings and that opens further avenues for career advancement. For others, the decision not to pursue partnership or the denial of partnership signals a downturn in professional prospects that diminishes potential earnings and that permanently reduces occupational opportunities. For women especially, the partnership decision can loom as a barrier in a fork in their professional lives, with one path leading to the continued development of a legal career in firm practice, and alternative paths leading to other occupational settings or away from remunerative work altogether. Partnership decisions also have important societal implications. Partners in prominent firms often assume important leadership positions in politics and business and become role models for others.

So partnership decisions can be fateful turning points or transitions that influence longer-term career trajectories of individuals and societal trends as well. One might therefore expect the transition to partnership to be extensively studied and well understood, but this is not the case. Writings about partnership are based more on speculation than on the analysis of empirical data. As we will see, the decision to grant partnership is highly discretionary but has nonetheless patterned outcomes that are important in understanding the lives of lawyers.

The Elusive Criteria of Partnership

If there is a single person and institution identified with the conception and operationalization of a philosophy of partnership for the legal profession, it is likely to be Paul D. Cravath, and his powerful New York City firm of Cravath, Swaine, and Moore. The philosophy is described by Cravath's colleague, Robert Swaine (1948), in his privately printed book, *The Cravath Firm and Its Predecessors, 1819–1948*. Now nearly a half century old, this volume articulates the tenants of "the Cravath System." Although pedantic and pretentious, this volume articulates principles and procedures that are in many ways descriptive of attitudes and practices that persist in contemporary firms. Swaine (1948) offers this overview of the Cravath System of choosing partners:

> Obviously not all the men competent to be partners can be taken into the firm — for that would make the firm unwieldy. The choice is difficult: factors which control ultimate decisions are intangible; admittedly they are affected by the idiosyncrasies of the existing partners. Mental ability there must be, but in addition, personality, judgment, character. No pretense is made that the ultimate decisions are infallible. Only infrequently have mistakes been made in taking men into the firm; more often, mistakes not so easily remedied have been made in not admitting others.

Of course, only men were considered a half century ago at the Cravath firm, and these were predominately if not exclusively white, Anglo-Saxon Protestant men (Smigel, 1969). So some important changes obviously have occurred.

Most notably, the ethnic and male exclusiveness of elite firm partnerships has diminished. Nonetheless, aspects of the Waspishness and maleness of this partnership culture have endured. These lingering ascriptive tendencies often blend tangible and intangible factors and objective and subjective considerations, making it difficult to pin down the criteria applied in partnership decisions. Even those who doubt the lingering effects of the overt discrimination that obviously once openly governed the granting of partnerships in law firms still acknowledge the possible effects of more subtly worrisome considerations. For example, Stewart (1983:16) writes in his popular account from nearly a decade ago, "If there is discrimination today, it is extremely subtle, even unconscious, reflecting a generalized preference for people who will 'fit in' and work well with clients." The latter "intangibles" were granted a legitimacy in the U.S. Supreme Court case of *Hishon v. Spalding* (1984).

Elizabeth Hishon was hired by the Atlanta firm of King & Spalding in 1972 and left seven years later when she was not elected to partnership. Hishon claimed in a suit against King & Spalding that her rejection for partnership was a violation of the U.S. Civil Rights Act of 1964. Her claim was denied in two lower court decisions before eventually being upheld in 1984 by the U.S. Supreme Court. The latter decision explicitly accepted the premise that the granting of partnership entails intangible factors, but also held that these factors cannot be used to shroud discriminatory criteria, including the tangible fact of being a woman. This decision also established that firm decisions about partnership were not distinct from other promotion decisions about employees, in that becoming a partner is a condition of employment.

There was strong circumstantial evidence of discrimination in the case of Elizabeth Hishon. The King & Spalding firm claimed that Hishon "didn't socialize much" and "just didn't fit in." However, gender interactions in this firm lacked the subtlety that a claim of intangibility implies. For example, during the period the case was pending, the partnership convened a student swimsuit competition that included an award to the female "body we'd like to see more of" (*Wall Street Journal*, December 20, 1983). *Hishon* therefore provides a case in which *in*tangible factors alone were not judged to fully account for the failure to grant partnership.

One might have expected that the Supreme Court decision in *Hishon* would have encouraged a wave of partnership discrimination suits against firms, but it was not until a federal district court's 1991 ruling in *Ezold v. Wolf* that another partnership case was adjudicated on the issue of gender discrimination. Although the suit of Nancy Ezold against her former Philadelphia firm initially was successful at the district court level, where it was held that the firm had engaged in unlawful disparate treatment, this judgment was reversed by the Third Circuit Court of Appeals. The court of appeals narrowed the issues considered in the district court decision and concluded that the firm had legitimately denied partnership on the gender-neutral basis of "subjectively" developed doubts about Nancy Ezold's legal analytical ability. These subjective evaluations were inferred from comments recorded in performance reviews.

Despite the reversal, the judgment in *Ezold* does explicitly endorse the position taken in *Hishon* that decisions based explicitly on gender or in ways that cause a disparate impact on women are illegal. Interestingly, although Ezold's counsel noted the small number of women admitted to partnership, this issue was not pursued further with statistical analysis or evidence of the kind developed in this chapter, and so the district court could not make findings on this issue. Meanwhile, references to "subjective" and "intangible" factors may more generally be a way of avoiding explicit consideration of barriers to the advancement of women in the private practice of law, camouflaging the role of these barriers in partnership decisions.

Structural Barriers to Partnership

There are more explicit factors noted in human capital theory that reduce the prospects of women obtaining partnerships in firms. The literature on gender stratification describes these factors as structural barriers to the advancement of women in nontraditional occupations and professions. Most conspicuously, in the aggregate, women's occupational careers have been characterized as bimodal or M-shaped, with reduced participation in economic activity during childbearing years that are interposed between periods of higher employment activity (Silverstone and Ward, 1980:10). These discontinuities in employment may affect advancement through "foregone appreciation" in experience and opportunities for promotion (Robinson, 1986:226), as well as through discriminatory treatment, so that, for example, individuals resuming occupational careers may not only encounter problems in returning to positions or resuming employment, they may also have to accept lower positions and pay than they held before leaving work (Nieva, 1985; Roos, 1985). Child care responsibilities join with these problems in jeopardizing prospects for advancement.

These and related differences between the careers of men and women may produce vulnerabilities and dilemmas or contradictions of status (Hughes, 1945). So that while being a woman lawyer is no longer considered "deviant" or a "status contradiction" in the way that the restriction of gender pronouns in the quote about "the Cravath System" implies, nonetheless, being or becoming a mother, especially during the period when most promotion decisions are made, may still present vulnerabilities and dilemmas in beliefs about the work and career prospects of women.

One powerful set of beliefs about the effects of parenting on the commitment of women to their careers is expressed in the assumption of human capital theory noted in chapter 1 that women invest less effort and over time accumulate less human capital than do men toward the advancement of their careers. Rhode (1988) describes the implications of the human capital perspective this way:

Although no professional can be accessible at all times for particular needs, inaccessibility related to family needs has often carried special stigma. The prevailing view at some firms is that "having a baby is a personal decision, rather like vacationing in Tahiti" and unworthy of organizational support. Individuals who make work the central priority in their own lives are often unwilling to accommodate those with divided loyalties. Even temporary suspension of normal working hours can create permanent professional risks. (1185; references omitted)

A respondent in a panel study of University of Michigan law graduates captured the gender-specific implications of the effects of pregnancy-related absences from work, when she observed, "I have taken three medical leaves for pregnancy-related disabilities. For career purposes, it would have been less detrimental to have suffered three heart attacks" (see Chambers, 1989:282n). From the human capital perspective, childbearing is often treated as a chosen inefficiency that can be expected to impede career advancement.

Fox and Hesse-Biber (1984:139) underline the significance of this perspective to the practice of law when they note that professional work often demands a "rapid and relentless pace — and performance is measured against time." The point is that conflicts between family responsibilities and work demands often produce barriers in ascending career ladders (Lopato et al., 1984), either through the reality of the demands of family, or through the imputation of their presumed consequences.

Viewed from a structural life course perspective, Elder (1985:3) notes that contemporary life patterns are organized by interlocking careers of family and work that vary in their "synchronization." For example, if women graduate from law school at about twenty-four years of age and take five or more years to "make" partner, then they must commit the most time to firm practice during the optimal years for bearing children (Menkel-Meadow, 1989b). The demands of private firms are therefore often "out of phase" or "asynchronous" with the needs and commitments of its members who are moving into their childbearing years (Riley, 1988).

Although we will see below that detailed analyses have yet to be undertaken in professions such as law, the larger research literature indicates that women are disadvantaged by discontinuities in their employment histories resulting from childbearing (Waite, 1976; Rosenfeld, 1980; Boyd, 1982; England, 1982; Sorenson, 1983; Robinson, 1986; Rosenfeld and Spenner, 1988; Jones et al., 1990). Our own analyses therefore will measure and analyze leaves from practice and investments of time in child care and work to consider how these factors might influence the advancement of women in law.

A further barrier to the advancement of women in law may involve areas of specialization in practice and the related development of corporate clients. There is a prestige hierarchy associated with areas of practice in law. Some higher ranking areas, such as civil litigation, tend to be male-dominated, while other, lower-ranking areas, such as family law, tend to be predominantly female. The higher-ranking areas tend to involve more corporate clients. As suggested in chapter 2, the development of client relations, especially corporate clients, is an important form of human capital, with a social/cultural dimension. The development and attraction of corporate clients, often called the "rainmaking" function in law, may be particularly important in the granting of partnership. Often women are at a disadvantage in developing the kinds of network ties that are useful in rainmaking with corporate clients. For example, a respondent in Epstein's (1981:287) study *Women in Law* says succinctly of the "drinking routine" for developing client networks, "There are a lot of mechanisms one can use to be informal that simply don't work in heterosexual situations, although in all-male settings they work very well." So women are more restricted than men in the development of client networks. We include in the following analysis measures of specialization and corporate clientele and their influence on attaining partnership.

Although the literature on women in the legal profession gives attention to issues of childbearing and the development of client networks, there is little empirical analysis of how these variables affect the transition to partnership.

Past Studies

Attempts to collect information on partnerships in law firms are largely anecdotal and descriptive. Some of this material is found in the growing circulation of legal periodicals. For example, a recent front-page story in the *Law Times* leads with the title "Study Shows Firms Lack Women Partners" (Kulig, 1990:1) and an article in the periodical *Trial* reports that "walk into almost any established law firm and you will still find, as you would have found a generation ago, that the majority of partners are white males from a middle- or upper-middle-class background" (Spire, 1990:57).

However, when results of counts of partners and associates by gender are reported, they usually are in a summary form that makes their interpretation problematic. For example, Fenning (1987) reviews three studies from Los Angeles, Maryland, and Michigan that collectively indicate that women represent from 4 to 8 percent of partners and from 25 to 30 percent of associates in firms. Although these figures are suggestive, they do not include controls for gender differences in experience in practice, or other differences between women and men lawyers.

Several studies by provincial law societies in Canada (see Buckley, 1993) and in the United States (for a review, see Curran, 1986) have further documented the overrepresentation of women among associates and their underrepresentation among partners. In 1980, the *National Law Journal* reported that across the United States, women accounted for only 14 percent of the lawyers in the fifty largest firms. When examining job descriptions, women accounted for 22 percent of associates and 2 percent of the partners at these firms. None of the firms lacked women associates, but one-fifth had no women partners (Fossum, 1981:582). Between the early 1960s and the mid-1980s, the percentage of women in the American legal profession increased from 3 to 14 percent, but women still represented only 5 percent of partners at the nation's one hundred largest law firms and a handful of key judicial and governmental decision-makers (Rhode, 1988:1179; see also Wolfram, 1986). A national survey of career satisfaction/dissatisfaction undertaken by the Young Lawyers' Division of the American Bar Association in 1984 reported that 13 percent of women were partners, compared with 44 percent of men (Hirsch et al., 1989:24). Again, these studies do not control for differences in years of practice or otherwise analyze their data in ways that allow secure conclusions about the gender disparity in partnership.

Abel's (1988b:203) work on American lawyers also reports that within private practice women are more likely than men to be associates in large firms and that women are less likely to be found in small firms or to be partners. Menkel-Meadow (1989b:307) observes that given the increasing proportion of graduating law classes made up of women, and the increasing entry of women into firms, we should expect a rapid growth in the representation of women in partnerships. There is some recent evidence that men and women experience mobility through large firms differently, with men more likely than women to move both vertically and horizontally into partnerships within and across firms (Hagan and Zatz, 1989; Menkel-Meadow, 1989b:307). There is also some evidence that women are disproportionately represented among new categories of legal professionals, such as "contract associates" (Kingston, 1988).

A study of the Harvard Law School class of 1974 revealed that although graduating women were more likely than men to begin working at large elite firms, only 23 percent of these women were partners ten years later, compared to 51 percent of the men. Over half of the forty-nine women who initially entered large firms had left within ten years (Abramson and Franklin, 1986). Nelson (1988) similarly reports from his research in Chicago that women are far more likely than men to leave firms without making partner. By focusing on cohorts of lawyers who enter practice at the same time, these studies control for differences in experience. However, other sources of differences in partnership outcomes still can vary, for example, parental leaves and corporate clientele. Nonetheless, the important contribution of these studies is their demonstration that over time many women are removed from the partnership ladder.

There is some optimism that things are changing. Epstein (1981:188) observed more than a decade ago that "blatant discrimination has been done away with. Where prejudice continues to exist, its expression is subtle." Chambers's (1989) study of graduates of the University of Michigan Law School from the late 1970s also suggests that the gap is narrowing between the attainments of men and women in private practice. However, Epstein also documents subtle sources of gender differentiation in firms, and Chambers is careful to note that his sample consists of elite law school graduates. A recent Canadian brief suggests that, "in fact, there is a growing number of incidents at large firms in which female associates have been financially downgraded, placed on probation or dismissed within six months to a year from returning from maternity leave" (National Association of Women and Law, 1993). Meanwhile, others argue that past gender inequalities in partnership are simply products of employee differences in work patterns (for a review of such arguments, see Rhode, 1988:1180). Such views remain plausible in the absence of detailed accounts and analyses of partnership practices drawn from recent data.

Participants' Accounts

Our own research revealed a widely based perception among women lawyers that discrimination persists in various forms in relation to promotion and partnership. This view often was expressed by older as well as more recent entrants to the profession, although some older women lawyers disagreed. For example, one early entrant to the profession observed, "The only sexual discrimination I have felt is not having anyone to lunch with. Other than that, being a woman has been an advantage, and people have always been willing to stick their necks out and give me a chance." In contrast, another older woman lawyer in our sample reported that

> I began practice when women were not yet common in the profession. My opportunities were unquestionably deleteriously affected by being a woman — in respect to work, advancement, personnel matters, and general well-being. In the thirteen years I have practiced law I have come to believe that for the most part the legal profession is a men's club. Misogyny, sexism, and sexual harassment are often

the norm and, surprisingly perhaps, not the preserve of older members of the profession. I suppose that eventually the profession will improve, but when I think of the disadvantage and pain that women have suffered, I know that any change has been purchased by women who have put their careers on the line and who often as not will never recoup for themselves what they have personally lost.

Another senior woman in the profession, no longer in firm practice, recalled, "The firm with which I was associated was hierarchical and male-dominated. The women who worked as secretaries, despite competence and long, loyal service, were spoken of with derision. There were no other women lawyers, and I often felt alienated from the corporate culture of the firm. Partners' meetings confirmed that decisions were not made on the basis of policy, but often as the outcome of a power struggle." A third early entrant to the profession observed,

> I find the practice of law is very much tied to the "old boys' network" and the profession is not willing to consider innovative changes to the traditional methods of practicing law even though clients' needs have changed. I find the trend towards "mega-law firms" sad because the emphasis is away from the client and his/her needs. Despite the slow increase of female partners in law firms, I feel that sexual discrimination still exists, except that now lip service is paid to the need to welcome women into the profession. Discrimination now takes a more insidious form but unfortunately is still prevalent.

The younger women in our sample consistently noted the pervasiveness of gender bias and discrimination in the profession. One young woman expressed the problem as involving a silencing of legitimate concerns, noting, "I find the profession to be intolerant of women's concerns in regard to family commitments but also in terms of worldview. I find it difficult to be heard with credibility rather than as a 'dizzy blond.'" This discounting of concerns often led women in our sample to indicate a sense of futility about registering their objections to common attitudes and practices. A second respondent observed, "Discrimination against women in the profession is extreme and depressing. In my office it is treated as something akin to bad breath: not nice, but so what? One of the men who has management responsibilities constantly makes remarks about there being too many women in my section, and management sees him as almost 'cute' in his openness. I now simply ignore this man and have told my immediate boss why." This sense of futility is also reflected in the comments of a third respondent: "Suffice it to say that I feel the legal profession is just as prejudiced as other segments of the population. . . . The sexism is incredible, and there is nothing you can do — you just have to live with it — you can't even explain it to the guilty parties, it being sometimes somewhat subtle."

The significance of these perceptions goes beyond the subjective feelings involved, because these feelings often are the basis of decisions to leave firm practice and sometimes the practice of law altogether. A woman lawyer who returned as an associate to the firm with which she articled reported, "I discovered much to my surprise that I was unhappy, with the area of practice (insolvency) and also with the sheer drudgery and hierarchy of life in a large firm. I resented the fact that my volunteer work (on the board of a social service agency), while admired by my colleagues, was no excuse for not being able to work late if a client required it. I didn't see the quality of life at a big firm getting any better as I became more senior, so I decided to get out before I became financially dependent on the pay cheque."

The issue of quality of life is clearly tied for many women to the problem of combining parenting with practice and the lack of accommodation that firms provide for women with families. One respondent articulated this view when she noted, "The reason women are not becoming senior partners in law firms is that the 'old boy' attitude in private practice does not allow a female lawyer with a small child any chance for advancement unless she basically has full-time child care or works eight to five and then does the 'mommy shift' (after the child goes to bed) from nine to midnight. This is no way to live — for the parent or the child — and this is why I am no longer in private practice." Again and again, this issue was raised by women in our sample. One woman lawyer remarked, "As a woman who is planning to have a family, I am concerned about my relationship with my child if I continue to work full-time. At this time, I am somewhat apprehensive how my employers will address my maternity leave and whether it will affect my consideration for partnership. We have only one woman partner, who had children about twelve years ago. There are no other women in our firm with children." Another respondent expressed her concern in these words:

> As a woman in private practice I do not see my career goals as being compatible with my hopes to have a family. I find the profession to be very male-dominated despite the increasing number of women. My firm is predominately male and no associate to my knowledge has ever had a child. The general sense is that in order to advance, make sure you don't have children. This has actually been said by one of our partners to an associate engaged to be married. Although it is certain that the male associates will become partners, I honestly believe that the women that choose to have a family will become permanent associates.

A third woman in the sample commented, "The profession continues to discriminate on the basis of gender: it is more difficult for female lawyers to obtain partnerships, and often the only way a female lawyer who is a parent can maintain her status in a firm is by denying the importance of her parenting responsibilities." A young woman associate in a large firm summarized the prevalence of these concerns among young women in firms when she reported, "The associates in our firm have just had a retreat . . . during which we discussed many of these issues. . . . We are concerned that the demands for hours and billings are ever-increasing. Many feel that the only choice is the 'fast-track' for partnership or 'no track' at all."

The factual basis for such fears is suggested by reports of women about their firm experiences with parenting and partnership. Stories reported by our respondents linked partnership decisions with parenting issues. For example, one respondent indicated, "I am sure the fact that I'm female and had two children in my eight-and-a-half year career were significant factors in my not attaining partnership in my first professional position. After I married in 1984, my employer's ideas of my aspirations and the firm's progressing hand-in-hand seemed to change! Things deteriorated to the point of me leaving there and joining another firm when I was eight months' pregnant with my second child." However, the following account is perhaps the most explicit illustration of the difficult problems that woman can experience in mixing parenting with partnership:

> Upon learning of my pregnancy . . . the partners of the law firm I worked for were not willing to assist me in managing my practice during my short maternity leave — they would not even consider hiring an articling student, which seemed to me the ideal option, as we would have to make only a short term commitment at a low cost, and the student could have assisted with my practice while I had my child and cared for him in the first few months. . . . I knew that I would not be able to continue a busy practice, the responsibilities of motherhood to my first child (who was three years at the time), and the physical strains of pregnancy and birth. I therefore decided to leave the firm. . . . When I advised the senior partner of this decision he suggested that a termination of the pregnancy was a better solution than terminating my employment and told me that if I wanted to be a mother that I had no business being a lawyer and taking up valuable space in law school. Although I gave ample notice (three months) of my departure, the partners insisted that I continue working until the due date and beyond (the child was due in early December, and they were not willing to grant my departure until the end of December). When I refused and left the office in October, they continuously harassed me by telephone and letter. One partner even telephoned me at the hospital, the day after my child was born by Caesarean section and I was heavily sedated, to inform me that there was a problem on one of my files that needed my immediate attention, and he insisted

that I have it resolved in three days. They also had delivered to the hospital a noncompetition agreement that I was forced to sign.

There is no doubt from the comments of respondents in our study that decisions about promotion and partnership are widely perceived to hinge on gender-linked considerations. The remaining challenge of this chapter is to modify or confirm these impressions on the basis of the extensive quantitative data we collected from women and men in our sample.

Analyzing Partnership Decisions

Analyzing partnership outcomes is a surprisingly challenging task. To begin, it is not obvious what kinds of samples are appropriate for analysis. For example, if we consider only those lawyers now in firms who have been there for a considerable period of time, we will ignore many lawyers who set out to become partners but have since left firms or the practice of law entirely. On the other hand, if we begin with undifferentiated samples of all lawyers who enter practice, our comparisons of outcomes will include entrants to the profession who have never practiced in firm settings and for whom partnership decisions are irrelevant. Further, if we consider only very recent entrants to the profession, there will have been little opportunity for partners to emerge. To meaningfully gauge prospects of becoming a partner, it is important to have a sample of lawyers who have started practice in settings with prospects of becoming partners, with at least some of these lawyers having been in practice long enough to be considered for partnership.

Our analysis makes use of both our Ontario and Toronto samples. For this analysis, we restrict these samples to lawyers who began their careers either at the articling or first-job stage in firms. Recall that the Toronto sample considers entrants to the profession before the first survey in 1985, who were then reinterviewed six years later in 1991, while the Ontario sample considers entrants to the profession from 1975 to 1990, who were interviewed once in 1990. Both samples are weighted to represent the respective populations of Toronto and Ontario lawyers.

The differences between these samples are important and complementary for the purposes of understanding partnership decisions. The Ontario sample is restricted to the period of great growth and rapid entry of women into the profession, while the Toronto sample assures that all respondents have progressed more than six years from entry to the profession to a stage when most lawyers who will become partners have done so. Our analysis is divided to consider all those lawyers who have entered practice through firms, and then those who have continued to practice full-time, in firms or elsewhere.

The former sampling allows us to consider attrition from practice altogether, by requiring no continuation in practice, while the latter sampling restricts attention to those who stay in practice full-time, including those who may have left firms for other settings. It can be argued that the Toronto sampling selects those with a more uniform commitment to law as a career, while the Ontario sampling allows a more comprehensive evaluation of partnership prospects.

Our within-sample analyses are weighted to represent the population of lawyers from which they are drawn. In Ontario, 158, or 11.3 percent, of the 1,394 lawyers who began in firms had left full-time practice by the 1990 survey; in Toronto, 101, or 15.2 percent had left. Nearly 80 percent of the lawyers who left full-time practice in Ontario were women, while in Toronto about 86 percent of these lawyers were. Clearly, the attrition of women from firm practice is extensive. These departures from law are the focus of a further analysis of "leaving law" in chapter 4.

A Picture of Practice

It is instructive to have a picture of the lawyers in the Ontario and Toronto samples with whom we will be working. Of all the Ontario lawyers who entered the profession through firms, 41 percent were partners by the 1990 survey; 42 percent of these lawyers who also continued to practice full-time were partners. The respective figures were about 57 and 59 percent for the Toronto sample interviewed for the second time in 1991. Of course, these samples differ in experience: the Ontario lawyers had on average about seven years of experience, compared to nearly sixteen years in the Toronto sample. These samples also were somewhat different in their gender compositions. Close to 80 percent of the Toronto panel who began in firms were men, a figure that increases to nearly 83 percent for those who continued in full-time practice in 1991. The respective figures for the Ontario sample were 71 and 74 percent, which reflects the increased representation of women in this more recent survey. Meanwhile, about 42 percent of the Toronto female lawyers were partners by 1991, compared to 60 percent of the Toronto male lawyers. The respective figures for the less-experienced Ontario sample were about 25 and 49 percent. Most of the analysis that follows in this chapter is organized to consider differences in experience and other factors that might account for these differences in partnership outcomes.

A range of variables beyond gender and experience may influence partnership outcomes. The additional variables we explicitly consider are indicated in the first column of table 4.1. To begin, five other background variables are included: grades in law school (measured in Toronto only) and graduation from an elite law school, as considered in the prior chapter; white, Anglo-Saxon, Protestant background; and being married and having children. Then variables are included to represent being in a smaller (fewer than ten members) or larger firm (twenty-one or more members). Lawyers in middle-sized firms (eleven to twenty members) serve as a reference point for considering effects of being in smaller or larger firms in the analysis.

A specialization status variable also is included. Respondents in the Toronto study were asked both to state their predominant area of specialization and to rank specializations on a ten-point scale of prestige. Areas like taxation, corporate and commercial law, and civil litigation were ranked higher, while family, criminal, real estate, debtor, and general areas of practice were ranked lower, with other areas between (see Hagan et al., 1988:26). These rankings probably partially reflect differences in the status of the clients served in these different areas.

Variables were also developed from questions about hours docketed, corporate clients, hours spent on child care, and parental and other forms of leave taken from practice. The Ontario sample was asked to report the number of hours they docketed per week, and the Toronto sample, for the year. Both samples were asked what proportion of their practice was made up of corporate clients, and these proportions were categorized into quartiles. Both samples were asked to report the hours per week spent on child care. The Ontario respondents were also asked to report if they took parental or other forms of leave, while the Toronto sample reported this information in the context of a job history. The former approach resulted in higher levels of reporting, while the latter perhaps reflected more formally arranged leaves, but also the fact that more of the women in the Toronto sample entered the profession before such leaves became more common. Both the maternity and child care variables were developed from the first and second waves of the Toronto survey to provide more complete coverage, while the partnership outcome is, of course, measured at the second wave in Toronto. Other variables were measured in the first wave of the Toronto sample. In the Ontario sample, an indicator is provided of whether the respondent practices in Toronto, to allow a point of comparison between the samples.

While it is by definition difficult or impossible to measure whether the intangible factors that we noted at the outset of this chapter might influence partnership decisions, it is both possible and necessary to measure tangible factors relevant to this process if we are to understand its outcomes better, especially in relation to gender. The variables we have described represent an attempt to comprehensively encompass this process in terms of the characteristics, conditions, and contexts in which partnership outcomes are determined. In particular, analysis of these variables should help to determine if the tangible factor of gender itself, or other tangible differences between men and women who enter into firm practice, can account for differences in success in partnership attainment.

Picking Partners

The coefficients presented in table 4.1 represent the results of estimating multivariate logit equations (discussed in the Appendix to this book) which simultaneously take into account the range of variables we have measured as influences on partnership outcomes in the Ontario and Toronto samples. These coefficients represent our efforts to estimate the net impact of potential explanatory factors on partnership outcomes with other variables taken into account. Parental leave is not considered in the Ontario part of this analysis, because it was so closely connected to gender that it could not be considered separately and because by itself it had no significant correlation with partnership. This is probably because the Ontario women in the sample are relatively young; significant effects are found and discussed in the older Toronto sample.

The most noteworthy finding in table 4.1 is that after controlling for the effects of other variables, especially the difference in experience between data sets, the effects of gender in Ontario and Toronto are of comparable strength and in three of four instances statistically significant. The one instance, among lawyers who continue to practice full-time in Toronto, in which the effect of gender dips slightly below the conventional level of significance, is considered in greater detail below.

There is also evidence in table 4.1 that the effect of corporate clientele is significant with all other variables held constant. This variable actually becomes stronger in the Ontario sample when other variables are considered, and it remains highly significant in the Toronto group. It is clear that having corporate clients enhances partnership prospects.

Another finding that appears in both data sets involves what might at first seem a counterintuitive positive effect of having children. This effect is substantial and significant, with its strongest effect among Toronto lawyers who continue to practice full-time. Recall that this is also the only context in which the effect of gender dips below statistical significance. These full-time practicing Toronto lawyers therefore merit more detailed consideration.

This further consideration is provided in table 4.2, where we estimate a series of equations that initially consider continuing full-time men and women Toronto lawyers together, and then separately by gender. The pur-

Table 4.1

Coefficients for Partnership Analysis of Ontario and Toronto Lawyers Who Began Practice in Firms and Continue to Practice Full-Time (Standard error in parentheses)

Variables	Ontario Sample Began in Firm (N = 1394) Logistic Coefficient	Antilog	Continue Full-time (N = 1236) Logistic Coefficient	Antilog	Toronto Panel Began in Firm (N = 665) Logistic Coefficient	Antilog	Continue Full-Time (N = 564) Logistic Coefficient	Antilog
Gender (male=1)	0.468(0.162)**	1.597	0.500(0.176)**	1.649	0.561(0.240)**	1.740	0.402(0.272)	1.501
Experience (years)	0.232(0.019)***	1.261	0.238(0.020)***	1.269	-0.014(0.011)	0.987	-0.006(0.012)	0.994
Elite Law School (1)	-0.236(0.145)	0.790	-0.242(0.155)	0.785	0.515(0.190)**	1.679	0.367(0.214)	1.449
Grades (A = 3; B = 2; C = 1)					0.500(0.172)**	1.652	0.616(0.190)***	1.850
WASP(1)	-0.040(0.143)	0.961	-0.078(0.153)	0.925	0.202(0.206)	1.220	0.223(0.229)	1.251
Married (1)	0.011(0.190)	1.011	-0.016(0.200)	0.984	-0.137(0.231)	0.864	-0.025(0.252)	0.970
Children (1)	0.628(0.199)***	1.874	0.647(0.223)**	1.910	0.829(0.287)**	2.307	0.989(0.316)***	2.693
Firm < 10 (1)	0.622(0.199)***	1.863	0.624(0.212)**	1.866	0.136(0.261)	1.143	0.074(0.285)	1.070
Firm > 20 (1)	0.072(0.237)	1.075	0.099(0.252)	1.104	0.138(0.263)	1.154	0.115(0.291)	1.120
Specialization (status)	-0.731(0.092)***	0.481	-0.709(0.098)***	0.492	0.091(0.093)	1.095	0.163(0.102)	1.177
Docket Hours (week/year)	0.012(0.006)*	1.012	0.009(0.007)	1.009	0.000(0.000)	1.000	0.001(0.003)	1.001
Corporate Clientele (quartiles, 4 = 76–100%)	0.667(0.072)***	1.948	0.665(0.076)***	1.944	0.320(0.071)***	1.379	0.359(0.079)***	1.435
Child Hours (week)	-0.005(0.004)	0.995	-0.008(0.006)	0.992	-0.000(0.005)	1.000	0.002(0.006)	1.002
Parental Leave (1)					-0.907(0.599)	0.301	-0.912(0.716)	0.370
Other Leave (1)	-0.235(0.227)	0.791	-0.240(0.249)	0.787	0.213(0.557)	1.126	-0.046(0.635)	0.925
Toronto Practice (1)	-0.166(0.155)	0.847	-0.223(0.165)	0.800				
Constant	-0.179		-0.212		-3.992		-4.389	
Log Likelihood	-692.860		-611.500		-412.82		-342.67	

$* p < 0.05; ** p < 0.01; *** p < 0.001$, one-tailed.

pose of estimating these different equations is to see if we can specify the role that individual variables emphasized in our earlier discussion — experience, corporate clientele, and parental leaves — have on partnership outcomes. The first equation in this sequence includes gender, background characteristics of experience, elite law school training, grades, WASP parents, marriage, children, firm size, and area of specialization. With these variables included, the effect of gender remains substantial and significant. So these variables do not account for much of the effect of gender on partnership outcomes.

The next two equations vary from the first in that each includes a single variable that is responsible for a notable reduction in the effect of gender. The first of these variables, introduced in the second equation, measures corporate clientele. This variable is itself highly significant, and it alone notably reduces the effect of gender; however, the effect of gender remains statistically significant, albeit at a reduced level. So the tendency for men to develop a greater proportion of corporate clients than women accounts for some of the difference in the partnership prospects of men and women lawyers, but not enough of this difference to itself account for the lower partnership prospects of women who continue in full-time practice. It is interesting to note further that the inclusion of corporate clientele in equation 2 reduces to nonsignificance the positive effect of specialization status on partnership. This supports the expectation that higher-status specializations lead to the development of corporate clients, who are important in the attainment of partnership.

In the estimates of the third equation shown in table 4.2 we remove the corporate clientele variable and now include the variable that measures taking parental leaves. This variable has a surprisingly high standard error (in parentheses), which we will see below apparently results from only women in this sample taking parental leaves. This results in parental leave not attaining statistical significance in this sample. Still, the effect of parental leave is large and in the expected negative direction, and it reduces the effect of gender to a low level of statistical significance. So the taking of parental leaves by women, more than gender differences in corporate clientele, accounts for a reduction in the statistical significance of the gender effect on partnership.

Nonetheless, both differences in parental leave and corporate clientele contribute to the overall reduction in the effect of gender on partnership prospects. This is reflected in the fourth equation results presented in table 4.2, which includes all variables considered in our earlier analysis and reproduces the set of results presented in table 4.1, produced again here for ease of comparison. When all variables are included in this model, the ef-

Table 4.2

Coefficients for Partnership Analysis of Toronto Lawyers Who Continue to Practice Full-Time (Standard error in parentheses)

	Equations (Eqs.)					
	Eq. 1	Eq. 2	Eq. 3	Eq. 4	Women Only	Men Only
Gender	0.586(.247)**	0.500(0.253)*	0.467(0.260)*	0.402(0.272)		
Experience	-0.007(.012)	-0.006(0.012)	-0.007(0.011)	-0.006(0.012)	0.048(0.033)	-0.011(0.017)
Elite Law School	0.365(.206)*	0.361(0.211)*	0.363(0.206)*	0.367(0.214)*	0.176(0.257)	0.462(0.328)
Law School Grades	0.648(.185)***	0.609(0.189)***	0.662(0.186)***	0.616(0.190)***	0.213(0.262)	0.722(0.283)**
WASP	0.274(.223)	0.211(0.227)	0.282(0.224)	0.223(0.229)	0.008(0.291)	0.263(0.345)
Married	0.026(.239)	-0.039(0.244)	0.055(0.240)	-0.025(0.252)	0.180(0.315)	-0.077(0.385)
Children	0.965(.291)***	0.988(0.297)***	0.994(0.292)***	0.989(0.316)***	0.287(0.378)	1.220(0.489)**
Firm < 10 Lawyers	0.021(.278)	0.075(0.285)	0.019(0.278)	0.074(0.286)	-0.350(0.375)	0.142(0.425)
Firm > 20 Lawyers	0.284(.281)	0.126(0.290)	0.281(0.281)	0.115(0.291)	-0.008(0.379)	0.128(0.433)
Specialization	0.304(.095)***	0.165(0.101)	0.302(0.095)***	0.163(0.102)	-0.065(0.158)	0.203(0.146)
Docket Hours				0.000(0.000)	-0.004(0.004)	0.001(0.004)
Corporate Clientele		0.362(0.079)***		0.359(0.079)***	0.304(0.102)***	0.377(0.118)***
Child Care Hours				0.002(0.006)	0.001(0.006)	0.003(0.010)
Parental Leave				-0.912(0.716)	-0.892(0.422)*	
Other Leave			-0.990(0.701)	-0.046(0.635)	-0.018(0.894)	-0.038(0.931)
Constant	-4.548	-4.364	-4.493	-4.389	-1.112	-4.744
Log-Likelihood	-354.360	-343.590	-353.290	-342.670	-193.020	-157.860

$* p < 0.05$; $** p < 0.01$; $*** p < 0.001$, one-tailed.

Note: This table includes the reduced form and structural series of equations discussed in the text, with the blank spaces in the columns representing the variables absent from the reduced form equations.

fect of gender is reduced to its lowest strength, which is slightly below statistical significance. As we note further in the concluding section of this chapter, the prominence of the parental leave variable in the last phase of this analysis is part of the larger pattern of findings which indicates that departures from, and discontinuities in, the involvement of women in private practice play a major role in their reduced prospects of attaining partnerships in firms. However, it should also be noted that even with parental leave and all other variables considered, the effect of gender remains notable and nearly statistically significant. There is considerable consistency in the effect of gender across our analyses.

The last columns of table 4.2 present separate analyses of women and men lawyers who continue to work full-time in Toronto. The first of these equations reveals that only corporate clientele and parental leave significantly influence partnership outcomes for women. Note that with only women now considered, the standard error (in parentheses) for the parental leave variable is markedly reduced, making the effect of this variable clearly significant for women. So the earlier nonsignificance of this variable in columns 3 and 4 was an artifact of the lack of variation in this variable among men, as suggested above.

Meanwhile, law school grades, children, and corporate clientele all positively and significantly affect the partnership prospects of men. The positive effect of children for men is especially interesting because it is absent for women, who in addition, of course, are disadvantaged in terms of partnership outcomes by parental leaves. The positive effect of children for men may reflect a benefit that occurs for them when spouses spend more time at home, allowing men to conform to the traditional approved role of the working man who concentrates efforts on law firm activities. Of course, women get no corresponding benefit and instead are disadvantaged by taking leaves. In this sense, having a family can be an asset for men and a liability for women. Gender-linked issues of having a family are pursued further in the following chapter.

Finally, we turn to a concluding part of our analysis, which allows us to make estimates of the probabilities of attaining partnership for respondents in our sample. The estimates presented reflect the probabilities of attaining partnership associated with variables (e.g., gender) when other variables in the equation (e.g., experience, corporate clientele, and parental leaves) are held at their mean levels. This simulates the effect of members of the sample being made equal on all variables other than the one being considered, so that probabilistic statements can be made about the net impact of particular variables.

Estimates can be derived from any of the logit analyses presented above, but for purposes of efficiency we will restrict ourselves to the equation in table 4.1 involving Toronto lawyers who began in firms. Only the variables in this equation that produced significant effects are considered, and the probability estimates (expressed as percentages) are presented in table 4.3.

The estimates in table 4.3 indicate that 47 percent of the Toronto male lawyers who began practice in firms could expect to become partners, compared to 34 percent of the women. This gap of 13 percent gives an estimate of the net effect of gender, with all other variables held at their mean levels in the analysis. Comparable gaps exist for other variables. For example, 49 percent of the elite law school graduates, compared to 36 percent of the nonelite law school graduates could expect to become partners; 56 percent with average law school grades of A compared to 32 percent with C; 47 percent with children, compared to 28 percent without; 56 percent with the highest quartile of corporate clients, compared to 32 percent with the lowest; and 45 percent of those who did not take parental leave, compared to only 20 percent of those (all women) who did. Women who took parental leaves were particularly unlikely to become partners.

Partings and Partnerships

The analyses presented in this chapter support the view that women are less likely than men to attain partnership positions. Even when a range of variables measuring experience and background are included in multivariate analyses of all lawyers who began practice in firms in the Ontario and Toronto samples, men are shown to be more likely than women to become partners. For example, when we simulate the effects of women and men having the same experience and background characteristics, nearly half of the men, compared to about a third of the women, in the Toronto sample are estimated to become partners.

When attention is restricted to lawyers who continue in practice full-time, it is still the case that men are more likely to become partners than women. This appears to be the case among Ontario lawyers even when all variables that might account for this difference are taken into account. However, in the more experienced panel of Toronto lawyers, the effect of gender is mediated by two variables, parental leave and corporate clientele. Of these factors, parental leave seems more salient, but corporate clientele also makes a difference. Indeed, the corporate clientele variable consistently has strong effects throughout our partnership analysis. Having corporate clients is clearly an important source of human capital in the practice of law.

However, we should also not be surprised by the effect of the parental leave variable. The risks of taking parental leave were often anticipated by

Table 4.3
Probability Estimates for Significant Variables in the Equation for Partnership among Toronto Lawyers Who Began Practice in Firms

Independent Variables	Probability Estimate [a] (percent)	Range (perrcent)
Gender		13
Men	47	
Women	34	
Elite Law School		13
No	36	
Yes	49	
Law School Grades		24
A = 3	56	
B = 2	44	
C = 1	32	
Children		19
0	28	
1 or more	47	
Corporate Clientele		24
≤ 25%	32	
26–50%	40	
51–75%	48	
> 75%	56	
Maternity Leave		25
No	45	
Yes	20	

[a] Estimated likelihood of partnership when scores on all other variables are
held at their mean. The logit response function of the probability of partnership
(P (partnership) $= 1/1+e^{-xb}$) is thus approximated by setting each independent
variable except the variable being estimated (b) at its mean value, in this case:
$$xb = c + b_1 x_1 + b_2 \bar{x}_2 + b_3 \bar{x}_3 + ... b_n \bar{x}_n$$

members of our samples. Several researchers as well have argued that as
long as partnership decisions coincide in time with the years of optimal
childbearing for women, women will be unable to succeed in numbers that
equal men. Even when firms permit maternity leaves or allow part-time
work, women who avail themselves of such "innovations" may find that
they are considered less committed to their work as lawyers (Stanford Law
Project, 1982; Abramson and Franklin, 1986; Fenning, 1987). Human capital
theory assumes that women specialize in family roles and reduce their investment in work roles. These women may be perceived as "opting out,"
without considering how presumably "neutral" rules of existing work structures have a "disparate impact" on women (Menkel-Meadow, 1989). The

effects of childbearing and child care may result for women in denial or delay of partnership, or departure from firm settings or the practice of law entirely. These potential consequences were perceived and commented upon by many women practitioners in our study.

From a gender stratification perspective, our findings can be viewed as indicating that the more women lawyers make themselves similar to men lawyers, for example, in declining parental leaves and in displaying undivided attention to their work, the more likely they are to be treated like men in partnership decisions. However, all of this underlines how different the decision to have children is for men and women lawyers. Having children for men may make it more likely that a spouse will care for the child and as well become a source of support for the development of the husband's career. So that while in our Toronto data we saw that parental leaves worked to the disadvantage of women, being married and having children actually enhanced partnership prospects for men. It is therefore unsurprising that women lawyers contemplate remaining childless or delaying family and children. As one woman lawyer in our sample commented, "Having no children is partly due to anticipated problems with care arrangements and managing household chores, as well as a perception that part-time lawyers who are mothers, even if such positions are available, . . . are perceived as having assigned a higher priority to home and children than work. In other words, I would continue to work full-time even with children, but I expect that this would be draining, so I haven't had any."

Despite efforts to adapt to the demands of private practice in firm settings, women are not progressing to firm partnerships in numbers and proportions that correspond to their entry into the profession and into early practice in firms. This finding lends further support to the argument made in chapter 2 that the growth of the profession associated with women has resulted in women attaining reduced shares in the cultural capital represented by partnerships in the profession. This finding is, of course, consistent with the expectations of gender stratification theory.

Galanter and Palay (1991) have explored the exponential growth of large law firms and the emergence of new patterns in what they call the "partnership tournament." As in our research, Galanter and Palay observe that the percentage of associates becoming partners seems to be declining in some firms, while years to partnership may be lengthening. In addition, law firms are increasingly making use of nonequity partnerships, paralegals, "temporary" attorneys, "second-tier" associates with no expectation of partnership, and the practice of retaining as permanent associates those passed over for partnership. As Galanter and Palay point out, while such practices may diminish demands on firm earnings, they simultaneously create difficulties in recruitment, compensation, motivation, and retention of productive young associates. The transformation of the partnership tournament is poignantly summarized by Galanter and Palay: "[A] cadre of permanent salaried personnel (paralegals, second-tier associates, and permanent associates/senior attorneys) now surrounds that promotion-to-partnership core. Within the core, promotion comes to fewer entry-level associates and it often comes later. For those who achieve promotion, the meaning of partnership has changed. The prospect of an orderly procession to unassailable eminence has been replaced by entrance to an arena of pressure and risk amid frenetic movement" (1991:76). Our data from this chapter indicate that the victims of these changes are especially likely to be women.

Indeed, we suggest that it is impossible to understand the fundamental changes that are occurring in the legal profession without taking into account that it is the addition of women to the profession that marks its most fundamental change. Often the practice of law as well as analyses of it attempt to treat women as if they were men and assume that outcomes can unfold as they would otherwise. However, because gender fundamentally stratifies social life, especially work and family life, in ways that are different and go beyond other factors, gender itself must be brought into the analysis.

In particular, the entry of women into the legal profession may force a reconsideration of many of the accepted ways of organizing private practice and relationships between work and private life. These kinds of issues will become increasingly important in chapters that follow on earnings and job satisfaction. They are at the core of the most important changes that currently confront private practice in law. However, before turning to issues of income and work satisfaction, we give further consideration to conflicts between career and family and departures from practice that were singled out for special analysis in the Ontario survey.

5

Careers in Conflict

I find the gap between my views and the male lawyers I went to school with to be growing as we have children. I don't understand why making so much money is so important to them that they are prepared to work long hours and participate in family life so little. These are thoughtful, intelligent men but they seem to be settling into very traditional fifties-style family patterns. It's only my women lawyer friends who question the value of the long hours and do something about it. Generally speaking, I can tell you I'm weary of breaking new ground as a woman. Maybe in my next life I'll go into a so-called women's profession.

Career and Family as Competing and Enhancing Domains

The kinds of questions asked of women in the job search and the kinds of concerns that often jeopardize their prospects for firm partnerships expose fundamental problems in combining family and work roles. At the core of these problems is the structural dilemma noted in the previous chapter: if women graduate from law school at an average age of about twenty-four, and if it takes women an average of about seven years to become partners or to otherwise establish themselves in their careers, then firms as well as other kinds of employers will likely expect that women devote their longest hours to their careers during the optimal years of childbearing and family responsibility (Stanford Law Project, 1982; Menkel-Meadow, 1989b). We further explore this issue in this chapter by considering demands placed on women in their family and work roles, and by analyzing the impact of these demands on decisions about changing jobs and about departing from practice altogether.

For many plausible reasons, research on gender roles usually has re-garded the multiple role responsibilities of women as having detrimental outcomes (Goode, 1960). These negative consequences are assumed to af-fect all categories of women, including highly educated professional women, such as lawyers. When women encounter problems in their work or family lives, their difficulties are often attributed to colliding constraints of career and family responsibilities, that is, to role overload and conflict (e.g., Houseknecht, et al., 1984).

Role overload is defined as having too many role demands and too little time to fulfill them (Rapoport and Rapoport, 1976; Baruch et al., 1985). *Role conflict* refers to "the extent to which a person experiences pressures within one role that are incompatible with the pressures that arise within another role" (Kopelman et al., 1983:201). Role overload leads to role conflict when the demands of one of the multiple roles make it difficult to fulfill the demands of another role (Lehrer and Nerlove, 1986:182; Houseknecht, et al., 1987:355; O'Connell, et al., 1989:37). In particular, role overload may lead to role conflict in a situation in which no alternative mechanism exists to help individuals fulfill their various roles (Coverman, 1989:968). For example, a woman lawyer with limited or unstable child care arrangements is more likely to experience role conflict than a woman lawyer in a setting that provides adequate child care facilities.

Several studies of the legal profession lend support to theories of role overload and conflict. In a study of employed lawyers in the United States, Spangler (1986) concluded that male and female attorneys generally spoke similarly about their work, but only women seemed concerned with the issue of accommodating career and family. The women lawyers felt role conflicts that men lawyers did not. This is easily understood.

The substantial body of research on women who work outside the home observes that women bear a heavier burden than men for the care of children. And, despite the increasing number of women working outside the family, women continue to be the primary child care providers within their families. Meanwhile, Liefland observes that "the traditional legal career track affords lawyers little time for non-work pursuits, especially those that involve a substantial, daily commitment of time outside the office" (1986:613). In a similar vein, Taber and colleagues note, "Torn by family pressures, it is often difficult for women to maintain the appearance of total dedication to their careers that is necessary to compete in settings such as law firms" (1988:1228).

A study of Stanford University law students showed that both male and female students expected child care to remain primarily a woman's responsibility (Stanford Law Project, 1989). Epstein (1981) also found that even when both spouses are professionals, women are more often the primary child care providers. Liefland's study of lawyers (1986) revealed that a higher percentage of women lawyers than men were not working full-time and that family responsibilities were the primary reason given by women lawyers for working part-time or for not working in the paid labor force. This study also showed that if one parent had to work fewer hours or leave the workplace to accommodate the family, that parent was more often the mother. There may also be an interplay between these factors and work problems, as women are subjected to greater pressure to interrupt their careers to care for children when they experience unfavorable treatment at their place of work (Liefland, 1986:617–18).

In addition, Liefland's study showed that, especially in the marriages of male lawyers, women were primarily responsible for child care. Male lawyers were also more likely to be married to women who either worked part-time or were not employed. As Liefland comments, "Common sense tells us that it is easier to single-mindedly pursue a career when someone else is overseeing the other aspects of one's life" (1986:614). There is also evidence that spouses of female lawyers are more likely to be high-status professionals than are the spouses of male lawyers. The spouses of female lawyers may therefore be less willing to make career sacrifices in order to share child care responsibilities (Liefland, 1986:614).

Furthermore, few law firms allow paternity leave, thereby implicitly endorsing the notion that child care is primarily a woman's responsibility (Taber et al., 1988:1228). Therefore, even men who would choose to take on greater responsibility for the care of their children may be unable to do so. Knowledge of the scarcity of leave and part-time opportunities for fathers may reinforce men's expectations that their wives must retain primary responsibility for child care. Rhode (1988) notes that the language and internal culture of the law is still male in a way that disadvantages females through the "biological clock" and through societal expectations that place non-work-related responsibilities more heavily on women than men.

Similarly, Epstein (1981:8) asserts that the profession "has been structured to mesh with the lives of men and the norms of society which encourage men's commitment to work." The all-consuming demands of early professional development, particularly in the private practice of law, allow little flexibility for large time commitments outside the workplace (Thorner, 1991:100). As Liefland remarks, "Women lawyers who choose to have children are caught between society's delegation of child care to women and a career structure that does not accommodate the family" (1986:613).

The power of societal and professional expectations about gender divisions in family responsibilities is reflected in the tendency to use the human capital language of "choice" to describe women's occupational decisions about family and their remunerated careers. The decisions women must make about remunerated work and a home life, professional advancement and interpersonal relationships, or career and family, often adversely affect both their private and professional lives, and it therefore may be more accurate to describe these decisions as adaptations than as choices.

Notwithstanding the salience of the preceding points, some researchers examining women in the labor force have more recently offered an alternative view of the combining of work and family roles: that of role enhancement. These researchers find that women often respond to multiple roles and their demands with expressions of satisfaction rather than distress (Barnett et al., 1982; Nieva, 1985). Marks (1977) argues that many individuals form strong commitments to multiple roles and happily sustain numerous, diverse involvements. Taylor and Spencer (1988) suggest that "career spouses may be enjoying fuller, though more hectic lives."

Increasingly, we see more women remaining in the workforce even when their children are very young (Smith, 1976). This "double tracking" rather than "sequential" approach to childbearing and employment implies, according to Nieva (1985:176), that either "satisfactory solutions have been developed to handle work-family conflict problems or that the satisfaction derived from role accumulation may override the conflicts."

However, the challenge of balancing career and family responsibilities requires considerable innovation and accommodation, and although many women are combining roles, many compromises also have been required. Women find they must establish priorities, eliminate some subroles, and rotate attention among roles (Hall, 1972). Considering the importance placed on the family role for women in our society, it is not surprising that many married professional women report "curtailing" their careers (i.e., separating their work and family lives) in various ways in an effort to reduce the role strain associated with carrying out their family responsibilities (see Macke, 1984).

This has led some women to eliminate roles and to make choices not traditionally required of men. For example, some women remain childless to reduce role conflict, especially in demanding careers (Nieva, 1985:176). Rebecca (1978) suggests that voluntary childlessness can be understood as a conflict-reducing mechanism. Early studies found that the marital role was also frequently sacrificed: the majority of professional women remained unmarried (Rossi, 1965; Epstein, 1981).

Dranoff's early study of Toronto lawyers (1972) highlighted how women combined law careers with marriage and motherhood in different ways. One of the ways that women lawyers chose to deal with their dual responsibilities was to limit family size. Fifty-six percent of her sample of Toronto women lawyers were childless and 74 percent had no more than one child (1985). Dranoff concludes, "This seems a rather high proportion in relation to the female population at large and possibly indicates that many women still believe that it is children *or* a career that is acceptable and possible in our society, rather than children *and* a career" (185). Similarly, an early study of Harvard law school graduates (Glancy, 1970:24) revealed that women lawyers were more likely than male lawyers to remain single, or if they did marry, to remain childless.

Dranoff (1972:185) also found that women planned their pregnancies to minimize conflict with their professional life. She reports that women differed in the strategies they adopted in response to this conflict. Some women started their families before beginning to practice while others delayed having a family until their law practice was established. Dranoff also found that most women who had established their careers returned to work almost immediately after childbirth and arranged for child care assistance in the home (187). Nearly three quarters of the women in Dranoff's sample of Toronto lawyers returned to their practices within a short period of time after the birth of their child. This led Dranoff to conclude, "There appears to be little justification for male lawyers' concern that a woman lawyer will be lost to the profession for an unduly long period of time" (186).

Nonetheless, a 1988 study of Stanford law graduates (Taber et al., 1988) revealed that women were more likely than men to have interrupted or slowed the progress of their careers. Women were more likely than men to have taken a leave for six months or more, to have stopped working completely (or never have started working), or to have worked part-time. This difference related to the greater frequency with which women took maternity leaves or time off to provide child care. In addition, 82.1 percent of the women, compared with 12 percent of the men, reported career interruptions or never having worked in order to care for their children. Although 76.8 percent of the women who had interrupted or slowed their careers indicated they had done so in order to take maternity leave, only 4.2 percent of the men who had interrupted their careers said they had done so to take a paternity leave.

Part-time work arrangements, at least for a period of time while children are young, is one strategy for balancing the demands of career and family. One woman respondent in Liefland's study (1986:614) who was working at a "bank or corporation" and was the mother of a child wrote that

> I hope that I will soon be working part-time. . . . My husband (also a ____ grad) is an associate with a large firm. It seems difficult (if not impossible) to raise a family with two full-time legal careers. Al-

though my job is considered to be less high-powered than my husband's, it still leaves me little time to be with my child. There is sadly
a dearth of serious part-time positions for lawyers. Other women lawyers jokingly wonder what a part-time job would be — forty hours a
week? It would be nice if my husband could spend time with our
child, too. Family life seems unimportant to the managing partners.

However, Liefland also found that while some women decided to work part-
time because of family responsibilities, even more women were committed
to practicing law on a full-time basis (616-17).

The research literature we have reviewed suggests that women lawyers are seeking to reconcile two roles, as mothers and as professionals, and
that younger women may be less willing than women of previous genera-
tions to accept either role at the expense of the other. According to Halliday
(1986), women often therefore pursue practices that satisfy at least two
criteria: "First, the time commitments must be fairly strictly and predictably
circumscribed so family responsibilities are not unduly complicated; and
second, they must follow paths in segments of the profession in which dislo-
cations of time and intermittency of career are least disruptive" (75). This
reflects conscious efforts to reduce role conflict and achieve role enhancement. However, many women also stretch themselves further and try to do it
all, working full-time in life-consuming practices that offer few accommodations to the combined demands of work and family.

Employers' Conceptions of Workplace Issues

While many women may sustain high levels of commitment to full-time
work and family roles, they may still find themselves disadvantaged in the
workplace because of assumptions employers make about women's commitment to work roles (Bielby and Bielby, 1989:778). Research on women
and paid work shows that employers, the human capitalists we introduced in
chapter 1, often perceive women with children to be less reliable workers
because they are assumed to have excessive demands from home. Employers may also assume that women will leave work at some point (for an
extended period of time) so that it is unprofitable to invest in their career
development (Menkel-Meadow, 1989a:221). Similarly, some women lawyers are assigned less desirable and less lucrative clients because firms assume that they will not be available over the long term; for similar reasons
women may be trained as "permanent associates" and removed from the
partnership track. Epstein (1970) has suggested that the discrimination that
women face at work is similar to that faced by ethnic minority groups, but
that it is compounded by the way in which women are "inexorably seen in

relation to their childbearing functions and . . . the delegation of family roles to them" (3). Rhode (1988) suggests that the conflict between "reproductive and productive rhythms" partially accounts for the rising number of professional women who remain single and/or childless (1187).

Based on cross-national research on the legal profession, Menkel-Meadow (1989a) suggests that as long as partnership decisions are timed to coincide with the years of childbearing, women will be unable to succeed in large numbers (210). The availability of maternity leaves and part-time work arrangements cannot alone solve this problem, because when women make use of these "innovations," they often are considered less committed to their work (Stanford Law Project, 1982; Fenning, 1984; Abramson and Franklin, 1986). These realities of the workplace add to the difficulties of balancing career and family roles.

The Work and Personal Lives of Ontario Lawyers

It is possible that research of the type we have reviewed is already dated. Work and gender roles are changing, and it could be argued that the research findings we have reviewed might already be superseded by subsequent changes and trends. In the following section we examine how the lawyers in our 1990 Ontario sample balance responsibilities in the home and demands of legal practice. A preliminary sense of the frustration and disillusionment recently experienced in this sample is reflected in the comments offered by three women lawyers. One respondent observed, "I love the practice of law but it kicks the hell out of you. Time and clients' demands require that you learn how to balance all other aspects of life against work. This is a skill unto itself." Another respondent reported, "Most employers expect a slave-master relationship with long hours for as little money as they can get away with. If you do not wish to spend sixty to eighty hours/week working you cannot expect a decent pay cheque either. There are two extremes — long work hours, no time for personal life, and a high salary or a regular work week with very little money, benefits, or security. There is no in-between consisting of a regular work week, a decent salary with benefits, and job security. Overall, this aspect of being a lawyer is very frustrating, if not depressing." A third respondent wrote,

> I work 9-5, which I believe is highly unusual for a lawyer in downtown Toronto. I also do not get the going rate. I wish there were more opportunity for regular working hours or part-time work in law. As a new lawyer in terms of experience and as a new mother I find the stress of combining both very difficult. Also, being a male-dominated profession, I do not think there is a very strong incentive for anyone

to change things. Law is meant for the young, eager, single-minded person willing to lose their life in it for five to ten years, not for someone who wants a life outside law.

It should not be surprising to find, then, that anticipated and experienced aspects of work affect decisions about parenting.

Timing of Parenthood: Research reported earlier in this chapter notes that women lawyers often delay marriage and childbearing until they have passed their major career hurdles. Furthermore, as a result of repeated delays, many women lawyers may forgo marriage and parenting roles altogether (Cooney and Uhlenberg 1989:757). Nearly two-thirds of the men (61.3 percent) compared to about one-third (37.6 percent) of the women in the Ontario sample had become parents. Numerous women in the Ontario survey described work histories in which they delayed starting a family until their career was established; others described strategies in the timing of childbearing so as to minimize conflict with the demands of early career development; still others decided to forgo any plans for children. Although women in this sample are still relatively young, a pattern of delay seems apparent. For example, one woman reported, "I accidentally fell into [the field of law] and really enjoy it and do well at it. However, more flexibility is required in work arrangements. I have delayed having children because of my career to some extent but also because both my spouse and I work so hard and long hours. When I have hearings or deals, work hours stretch to 50-60-80 hours a week. I was originally headed for medical school and I often feel I would have had more flexibility and better quality of life had I done so." Another respondent commented, "Maternity leave . . . is a big problem. I took only two weeks and this has seriously deterred me from having a second child."

To test a hypothesis that pressures of larger firms in particular play a significant role in delayed parenting, we analyzed the timing of first births among the women and men lawyers in small (fewer than ten lawyers), medium (ten to forty-nine lawyers) and large Ontario firms (fifty or more lawyers). Recall that the majority of the Ontario women lawyers have not had children, while the majority of the men have. The timing of first births is measured in terms of the average number of years before or after being Called to the Bar. Among lawyers, as elsewhere, women who have children tend to have them at younger ages than men. However, as shown in table 5.1, this difference is largest in small firms and smallest in large firms. For example, women who have children in the small firms of the sample on average have them about four years before being called to the bar, compared to men who have them on average about one year after their calls.

This difference of five years shrinks by about half in large firms. Here women who have children have them on average at about their time of call, while men have them about two and one-half years later. So both men and women in large firms in Ontario postpone parenting, but women do so more than men. Women in medium-sized firms are more like their counterparts in large than in small firms, but the expected gradient is nonetheless apparent in table 5.1 from small to medium to large firms. These findings indicate that large firms have their expected effects in delaying parenting.

Child Care Responsibilities: To explore how lawyers in the Ontario sample who have children balance their work and family responsibilities, we next considered the allocation of child care responsibilities. Respondents with children were asked the proportion of responsibility they and others assumed for child care (including meals, supervision, attendance at sporting and school events) and how many hours per week on average they spent on this care.

Women reported a much greater proportion of the responsibility for child care as their own: the proportion they reported bearing by themselves averaged 49 percent, compared to 26 percent reported by male lawyers.

Table 5.1

Differences among Men and Women Lawyers in Firm Practice in the Timing of First Births, Ontario, 1990

Setting	N	Mean	Standard Deviation	Standard Error	F-Value	2-Tailed Probability
Small Firm [a]						
Women	36	−3.95	10.59	1.77	5.09	0.000
Men	206	1.08	4.70	0.33		
Medium Firm [b]						
Women	9	−0.58	7.26	2.41	2.67	0.039
Men	39	1.73	4.44	0.71		
Large Firm [c]						
Women	35	−0.21	7.06	1.19	4.92	0.000
Men	148	2.41	3.18	0.26		

Time from Call to Bar to First Birth (in years)

[a] Fewer than 10.

[b] 10–49.

[c] More than 50.

Women lawyers also reported a lower proportion of responsibility for child care to be assumed by the person with whom they lived: women reported their partners averaged 21 percent of child care responsibility, while male lawyers reported the person they lived with assumed about 61 percent of this responsibility. Women lawyers were also more likely to report the presence of a paid child care worker: they reported that a paid worker assumed on average 26 percent of the responsibility for child care. In contrast, male lawyers were more likely to report that their spouse assumed most of this responsibility, with about 10 percent assumed by a paid child care worker. In terms of hours per week, we found women lawyers invested considerably more time than men on child care: women with children averaged the equivalent of a second full-time job, spending an average of forty-eight hours per week on child care; men with children averaged twenty-one hours per week.

These patterns were reflected repeatedly in the comments of respondents. One observed, "Since becoming pregnant in 1986, I spend approximately 90 percent of my working hours trying to figure out how to combine my practice with my family life." Another noted that, "I don't have a personal life as such. Since both my spouse and I are in private practice, all personal life issues tend to take place in our two weeks of holidays each year." A third wrote, "Being a lawyer and a mother, I have simply had to give up my personal life. I have virtually no time for myself." Another commented that "family dinner times are nonexistent and all household tasks must be squeezed into a weekend."

Research reviewed earlier also indicated that the psychological as well as instrumental locus of responsibility for child care resides with women, who are accordingly expected to give family demands priority over paid work when unexpected problems and small emergencies arise (Blau and Ferber, 1985:30). Hence, researchers have referred to women's paid employment and family demands as simultaneous, and men's as largely sequential. For example, women are more likely to be contacted at their place of employment regarding an ill child (simultaneous demands), whereas unless the demands are urgent, the father is able to fulfill role obligations after work hours (sequential demands). We therefore asked lawyers to describe who leaves the place of paid work when their children are in need of assistance: "When the children are at home [for medical reasons, school holidays or require transportation to activities], who leaves work most often?"

Women are much more likely to leave work to attend to their children's activities than their spouses. Fifty-two percent of women, compared to 8 percent of male lawyers, said they leave work most often. Similarly, more than a third of male lawyers report that the person they live with

leaves work most often (39 percent), while only 7 percent of women lawyers said the person they live with leaves work most often.

Child care responsibilities may also affect lawyers' availability for
work-related involvements outside "regular" working hours. Respondents
were asked to report the average frequency of attendance at activities (that
is, related to business or client development, including lunches, dinners,
meetings, conferences, receptions, and continuing educational programs)
during different periods of the workday and night and on weekends. Men
and women reported similar attendance at activities during the workday.
Women were more likely to curtail non-work hour business activities.

A common result of compromises made in satisfying competing demands of work and family involves feelings of inadequacy and a preoccupation with efficiency. A respondent worried, "I have had much soul searching on this matter since the birth of my second child. It is difficult to predict
how much longer I will remain a partner in private practice due to my
inability to meet my family commitments." Efforts to save time and work
more effectively were commonly reported: "I have learned to be efficient
— not waste one minute. . . . I have two computers at home and three
briefcases so that I can work at home."

Notwithstanding the extent of these efforts, feelings of guilt were commonly mentioned by respondents. One woman lawyer commented, "I es-
chewed private practice because I didn't want the guilt and fear attached to
my time with family and in recreation." Another woman in the sample
noted, "One always has a sense of guilt. While at home, one feels the stress
of undone things at the office. When at the office, one feels the guilt of not
being home with young children/husband. There is no time left for oneself."
A third woman commented, "The solitary priority for career, career advancing activities and hours of work takes priority over every other interest
and you are made to feel uncommitted and not serious if you don't have this
tunnel vision. The quality of work takes second place to quantity. You are
left feeling guilty if there are other things in your life besides law." These
problems extend beyond child care to include housework and other
unremunerated obligations.

Distribution of Labor in the Home: Lawyers currently practicing
law in Ontario and either married or cohabiting with someone were also
asked two questions regarding housework. The first question asked: "Thinking about the jobs that need to be done to keep a home running (such as
shopping, cooking, cleaning and planning, but excluding child care), how
much of the work is shared between you and your partner?" Answers to
this question revealed that a far greater proportion of women legal practi-

tioners took responsibility for housework (39 percent) than their male colleagues (4 percent). A greater proportion of male than female respondents also reported their partner did most of the housework (58 percent and 5 percent, respectively). Women lawyers were more likely than their male colleagues to report an even distribution of housework between themselves and their spouse (49 percent and 35 percent, respectively) and they were slightly more likely than their male counterparts to report someone else (i.e., relative or paid employee) fulfilled most of the housework demands (7 percent and 3 percent, respectively).

A number of women respondents in the Ontario sample reported that in principle their spouses were willing to take on household chores, but that in practice the actual division of responsibilities still devolved more heavily on the woman member of the household. For example, one woman lawyer reported, "My partner is also a lawyer and that helps tremendously in understanding how we both feel at times when the work is heavy. At those times my partner takes over the household responsibilities, except for laundry or vice versa. But my standard of cleanliness is unrealistic for most men. As it drives me crazy to see a mess, not my partner, I do the cleaning most of the time. The problem I have sometimes is that I don't want to be a nag and I don't always ask him to do things. I find it easier to do them myself." The same kind of point is made in a different way in the following report of a respondent: "I work hard at my job, I spend almost all other available time with my child; I work hard managing my household. My spouse is great and perceives that he helps as much as I do, but he doesn't. His standards of tidiness, etc. are much lower than mine. I never have any time to myself, I'm exhausted, cynical and cranky. Somehow it seems that practicing law and raising a family (at least for the mom) doesn't work very well!" Added to this, some respondents noted that the imbalance in the gender division of family responsibilities extends beyond child care and housework. For example, a woman lawyer in our sample commented, "You restricted 'household' duties to housework and child care — if you were to ask about social responsibilities, for example, entertaining, caring for other family members and friends and elderly acquaintances — you would find that women put in even more time." The bottom line to this accounting is, as noted earlier, that woman lawyers often find they have little time left for themselves.

Schedules and Leaves Available in the Workplace: The combined burden of responsibilities in the home and work in the labor market leads logically to a consideration of possible compensatory supports offered in the workplace. To examine flexibility in work arrangements and availability of leave benefits, we asked lawyers to identify the supports offered by their firm or employer. A total of nine types of arrangements were listed for consideration, including: disability insurance, part-time work, flexible hours (full-time), job sharing, maternity leave, paternity leave, part-time partnerships, child care, and leave of absence/sabbatical.

The most widely offered benefits included disability insurance (64 percent) and maternity leave (60 percent). Only 7 percent reported that their firm or office offered paternity leave benefits. Also, the majority of employers and firms did not offer any child care arrangements to their lawyer-employees (79 percent).

Twenty-four percent of lawyers reported that part-time work arrangements were available at their firm or office. Flexible work hours (on a full-time basis) were reported to be offered at firms and offices by 39 percent of respondents. However, only 7 percent reported that job-sharing arrangements were offered by their firm or employer. Even rarer were part-time partnerships, reported to be offered through law firms by only about 5 percent of the lawyers. Nor were leave arrangements widespread: only 31 percent of respondents indicated that their firm or employer provided such benefits as leaves of absence or sabbaticals.

The lack of flexible work arrangements surfaced not only in the quantitative data, but also in the comments offered by participants in the survey. For example, one woman lawyer commented,

> I enjoy law and intend to continue my career in it. I also have two children and I'd like to participate in bringing them up. So I am constantly looking for a balance between career and family. In a few more years, my kids will both be in school full-time and I'll be working real 'full-time' again. But I'd always like evenings and weekends for my family, and I will just have to find my niche. I see things changing slowly but surely. More and more firms may have positions available which are less demanding than the traditional practice of law. People are more aware now than was the case eight years ago when I first started to practice. A person must have time in her life for work, family, exercise, reading, and self. Yet law is usually a business and making money requires a certain degree of commitment. I hope we will be able to find a balance so that all of these goals can be achieved.

Another respondent offered a less hopeful assessment: "The practice of law is inflexible with respect to the accommodation of a person's 'lifestyle,' which is largely dictated by the 'stage-in-life' of that person (e.g., stages of no family obligations, heavy obligations when children are young, light family obligations when children are grown). Most law firms do not accommodate lawyers who are not willing to commit to long hours of work, the 'all-or-nothing' principle." This all-or-nothing principle derives from a standard that at least in the past seemed suitable for men who often could rely on support from their wives who were not working outside the home. As one woman lawyer noted, "With men, there seems to be less stress because of full-time wives. It's not the same for women lawyers."

Even when law firms and organizations permit maternity (and more broadly, parental) leaves, or allow part-time work and job sharing, women who opt for such arrangements may find themselves removed from promising promotion ladders, challenging work assignments, and generally treated as less dedicated lawyers (Fenning, 1985; Abramson and Franklin, 1986). We saw in the last chapter that women who took maternity leaves were less likely to be made partners. The alternative path is often a transition to forms of legal practice or government employment, which offer greater flexibility in work arrangements and improved benefits. One woman lawyer describes her work this way:

> Ultimately, I bit the bullet, left the legal profession, and entered a government job in a supervisory capacity. With my maternity, pension, and other benefits, I am in a position to control my own destiny. In the future I will be able to work part-time if I choose to do so (and will be supported in doing so by my employer) and be able to rise as quickly or slowly in my career as I wish. Unfortunately, most of my female friends who are still practicing do not have these options, and although they are earning more now than I ever will as a government employee, they are envious of the flexibility my career path holds. The legal profession still has miles to go to come to terms with the fact that it must accommodate women in the profession (e.g., "part-time" litigation work — 8-hour day instead of 18, free lance lawyers who can contract to complete *x* number of projects/ week, lawyers who can job-share, etc.). These types of options will make the profession more attractive to women in their child-bearing years and will keep them in it rather than forcing them to look elsewhere as I did. The bottom line is, we all spend too long a period of our lives to qualify as lawyers to throw it all away (as I did, in a sense) in order to fulfill the other needs in our lives.

Another woman lawyer, having left private practice to work in government, commented: "I am now a government lawyer, well paid, with challenging work and hours that allow me to lead a balanced life. . . . One just cannot live a balanced life in the private practice setting. I hope these views, which I anticipate will be reflected in other responses, percolate into the management committees of . . . law firms. I would like to see our society, including the legal profession, embrace or at least approve of a healthy work ethic."

One woman lawyer in the sample summarized her frustration with the profession this way: "I wish someone had told me it was not realistically possible to become a very successful lawyer and also a very successful wife and mother, because if they had I would have chosen a different profession. I don't think law is a very convenient occupation for a woman who also wants to have a family."

Further Effects of the Balancing Act

Clearly, women lawyers bear heavy burdens in attempting to balance demands of work and family. One of the most common observations recorded in our research involved the perceived difficulty for lawyers of balancing family and work roles. Men as well as women expressed this concern. A common kind of observation expressed by a male lawyer was, "In general I find the practice of law very exciting and rewarding; however, what I find quite disturbing is the lack of balance between professional (i.e., career) and personal (i.e., home) life." Another male lawyer commented, "Although I generally find my work challenging, interesting and varied, I find it difficult to find the time to do much else. Balancing a rewarding career with a rewarding personal life is difficult. Ironically, being a well-balanced individual with varied and numerous outside interests is an asset which enhances your ability to be a good lawyer. However, once you become a lawyer and begin to practice law full-time, those outside interests are very often sacrificed for the sake of your professional career." A third male lawyer summarized the dilemma for himself and his wife, also a lawyer, this way: "I work long and hard; my wife works long and hard. Each of us thinks the other works too long and hard and doesn't have enough time for the other. How does one spend less time at work, without either refusing clients who will go elsewhere (never to be seen again) or performing slowly (disappointing clients as well) to free time for family (and living in general) without risking financial harm? This is obviously a rhetorical question!" A final male lawyer comments, "I wish there was more time to pursue non-professional activities and to spend with my children and wife. There is too much to do in one life, and the law takes up too great a proportion of it, leaving me less rounded and involved than I would choose to be."

The crunch, of course, comes for many lawyers as they begin to have children. A woman lawyer in the sample noted, "I'm happy with my professional life now, but I'm afraid that when I have children in the near future, my career will conflict with my family obligations and goals. Law is unforgiving and unwelcoming to mothers." While having children obviously presents much greater challenges for women than men lawyers, it is interesting to note that a number of men in the Ontario sample perceived this problem as well. One male lawyer commented, "My wife and I are expecting a child in the coming months, and I am very concerned about increasing pressure in our firm and others to increase the number of hours docketed. Time with family will be a priority for me and if my career interferes too greatly, I will seek alternative employment, perhaps as in-house counsel." Another male lawyer again raised the issue of balance and observed, "[I am] considering a move to some area of law that is less demanding of my time. I want to be home more with my family. There is too much pressure in a large firm. My life is not balanced enough, and I know it."

The final parts of this chapter further assess the effects of this balancing act by considering the decisions of lawyers to make changes in their careers and, in some cases, to leave law entirely. Our Ontario data oversamples lawyers who have recently left law, providing an important opportunity to consider this group. Departures from law in the Toronto sample are considered in chapter 7.

Career Moves

We begin by providing a descriptive picture of the early career moves traced in the survey of Ontario lawyers. Several aspects of these lawyers' work histories are examined: the number of positions occupied, the type of employment pursued, and the level of employment at each stage (i.e., full-time, part-time, not in practice). We consider up to the first five professional positions occupied in the careers of lawyers; we chose this limited number of positions because the sample is restricted to the first fifteen years of practice.

First, we enumerated the actual number of professional positions held by men and women in our sample of Ontario lawyers. The amount of stability as well as movement in the legal profession is reflected by the fact that while more than a quarter of the lawyers in this sample were still in their initial professional positions, nearly three-quarters had experienced some movement. The average number of positions is slightly but nonetheless significantly higher for women than for men (2.35 and 2.27, respectively).

Next we examine the distributions of male and female lawyers by level and type of employment across up to five professional positions in table 5.2. Although the great majority of both men and women initially worked on a full-time basis, a slightly greater proportion of women compared with men started their first professional position on a part-time basis. As well, the proportion of women working part-time increased substantially with shifts in positions across their careers. For example, about 3, 5, and 11

Table 5.2
Characteristics of Lawyers' Work Histories, by Gender, Ontario

	Positions Held (Men Lawyers)					Positions Held (Women Lawyers)				
	1st	2d	3d	4th	5th	1st	2d	3d	4th	5th
Level of Employment (percent)										
Full-time	96.2	92.9	93.5	87.9	76.6	93.0	86.0	73.0	61.3	63.5
Part-time	0.9	1.3	0.6	0.0	3.4	2.6	5.1	11.3	16.4	9.3
Not Practicing	2.9	5.8	5.9	12.1	20.0	4.5	8.9	15.7	22.3	27.2
Type of Employment (percent)										
Government	7.3	10.1	14.8	11.8	12.7	10.8	15.8	17.5	24.5	17.4
Corporation	3.5	5.5	8.5	11.3	3.4	3.9	7.8	8.6	4.8	3.8
Legal Aid/Law Clinic	1.2	1.7	2.8	5.3	3.4	3.0	4.6	3.8	1.6	0.6
Private Industry	0.4	0.7	0.5	0.0	0.4	0.2	1.7	1.3	1.5	0.0
Associate	60.0	28.9	22.6	24.0	13.4	58.4	32.4	20.6	16.5	16.9
Partner	12.1	26.3	29.4	24.3	21.5	3.5	12.7	9.9	10.2	16.9
Solo Practitioner	8.6	15.2	12.0	7.5	18.5	7.2	8.2	12.6	10.4	10.6
Other	4.0	5.8	3.5	3.7	6.7	8.5	7.9	10.1	8.1	7.9
Not Practicing	2.9	5.8	5.9	12.1	20.0	4.5	8.9	15.7	22.3	27.2
Number of Lawyers	1,110	785	388	149	58	467	329	173	77	33

percent of women, respectively, worked part-time in their first, second, and third positions. The figures for men are 0.9, 1.3, and 0.6 percent (for first through third positions, respectively). But most striking is the proportion of men and women who are not practicing. The difference peaks by the fourth position, when 22 percent of women are not practicing, compared to 12 percent of men.

Distributions of women and men across types of employment are also detailed by position in table 5.2. The initial four positions are described, since these contain the largest number of respondents (94 percent). The largest proportion of Ontario lawyers started their careers as associates of firms, with close to 60 percent of Ontario men and women lawyers in 1990 beginning their careers as associates. The percentages of lawyers working as associates declines in later positions, partly because of their success or failure in becoming partners, examined in the previous chapter. Twelve percent of male lawyers began their careers as partners, while less than 4 percent of female lawyers started as partners. Consistent with our findings in the previous chapter, nearly three times the proportion of men (29.4 percent), compared to women (9.9 percent) became partners within three moves from entry into the profession.

Outside the private practice of law, we find that women are more likely than men to begin their careers as government employees, and at each successive position they are more likely than their male counterparts to find employment with government. About 11 percent of women compared to about 7 percent of men started in a government position. By their second position, nearly 16 percent of women compared with about 10 percent of men were employed in government, and by their fourth position, the comparison peaked at about 24 and 12 percent, respectively. This table confirms that women are much more likely than men to both leave the practice of law and seek positions in government. These are often alternative adaptations to the problems of balancing work and family demands.

Leaving Law

The overrepresentation of women among those lawyers leaving the practice of law prompts us to examine further the nature of this transition. Specifically, from where in the profession of law are these departures occurring? And why have these individuals left the practice of law?

Interestingly, we saw above that a large percentage of lawyers never entered the practice of law following bar admission. For instance, 16 percent of lawyers who reported having "departed" from the practice of law stated their first professional position after being called to the Ontario bar was outside the practice of law. Of those who did not practice law immediately after being called to the Bar, 43 percent were women. This is more than double the representation of women in the profession.

We further considered from where in the profession of law these departures were most likely to occur. The largest percentage of those having departed from the practice of law reported that they began as associates in law firms (45 percent); in addition, 12 percent were solo practitioners and 6 percent were partners. Overall, 63 percent of those having left law started their careers in private practice. Departures were most common in the first two positions occupied, and most frequently from the fields of civil litigation and real estate for men and civil litigation and family law for women.

In table 5.3 we model the decision to leave firm practice using a technique called event history analysis, which is discussed in the Appendix at end of this volume. Here we can simply note that the purpose of this methodology is to assess the probability of experiencing an event, such as leaving law, at some specific time by combining consideration of timing and risk. For example, the analysis we present in table 5.3 models the effects of the kinds of variables considered in the previous chapter on the rate of transition or movement from the first professional position in a firm to a decision to leave the practice of law. That is, we model the timing of decisions of women and men lawyers to leave firm practices and the practice of law entirely.

The results in the first column of table 5.3 suggest that male lawyers and lawyers who are married, have children, and practice in smaller or larger firms are least likely to leave law and do so most slowly. Of course, we are most interested in the fact that women are more likely to leave law and do so more quickly. The second column of table 5.3 introduces the measure of the number of hours spent on child care. Recall that women lawyers with children spend the equivalent of another work week on child care, more than double the time spent by men lawyers. In the second column of table 5.3 we see that the more hours spent on child care, the greater is the likelihood and rate of leaving law. Further, the introduction of this variable in column 2 reduces the effect of gender below statistical significance. The clear implication of this model is that women are leaving law to care for their children. However, this may too simply portray the reactions of these women to their work and family experiences.

A fuller sense of the motivations underlying departures from the practice of law emerged when we asked our respondents why they did so. Respondents who left legal practice were asked to rank their top three reasons for leaving law. The largest percentages of men who departed from the practice of law reported the following as their first reason for leaving:

• improved career opportunities elsewhere (26 percent),
• general dissatisfaction with the practice of law (25 percent),
• "other" reasons (18 percent).

In contrast, the main reasons for leaving practice among women were:

• general dissatisfaction with the practice of law (30 percent),
• to look after my children (15 percent),
• improved career opportunities elsewhere (12 percent).

So there are similarities as well as differences in the reasons that women and men indicate for leaving the practice of law. Both women and men expressed dissatisfaction with various aspects of work. Areas of displeasure included occupational tasks, number of work-related hours, quality of life, as well as a more general dissatisfaction with practicing law. Typical of women who had left practice in the Ontario sample was the observation,

Table 5.3
Antilogs of Estimated Effects of Variables on Rates of Transition from First Position in Firms to Departure from Practice, Ontario (Standard error in parentheses)

Independent Variables	Equations (Eqs.)	
	Eq. 1 Antilog	Eq. 2 Antilog
Gender	0.655 (0.145)**	0.852 (0.152)
Age at Call	1.003 (0.001)**	1.005 (0.001)***
Elite Law School	1.201 (0.142)	1.213 (0.142)
WASP	0.834 (0.151)	0.876 (0.152)
Married	0.660 (0.161)**	0.630 (0.161)**
Children	0.433 (0.166)***	0.231 (0.184)***
Lawyers in Firm		
< 10	0.526 (0.160)***	0.536 (0.161)***
> 20	0.242 (0.257)***	0.257 (0.258)***
Specialization Status	1.115 (0.100)	1.139 (0.104)
Child Care (hrs./week)		1.017 (0.002)***
Model χ^2	112.277***	167.768***
Degrees of Freedom	9	10

** $p < 0.01$; *** $p < 0.001$.
Note: Antilogs of estimated parameters are reported in this table because they are more easily interpreted than the parameters themselves. Antilogs can be interpreted as multipliers of rates. Values greater than 1.0 reflect increases in these rates, and values less than 1.0 reflect decreases.

"I feel the profession of law demands too much of my time, concentration, energy, and focus. Very little was left to lead anything close to a balanced life. It's not balanced yet, but much improved having left." Overall, when all reasons were combined, about two-thirds of the women who left law expressed some kind of dissatisfaction with working in the legal profession, compared to about half of the men.

Meanwhile, about 15 percent of women additionally cited looking after children as a first reason for leaving the practice of law. Another 8 percent of women listed child care as their second most important reason, and 4 percent as their third most important reason. Few male respondents identified children among their reasons for leaving the practice of law.

Although termination of employment or lack of promotion were not often selected by respondents as important reasons for leaving law, by either men or women, improved career opportunities elsewhere were an important reason for men.

Choice or Constraint?

The results of this chapter indicate that career patterns and experiences vary considerably between men and women lawyers. Women are likely to have held more professional positions than their male counterparts, and they are more likely to be employed in government. They are less likely to be partners and are more likely to be among those leaving the practice of law. Women who leave law are more dissatisfied than men, who are more likely to leave for better opportunities. It seems clear that women see these gendered outcomes as constrained rather than chosen.

In general, the careers of women are more diverse and complex than mens'. The diversity of women's careers and the difficulty of studying such diversity is illustrated in the following comment by one woman: "I did a number of legal tasks before being called to the bar. For example, I taught at a law school and worked on two government task forces between graduation from law school and being called to the bar. I also dropped out of law school completely for five years, farmed, and had a child between law school and my call. Your questionnaire seems to assume a more typical (and maybe male) career path."

As Halliday (1986) suggests, the effects of home and child care responsibilities encourage women to maximize employment characteristics other than status or earnings (e.g., more flexible working hours, more convenient job location) (see also Roos, 1985:120). The "push" factors involved in leaving private practice and the "pull" factors involved in attracting lawyers to nonprivate practice can be seen in the following: "I left private practice of criminal law in part because it was wearing on me and I wasn't making enough money for the time I put in. . . . I found that as a 'single mother,'. . . I had to spend some time with my son. . . . I like the variety that practice offers; I want the resources that government offers. The stability of my present position is something that is certainly very attractive."

The complete departure by many women from the practice of law is a more troubling development. Several writers have termed this a "flight from law" (See Hirsh, 1989; Menkel-Meadow, 1989b; Otvos, 1992). One woman's response suggests what the factors are that encourage departure from the practice of law by both men and women.

> The time method of billing places constraints on a lawyer's earning abilities. There are only so many hours a person can work in a week. I now run my own business and make far more than I could have earned as a salaried associate. More importantly, I can decide on critical lifestyle issues without stigma. I feel that I have escaped a pressure cooker environment where no one I worked with had time to read literature, attend cultural events, listen to music, or simply enjoy life's smaller pleasures. There is much more to life than bringing in clients, managing files, dealing with other counsel, serving ever-demanding clients, and battling the judicial system. Not to mention potentially crushing liabilities and responsibilities. Too many young lawyers are stressed out and have lost a sense of perspective. But, senior lawyers have cultivated this paranoia. They look at juniors as "revenue generating units" and do not put enough effort into cultivating character, self-confidence, and integrity.

These concerns with earnings, quality of life (particularly the balance between personal and professional lives), and career satisfaction affect both men and women, but they are especially salient for women.

There is much evidence in the findings of this chapter that women experience role overload and conflict in attempting to balance work and family, and many of them leave the practice of law or seek alternative positions to reduce this conflict. Human capital theory sees leaving of private practice or of law altogether by many women as an efficient choice in resolving this conflict. Many of these same women would regard this view as too comfortable. It smooths over the way in which the gender stratification of legal careers constrains opportunities for men to contribute more to family life and for women to continue to contribute to firm and legal life. We have seen in this chapter that many men as well as women would prefer to better balance these contributions, that is, to redistribute family and practice roles in a more gender-neutral fashion.

Meanwhile, an increasing number of women are continuing to work full-time in the private practice of law, often with young children. The motivation that animates the careers of many such women is expressed by a respondent who observes, "Maybe the most accurate way of stating it is that I could not imagine life without a career. . . . Without doing something with myself and my talents, I can't imagine life at all. I only wish I had more time for personal relationships and family." The combination of work and family roles may be uniquely experienced by these women. Human capital and gender stratification theories make quite different assumptions about the impact of parenting on women and men in full-time private practice. We explore these assumptions in the next chapter, in the context of an analysis of lawyers' earnings.

6

Born to Bill?

I put up with people (including clients) that in other circumstances I would avoid like the plague. Over the span of 33 years in practice the firm has grown from a "gentleman's club" to a "factory." Regrettably, this is the price of progress, but some of the attraction of practicing law has gone — leaving one to worry about hours billed, clients with increasingly unrealistic demands, and a general feeling of malaise. I should have taken my father's advice and stuck to medicine!

The practice of law has changed drastically over the last ten years and is still changing. Many of us have become greedy, the only focus being the bottom line at the expense of human values. Billable hours have become too important.

Billings and Earnings

The last several decades have brought a sea change to the private practice of law in firms. Firms that were once largely governed by principles of seniority, with older partners expecting and receiving a highly disproportionate share of practice earnings, today are increasingly concerned with productivity, with partners of all ages staking claims to practice earnings based on credit expected and received for the accumulation of billings. This credit is usually grounded in accounting regimes whose currency consists of billable hours, the units in which everyday lawyering activities in firms often are calibrated. The notion of a billable hour turns out to bear an affinity to human capitalist conceptions of the earnings process, and we will see in this chapter that these billable units play a key role in this theory's explanation of differences in the earnings of men and women lawyers. We will also see that gender stratification theory offers a rather different and well-supported alternative understanding of the role billable hours play in determining the earnings of men and women lawyers.

Explaining Gendered Outcomes

The chosen spheres argument of human capital theory introduced in the first chapter of this book asserts that intrinsic differences between the genders in bearing and caring for children can account for differences in employment outcomes (see Epstein, 1992:269–74), including gender differences in earnings. This version of human capital theory is of more than academic interest because it has played a key role in judicial decisions about gender discrimination in white-collar and professional settings.

Gender differences in blue-collar jobs, such as fire fighting, often have been attributed to differences in physical abilities to meet employment requirements. However, such arguments cannot be applied to the mental abilities required in professional jobs such as law. Instead, the focus shifts in cases involving professional and white-collar work to the role played by interests, preferences or choices involved in decisions to specialize attention on the family rather than work, or, in the language of human capital theory, to invest in the development of one's family rather than work resources. A U.S. court decision in the Arkansas case of *Gillespie v. Board of Education* (1981) exemplifies a judicial variant of this theory, reasoning that women are less likely to want administrative positions in schools because "[m]ales who are pursuing careers in education are often the principal family breadwinners. Women . . ., on the other hand, have frequently taken teaching jobs to supplement family income and leave when this is no longer necessary or they are faced with the exigencies of raising a family. We regard this as a logical explanation and find as a matter of fact that there has been no discrimination" (cited in Schultz, 1990:1803). Such decisions lend legal legitimacy to the underemployment and reduced remuneration of women in white-collar occupations and professions.

Research into gender inequalities in earnings demonstrates that income differences between women and men lawyers are larger than in most other occupations (Hagan, 1990). White (1967) sampled men and women from the graduating classes of 1956 through 1965 of 134 American law schools and discovered that "the males make a lot more money than do the females" (1057). A study of Harvard law school graduates (Glancy, 1970:25) found that fewer than 12 percent of the women, compared to 57 percent of the men earned in excess of $20,000 annually. A five year follow-up study (Adam and Baer, 1984:39) of the 1974 graduates of Ontario law schools reported that women graduates earned on average about $3,000 a year less than their male counterparts. A study (Vogt, 1987) conducted in seven north-eastern U.S. law schools in 1985 reported that among graduates eleven years out and in the same size firms, men earned on average $75,000 and women $46,500. At a minimum, these studies suggest that women lawyers have yet to break through the glass ceiling of legal practice.

The chosen spheres argument of human capital theory explains the gender gap in employment outcomes such as lawyers' earning as the combined product of efficiency and choice: the higher earnings of men are seen as an efficient reward for the investment of greater effort and therefore better developed human capital by highly committed men who have chosen to give priority to their careers (e.g., Mincer, 1985; Becker, 1991). The implication is that if women made similar choices and efforts as men, they would achieve comparable earnings. This version of human capital theory regards having a child as a choice to invest in family and child care, and these choices are assumed to reduce career commitment and effort necessary for occupational advancement.

Because human capital theory regards the division of labor between home and other work as an efficient investment in specialized human capital, it does not emphasize the issue of sex discrimination (see Becker, 1991:4), and this theory is used more generally to question the utility of discrimination law (e.g., Epstein, 1992). However, Becker (1991) also acknowledges that the greater investment of women in home and family, and a resulting reduction in occupational investment by women, can produce exaggerated differences in the payment to women for their employment outside the home that could be understood as discrimination. Indeed, Becker goes so far as to note that discrimination could alone conceivably produce these differences through male exploitation of the comparative specializations of women in the home and men in other work. We have called this the restricted spheres version of Becker's human capital theory. But this possibility in human capital theory is not Becker's primary concern, and his emphasis on the implications of the chosen spheres argument actively discourages research and litigation using statistical evidence to establish discrimination along gender lines.

Becker focuses instead on assumed "intrinsic" biological differences that comparatively advantage women at home and men elsewhere, and on the manner in which these initial differences are magnified by subsequent investments of human capital in these separate spheres. Becker's central concern is that "a small initial difference can be transformed into large observed differences by the reinforcing effects of specialized investments" (1991:63). This leads to a rejection of the kind of evidence used in racial cases to demonstrate discrimination based on gender, with Becker reasoning,

> This magnification of small differences in comparative advantage into large differences in earnings distinguishes differences between men and women from those between blacks and whites or other groups. A little market discrimination against blacks would not induce a large reduction in their earnings, because there is no racial division of labour between the market and household sectors. . . . Consequently, the empirical decomposition of earnings differences into discrimination and other sources should be interpreted more cautiously for men and women than for other groups because of the division of labour between men and women. (63)

Statistical "decompositions" of data on earnings are a common procedure in gender stratification research and in the presentation of evidence in employment discrimination cases (see Fisher, 1980).

In contrast with the chosen spheres version of human capital theory, gender stratification theory emphasizes that differences between men and women in earnings are the combined product of inefficiency and constraint: the lower earnings of women inefficiently penalize the comparable efforts of committed women who often in spite of constraining demands of family and inadequate rewards in earnings invest heavily in their careers (e.g., England and Farkas, 1986; Tienda et al., 1987; Bielby and Bielby, 1988). According to this theory, women who are similar to men in their career commitment are not rewarded at levels similar to men. This theory is also sensitive to the experiences of women who have children and are expected to devote more time than men to family and child care, because according to this theory these investments may commonly be made without reducing career commitment and investments on the job, and without corresponding rewards in earnings. Gender stratification theory sees hierarchical work structures as inflexible and unyielding sources of disparities in the opportunities and rewards open to women. These work structures are seen as discriminatory, and without change they are understood to perpetuate the subordination of women.

It is significant to note that the chosen spheres version of human capital theory implicitly adopts the role overload and conflict understanding introduced in chapter 5 of the multiple-role responsibilities of working women. It is this overload and conflict that presumably leads women to specialize in the home while men specialize in work outside the home. Alternatively, while gender stratification theory acknowledges conflicts between home and other work roles associated with unyielding job environments, it is nonetheless more likely to see the work of women outside the home as a source of role-enhancing diversity. If this is so, the expanded role requirements that come with the bearing of children should not result in a long-term decline in commitment to work outside the home. We explore this issue later in this chapter.

While human capital theory is a powerful paradigm for the development of provocative hypotheses about gender differences in employment and earnings, its key assumptions are seldom operationalized or subjected to serious measurement and empirical test by its proponents, and little or no attention is given to the restricted spheres variant of Becker's theory. As well, the presentation of the theory often incorporates a reasoning that shifts between classes of cases, for example, between women who pursue part-time and/or discontinuous employment and women who work full-time and continuously in careers outside the home. In doing this, there is a danger that human capital theory conflates a range of home and other work relationships and justifies policies that differentially reward men and women for their employment outside the home, implying that women are generally less committed to their occupational careers than men, and that therefore they differ in their accumulation of human capital and accompanying rewards.

Human capital theorists therefore are often understood as arguing that the solution to women's inequality in the professions and elsewhere lies with women themselves, implying, "if they want positions offering more pay, prestige, and power, female professionals must become more willing to make the personal sacrifices that such positions entail" (Rhode, 1988:1181). So that even while the human capital account might seem to be contradicted by the large number of women who are today "investing" heavily in legal education, and even though Becker's acknowledgement of a restricted spheres argument suggests alternative possibilities, "human capitalists" who manage law firms can invoke this theory, "particularly the assumptions about commitment to work, in . . . justifying the lower salaries paid to women" (Menkel-Meadow, 1989a:220). The issue of gender discrimination is deemphasized by some human capital theorists in a way that implies that a concern with this issue may be inefficient, and even "a source of mischief for ordinary employers and workers in the marketplace" (Epstein, 1992:282).

If the assumptions of the chosen spheres version of human capital theory are correct, they can justify differential treatment of women and men as fair and efficient aspects of professional life. However, if some of these assumptions are shown to be false, the differences associated with them can be better understood as discriminatory, as consistent with an alternative restricted spheres version of human capital theory as well as gender stratification theory, and therefore as abuses of an increasingly recognized "duty of nondiscrimination" that is in need of enforcement.

Assessing the Claims

Empirical efforts to resolve differences between chosen and restricted spheres versions of human capital and gender stratification theories confront demanding design and measurement requirements. For example, to avoid conflating or neglecting individuals pursuing different combinations of family and other work, separate as well as combined attention must be given to individuals who do and do not pursue continuous, full-time employment (Fligstein and Wolf, 1978; Tienda et al., 1987). As well, because concerns about the career progress of women compared to men and about breaking through the glass ceiling explicitly focus on change over time, panel data are needed to assess the effects of career movements and to establish causal sequences assumed to lead to success or failure in professional work. Furthermore, measures must be developed of commitment to work and applied across individuals and career experiences, with special attention to changes in family roles.

Bielby (1992) has noted that serious efforts to assess gender differences must measure both *subjective* and *objective* components of work commitment. Considerable progress has been made in measuring subjective commitment to work (Bielby and Bielby, 1984) and perceived work effort (Bielby and Bielby, 1988). However, more objectively focused measurement of work commitment, effort, or "productivity" is in some ways more challenging. Of course, part of the difficulty lies in determining by whom and how such measures are assumed to be objective. But putting these problems temporarily aside, there are even more obvious and immediate problems. Common indicators of hours/weeks/months of employment only crudely measure the kinds of investment made in work across occupations. Productivity measures probably come closer to the task, but they vary widely across types of employment. For example, while volume and prestige of publication and/or teaching evaluation scores are widely recognized measures of productivity in academia, these measures have little meaning for other occupations. This may be one reason why little systematic attention has been given to measuring productivity across occupations. However, measures of the productivity of work efforts are necessary to consider meaningfully the claims of human capital and gender stratification theory, and this may therefore require occupation-specific treatment.

The Billable Hours of Privately Practicing Lawyers

While women lawyers attain earnings far higher than women in most other occupations, studies noted above indicate that with experience and other human and social capital variables held constant, the income gap between men and women lawyers is substantial (Hagan, 1990). As we have seen, human capital theory does not doubt this disparity, but explains this gap by assuming differences in productive investment in work. The "billable hour" is a key part of this argument for privately practicing lawyers.

For many years law firms were somewhat casual about monitoring the hourly work of lawyers and their methods of charging clients. Large firms seem not to have kept accurate time records prior to the end of World War II (Earle and Perlin, 1973:354), and although diary and time sheets were used to keep track of time in some firms in the 1950s (Klaw, 1958), it was not until the middle 1960s that billing for lawyer hours became a standard method of calculating fees (Smigel, 1969; see Galanter and Palay, 1991:34–35).

Attention to time spent on particular files and cases was in the beginning largely for the purposes of charging clients. Nelson (1988) found little evidence of reliance on billable hours in the division of partnership profits in his study of four Chicago firms, but he nonetheless observed an outpouring of consultants' recommendations, sometimes connected to intergenerational conflicts among partners, that pointed in the direction of change; he predicted that "as firms adopt a more entrepreneurial approach to management, the trend toward compensation formulas emphasizing client production will gain momentum" (203).

Indeed, as the billable hours method of calculating fees took hold, its use as a device to simultaneously track productivity became increasingly pervasive. By the mid-1970s firms began to set targets for partners and associates that ranged from 1,500 to 2,000 billable hours per year (Bernstein, 1978:104–12; Hoffman, 1973:130–31). These targets were used in latent and then more manifest ways to stimulate and monitor productivity in firms. Epstein (1981:212) succinctly notes that "time diaries and the billing system are watchdogs."

Galanter and Palay (1991; see also Gilson and Mnookin, 1985) similarly emphasize a turn toward monitoring productivity and accountability in an era of new competitiveness: "[F]irms rationalize their operations;

they engage professional managers and consultants; firm leaders worry about billable hours," causing a shift in emphasis from seniority to the direct production of profits: "'Eat what you kill' compensation formulas emphasize rewards for productivity and business-getting over 'equal shares' or seniority" (Galanter and Palay, 1991:52). Spangler (1986) writes, "New lawyers must not only learn to be partisan, but also to be economical. . . . They must remember that the practice of law is 'first and foremost' a business" (43). A well-socialized young woman lawyer in our sample reported, "I value everything in terms of time. My free time seems to have a dollar value. I will pay for something to free up time because I've been trained to believe every minute has a financial value." Another respondent commented, "Helping people and talking to them is replaced by 'got to get the billings up,' like a rat on a treadmill." Billable hours have become a centerpiece of contemporary life in private practice.

Measuring the Work of Men and Women Lawyers

As we have noted, human capital theory assumes that women work less than men in the private practice of law. Such behavior is more generally and evocatively described in the human capital literature on law firms as the problem of "free riding" or "shirking" (Leibowitz and Tollison, 1980). Billable hours are regarded by human capital theory as an efficient device for monitoring these behaviors, although because lawyers are "mental workers," monitoring their time is more costly than simply installing a punch clock.

> It is true that lawyers' inputs are more cerebral than those of many other workers, making input monitoring more costly, ceteris paribus. All things considered, however, the marginal cost of reducing shirking by monitoring time inputs may actually be lower in law firms. Lawyers quote fees and bill clients on the basis of time inputs. . . . Lawyers in a typical day work for several different clients, which requires that they keep better records than nonprofessional workers, whose time is not billed directly to customers. The marginal cost of input monitoring to reduce shirking is lower when firm owners already collect and monitor input data for other purposes like billing. (McChesney, 1982:383)

Observers of law firms note that this record keeping can be precise, to the point that "hours may appear as quarters or as six-minute bits," with lawyers keeping accurate timed accounts of "telephone calls, letters dictated, cases looked up in the library, as well as meetings, court appearances" (Mayer, 1966:20). When lawyers are dilatory about this responsibility, "they become diary delinquents, and firms devise various penalties to enforce record keeping" (Spangler, 1986:52).

Nonetheless, the existing empirical literature is uncertain in its assessment of the time investment that women lawyers actually make in their work. Epstein (1981) reports that "most women interviewed in New York firms said that they devoted the same amount of time to work as their male colleagues and some even claim to work harder in order to prove themselves" (210). Similarly, Rhode (1988) reports that "folklore abounds with examples of the dedicated professional who bills 2,000 hours while pregnant or is back 'faster than a speeding bullet' after childbirth" (185–86). Yet, when Epstein (1981:315) turned to census measures from 1970, she found that women lawyers worked an average of 38.7 hours a week, while male lawyers worked an average of 45.8 hours a week. Menkel-Meadow (1989:218) similarly reports that the 1980 U.S. census data indicate that "women . . . work for fewer hours . . . and women's hours drop when children are born." Epstein also reveals that in her own interviewing, "[i]t was difficult to learn the precise hours worked . . . because the women themselves did not always have a clear idea of what they were" (315).

Some of this confusion follows from uncertainty about what is meant by *hours worked*. Not all hours spent at work are billable hours. Indeed, women lawyers often complain that men lawyers spend many useless office hours "showing the flag" and wastefully engaging in what Goffman (1971) calls "interaction rituals." In any case, many hours spent at work are distinct from hours more specifically *docketed* for firm committee assignments, pro bono obligations, community activities, and firm promotional efforts, as well as for clients. Hours *billed* to clients, the ultimate measure of productivity for the human capitalists, are a crucial subset of both hours worked overall and docketed hours. One of our respondents notes, "Almost everyone works a ten-hour day to bill seven hours." Another remarked that, "though I bill about forty hours a week, I routinely work over seventy." Spangler (1986:53) reports that in the Boston firms she studied there was an understanding that time billable to clients constitutes about two-thirds of the total hours worked, a figure very close to what we report below.

However, this is only part of the problem, and our point is not that the recording of billable hours is an unprejudiced check on free riding or shirking, as assumed by the human capital theorists, for we do not assume that hours are billed in a one-to-one fashion with hours spent on a case or file, or that these counts are in any sense perfectly accurate. Galanter and Palay (1991) note that "'billable hours' is a product not only of actual time spent but of recording and billing practices, which may change independently of the former" (35n). More generally, Granovetter (1992) notes that productivity is rarely measured well except in certain well-defined and individualized jobs, and, more importantly, that the difficulties are more than merely technical. "Rather," Granovetter notes, "the productivity of individual workers is inextricably intermeshed in a network of relations with other workers" (251), which he calls the "social context of production" (252). The potential importance of this context is well illustrated by considering social aspects of the production of billable hours in legal practice.

First, there is likely an important element of hierarchy in who obtains credit for the difference between actual time spent and time recorded and billed, for lawyers in our research spoke of the need to exercise discretion in "writing up" or "writing down" hours. Thus, Spangler (1986) notes that while partners are rewarded primarily for their own work, they also are rewarded for "coordinating and supervising the work of others" (40). She goes on to note that "[o]nce a client, or a particular case or matter, has been accepted, the partner managing the work is also free to staff the project as he or she sees fit, . . . the partner in charge is free to bill for the firm's time at exactly the number of hours logged; at a discount if a young associate was trained on the project or if an error was made; or at a premium if the client concluded a very lucrative transaction or if extraordinary efforts ('all night at the printer's') were required." Lawyers in our own Toronto research spoke of "power billing" to refer to situations in which they felt free to increase the numbers of hours they charged clients for services that they felt able to perform with unusual efficiency. Spangler (1986) notes that on all such issues of billing "partners are the final arbiters" (48), so the reference to power billing may be appropriate in a number of ways.

These may not be small or idle points, for women may be greatly affected in the credit they take and receive in billing for hours they work. The problem partly derives from power relationships between men and women in the professions, as elsewhere. The legal profession has a hierarchical structure that we documented with our typology of practice in chapter 2, and this hierarchical structure advantages men (Hagan, et al., 1988; Martin, 1992). Meanwhile, Bielby and Bielby (1988:1034) cite experimental evidence that women in general undervalue and underreward their own work efforts relative to men. A male respondent in our study remarked of women, "They seem less aggressive on their own behalf." This may make it less likely that women will use the hierarchical positions they attain to reward their work in the same way as do men (Menkel-Meadow, 1989b). And if they do not take their fair share of credit, it is less likely that it will be received, for as Martin (1992) notes, "power relationships become apparent when the important and often unspoken question of given, allowed and permitted by whom is asked" (9).

A number of women lawyers in our research commented on the problems of obtaining access to good files and promising cases. One woman lawyer observed, "The interesting work seems to be decreasing at my large firm, and I am typically supporting work of seniors with little involvement or control." Another remarked, "The discrimination is very subtle, and related to the type of work assignments." A third respondent reported, "Senior male partners prefer to work with male associates. As a result the quality of work that a female associate receives is well below the quality of work a male associate receives. . . . Male partners welcome male associates into the corporate fold."

There are related problems in obtaining fair credit for work that go along with women being underrepresented, such as their work being more heavily scrutinized and assessed against especially rigorous standards, while at the same time being asked to take on special burdens, such as increased committee work that decreases time available for more instrumental tasks: namely, developing promising files and billing clients (see Rhode, 1988:1,191; also Kanter, 1977a, 1977b).

Women may also be channeled into specializations that demand fewer hours and away from cases and files that offer greater opportunities for extended, profitable billing (Epstein, 1981:318); and they may be excluded from informal networks that can enhance the flow of billable work and the opportunity to assume credit for it (Menkel-Meadow, 1989a:222). A respondent in our study reported that "[w]omen are usually channelled from the start into the less lucrative, more service-oriented areas of practice which are less productive of large billings." Another observed, "In corporate and litigation areas, women are not 'plugged in' to major transactions and cases." And a third respondent noted that "[f]rom an early stage men are groomed and promoted and are seen as more able because of their exposure to files. . . . Women often do not get major responsibility on files."

Lawyers on several occasions in our research referred to "pink and blue files" in response to questions about channeling productive cases to men and away from women lawyers. This practice was illustrated in the case of *Ezold v. Wolf,* discussed briefly in chapter 4. The federal district court judge's "summary of facts" in this case illustrated how the channeling of cases can occur:

> During her 1983 hiring interviews, Ms. Ezold was told by the then Chairman of the Litigation Department, Mr. Kurland, that it would not be easy for her at Wolf, Block because she was a woman, ... Ms. Ezold was primarily assigned cases that were small by Wolf, Block standards. Ms. Ezold did not work more than 500 hours on any one matter in any year, whereas virtually all the male associates

in the department worked on major matters for which they logged at least 600 hours per year. Ms. Ezold complained about the quality of her assignments and the limited number of partners she was assigned to work with. The Litigation Department Chairman acknowledged the inferiority of Ms. Ezold's work opportunities. (304)

Such problems are not restricted to larger firms and actually may be more severe for women in smaller firms.

Epstein (1981:166) makes this point when she observes that women in small practices must depend more exclusively on relationships with men, and that obviously "women who do not have such relationships are at a distinct disadvantage." Further, such relationships often involve strong ties, including those of family and marriage. Granovetter (1992; See also 1973; 1983) notes that such ties can be restrictive because "strong ties within highly interdependent groups close the group off, making difficult the formation of weak ties to other groups of the sort that have the potential to channel activity from one part of the social structure to another" (1992:247). Having wider access, albeit through weaker ties, to a larger firm's referral base, and therefore also to more women as sources of referrals, increases opportunities for productive work.

Of course, all of the above factors may be influenced and reinforced by the hierarchical power relationships that subordinate women to men in private practice. These points are important to the gender stratification position because they underline the likelihood that allocations of work and the taking of credit for it are not entirely efficiency- or choice-driven. Rather, a central point of this theory is that opportunities for women in firms are constrained by sex-specific conditions within markets that are segregated by gender (England, 1982; Reskin, 1984; Tienda et al., 1987). Menkel-Meadow (1989a) argues that the system of billable hours itself intensifies this stratification, because "in a legal culture where billable hours increase . . . and competition intensifies for good lawyers and clients, the demands of work increase sex segregation" (221). This point, which has not benefited from empirical assessment, is central in the analysis of billings and earnings undertaken next to address competing claims of the human capital and gender stratification positions.

Assessing Billings and Earnings

The Toronto panel survey of women and men lawyers provides a unique opportunity to assess competing claims of human capital and gender stratification theories. Most of the respondents in this panel who continue to work full-time in private practice have reached partnership positions by the second wave of the panel and many have had children. Enough time has passed for children born before the first wave of the survey to reach school age, while all pre-school-age children at the second wave of the panel were born between waves. This allows inferences about important effects of parenting below.

In the analysis presented below we give some consideration to all 815 members of the Toronto panel, but particular attention is focused on 375 respondents who were in full-time private practice. We focus our analysis in this way because it is only among privately practicing lawyers that the measure of billable hours that is central to our analysis occurs. Although private practice is the most common form of employment among lawyers, it is frequently noted that this is also the most competitive type of legal employment, and it is therefore likely that there is a selection process that leads different kinds of individuals into this sector of the profession (see Berk, 1983). We report an analysis of this selection process below. Although we find differences between those who are and are not in private practice, this does not have a notable substantive influence on our results.

We apply standard multiple regression techniques (discussed in the Appendix to this volume) that parallel the presentation of statistical evidence in the case law and research literature on employment discrimination (see Fisher, 1980; Finkelstein, 1980; Campbell, 1984; Epstein, 1992). The analysis presents pooled (i.e., men and women) as well as gender-specific models of earnings in 1984 and 1990, the immediately preceding years for which income is reported in the waves of the panel. The initial pooled model is important because it shows the effect of gender on earnings, overall and net of other variables such as experience. However, an analysis that stops with pooling men and women together implicitly assumes that women and men move freely between positions in a legal profession that efficiently rewards their employment choices. Alternatively, Becker's human capital theory argues that small gender differences in work commitment deriving from family relationships are magnified by human capital investments, so that income returns on time investments will occur differently for men and women, with the earnings for every hour worked by men increasing faster than those of women. Gender stratification theory also assumes that outcomes in the profession differ by gender, because men and women move within markets that are differentially constrained by selectively contingent competitive processes, for example, as associated above by Menkel-Meadow with differences in billable hours. This issue is addressed by adding interaction terms which specify effects by gender in pooled models and by estimating separate models for men and women below.

By focusing on the incomes of privately practicing lawyers in the years immediately preceding the waves of our survey, in 1984 and 1990, we are able to consider both good and bad times for lawyers. We noted in chapter 1 that the 1980s began and ended with recessions. These recessions had implications for all kinds of lawyers, including lawyers in larger firms. For example, the explosive period of growth that characterized the mid-1980s saw merchant bankers, stockbrokers, and corporate lawyers playing central roles in major mergers and acquisitions. These transactions often involved large amounts of time and many lawyers, and this should have made the middle part of the decade a period of rising incomes. When the deals began to decline, many Toronto lawyers had to find alternative kinds of work. In some larger firms this could occur through reassignment of lawyers from a shrinking corporate area to insolvency and litigation activities, which traditionally increase in recessionary periods. However, even this transition may have involved longer hours of work at reduced profit margins. A respondent in our sample observed that "[t]he trend seems to be toward the extremes — you try to bill two thousand or more hours per year or you don't work at all." The early 1990s was a period of retrenchment, and this may have hurt some lawyers more than others.

Preliminary Gender Differences

Lawyers were asked in both waves of our study to report within twenty-five grouped categories (from $10,000 to $500,000) their earnings from the practice of law during the preceding year (1984 and 1990, respectively) before taxes and other deductions. Dollar amounts were calculated by assigning category midpoints, with the 1990 amounts deflated to 1984 dollars, and the amounts divided by 1,000, so that results could be discussed in terms of thousands of dollars of income. As indicated in the right hand columns of table 6.1, in 1990 men were on average making about $157,000 in 1984 dollars (more than $180,000 in 1990 dollars), while women were averaging incomes of about $116,000, adjusted for inflation (more than $125,000 in 1990 dollars). As indicated in the left-hand columns of table 6.1, these figures had increased from about $95,000 for men and about $50,000 for women in 1984. So that while in deflated dollars men increased their earnings by about $62,000, women increased their earnings by about $65,000 (cf. Sander and Douglas, 1989). However, these relative gains are somewhat misleading, because there are steep increases in salaries in the early stages of the private practice of law, especially as lawyers move into the early years of firm partnerships. Because of the relatively recent large-scale entry of women into practice they are on average younger than male lawyers; they are therefore entering in larger proportions than are men the years when they should achieve their maximum gains in earnings. As these early income gains decline, it will prove difficult if not impossible for women to collectively catch up to men in absolute earnings. So that even though most of the women in our sample may have gone through the years of their biggest gains in earnings by the second wave of our panel, they still remain nearly as far behind men in their incomes in 1990 (the gap is about $41,000) as they were in 1984 (when the gap was about $45,000).

It is crucial in analyses of income to take age and experience into account. These variables are so closely related that only one or the other can be included in the analysis. We include measures of age and "age squared." Both are included in the models of earnings to take into account the tendency of incomes to increase into middle age, and then the tendency to decline with advancing age. The linear term (i.e., age) picks up the ascending effect, and the quadratic term (i.e., age squared) captures the later decline.

Several background variables considered in previous chapters are also included in this analysis of earnings. These include gender, elite law degree (University of Toronto or Osgoode Hall law schools), self-reported average law school grades, and self-identified white, Anglo-Saxon Protestant background. Men and women are similar with respect to these variables, with the exception that, as indicated in table 6.1, slightly more men have elite law degrees. This reflects the fact that the more elite schools are older and have trained a larger share of the profession before the more recent large-scale entry of women.

A number of variables are next included in our analysis to reflect the intersection of work and family experiences emphasized in human capital and gender stratification theories. These include marital status and having children. The age of children was asked only in the second wave, and this made it necessary to collapse the age categories of older children in the first wave. Respondents without children form the omitted comparison category for these variables in both waves. Although the older men of our sample are more likely to have children, more than a third of both men and women have pre-school-age children by the second wave, while substantial proportions of men and women have older children as well. This provides ample opportunity to assess the effects of children. As noted above, pre-school-age children in the second wave of data collection were born between waves, and this allows the timing of these births to be linked to other changes we can observe in these panel data.

Table 6.1

Means for 1984 and 1990 Income Analysis of Toronto Lawyers, Pooled and by Gender (Standard deviation in parentheses)

Variables [a]	1984			1990		
	Pooled Mean	Male Mean	Female Mean	Pooled Mean	Male Mean	Female Mean
Income/1,000s (1984$)	73.42(62.46)	95.13(75.35)	50.88(32.79)	136.96(81.23)	157.16(92.37)	116.00(61.33)
Age (years)	33.49(7.82)	36.50(9.32)	30.37(3.92)	39.49(7.82)	42.50(9.32)	36.37(3.92)
Age Squared (years)	1,182.73(642.08)	1,418.54(793.80)	937.95(264.70)	1,620.70(734.91)	1,892.50(904.59)	1,338.50(311.47)
Elite Law Degree	0.67(0.47)	0.70(0.46)	0.65(0.48)	0.67(0.47)	0.70(0.46)	0.65(0.48)
Law School Grades	2.05(0.54)	2.09(0.57)	2.10(0.51)	2.10(0.54)	2.09(0.57)	2.10(0.51)
WASP	0.28(0.45)	0.28(0.45)	0.27(0.45)	0.28(0.45)	0.28(0.45)	0.27(0.45)
Married	0.74(0.44)	0.83(0.38)	0.65(0.48)	0.80(0.40)	0.83(0.37)	0.76(0.43)
Child 0–5	0.30(0.46)	0.33(0.47)	0.27(0.45)	0.38(0.49)	0.37(0.48)	0.39(0.49)
Child 6–12	0.13(0.34)	0.16(0.37)	0.10(0.30)	0.30(0.46)	0.33(0.47)	0.27(0.45)
Child 13+/13–18	0.12(0.32)	0.18(0.38)	0.06(0.24)	0.13(0.34)	0.16(0.37)	0.10(0.30)
Child 19+				0.12(0.32)	0.18(0.38)	0.06(0.24)
Housework Hours				5.98(8.27)	4.96(5.80)	7.03(10.13)
Parental Leave	0.04(0.19)	0.00(0.00)	0.07(0.27)	0.05(0.21)	0.00(0.00)	0.10(0.30)
Child Care Hours				16.17(21.14)	10.88(13.82)	21.66(25.60)
Work Commitment	37.86(2.62)	37.96(2.70)	37.75(2.54)	36.06(3.99)	36.61(3.82)	35.49(4.09)

Internal Market [b]	0.46(0.50)	0.40(0.49)	0.52(0.50)	0.50(0.50)	0.47(0.50)	0.53(0.50)
Internal to External Market	0.11(0.31)	0.11(0.32)	0.09(0.30)	0.04(0.19)	0.03(0.17)	0.04(0.20)
External to Internal Market	0.07(0.26)	0.09(0.29)	0.05(0.23)	0.15(0.36)	0.16(0.36)	0.14(0.35)
Partner	0.48(0.50)	0.61(0.49)	0.35(0.48)	0.88(0.32)	0.90(0.30)	0.86(0.35)
Works Own Cases				0.40(0.49)	0.51(0.50)	0.29(0.45)
Autonomy	3.26(0.91)	3.45(0.81)	3.07(0.96)	3.58(0.79)	3.60(0.81)	3.56(0.77)
Decision Making	3.18(1.55)	3.55(1.50)	2.79(1.51)	3.88(1.34)	3.94(1.31)	3.81(1.36)
Hierarchical Position	2.52(0.88)	2.69(0.96)	2.34(0.74)	2.96(1.00)	3.00(1.02)	2.91(0.99)
Corporate Clients	2.86(1.23)	2.84(1.20)	2.87(1.27)	2.80(1.30)	2.80(1.25)	2.81(1.35)
Specialization Status	6.27(0.93)	6.25(0.97)	6.30(0.90)	6.12(0.98)	6.12(1.02)	6.12(0.94)
Docketed Hours	1,621.44(461.18)	1,636.63(443.34)	1,605.68(479.71)	1,721.27(41.86)	1,769.25(446.65)	1,671.47(369.23)
Billed Hours				1,564.80(377.23)	1,627.26(396.51)	1,500.00(345.40)

[a] See text for description and discussion of variables.

[b] Market variables refer to job location within and movements between firms with 20 or more lawyers.

We also have measures of hours spent on housework at wave 2, parental leave measures for both waves, hours spent on child care at wave 2, and measures of work commitment at both waves of data collection. Women lawyers spend more time on housework and nearly double the time on child care than men, while only about 10 percent of the women reported taking maternity leaves. This tendency of women in full-time private practice not to take parental leaves is striking, and in itself may question assumptions made by human capitalists about the work commitment of women. A common explanation for not taking a maternity leave is summarized in the comment of a new mother in our sample that "it seems the best way to show you are still to be taken seriously as a lawyer is to return to the office as soon as possible and act as if the fact that you have a child or children has no impact on your life."

Our measure of work commitment uses multiple indicators developed by Bielby and Bielby (1984; see also Hagan, 1990) to increase the reliability with which this important variable is measured. Respondents were first asked separately about career preferences and expectations: "In the long run, which one of the following do you really prefer and which one do you realistically expect?" Possible answers ranged from full-time to no employment and were coded from low to high to reflect strength of work orientation. Respondents were then asked, "For each of the following periods of your life, circle whether you expect to be working full-time, three-quarters time, part-time, not at all or don't know?" Answers were included for when the respondent's youngest child is of pre-school-age, or six to twelve years old, or when children are all working or married. Finally, respondents were asked, "Imagining yourself ten years from now, how would you rate your work or career in terms of its importance to you?" Responses were coded from low to high, as not at all important to very important. As indicated in table 6.1, men and women lawyers scored quite similarly on the summed responses to these items on the wave 1 survey (both had scores of about 37), and both decreased slightly by wave 2, with men decreasing a little more than one point, and women a little more than two. As Bielby and Bielby (1984) also found, these scores become somewhat more stable over time. This was reflected when we calculated Chronbach's (1951) alpha reliability coefficients, which came to .616 in wave 1 and .769 in wave 2.

Our next measure is of the sector(s) within which individuals have moved while in the profession. This measure is intended to capture the advantages of moving within or into larger-firm private practice settings. Sociological research (e.g., Kalleberg and Berg, 1987) often stresses the advantages that job ladders provide for advancement in larger-firm settings, and this may be important for women in general (see Felmlee, 1982) and in law more specifically (Epstein, 1981). However, the issue may not only be one of job ladders, but also of access to the work that makes climbing a ladder possible. Following the arguments of Epstein and Granovetter (summarized above), we expect that women will be better located to obtain billable work in the larger firms that we identify as the core internal market.

We created variables based on wave 1 and 2 measures of being in the core internal (i.e., a firm with twenty or more lawyers) or external (i.e., all other settings) markets. These variables distinguish respondents during the time of the panel who have a job history that is entirely within the internal core of the profession (internal market), who have moved into this sector (external to internal), and who have moved out (internal to external). Those entirely outside the internal sector are the omitted comparison group. Because firms grew during the time of the panel, the proportion in the internal sector of the profession increased between waves. Nearly two-thirds of the private practice sample were within the internal market by the second wave, and about half of the men and women moved entirely within this sector.

Measures are also included of partnership at waves 1 and 2 of the panel. By wave 2, about 90 percent of the men and 86 percent of the women who continued to practice full-time and privately were partners. Since it is often suggested that men are better able than women to play a "rainmaker" role in firms by bringing new business into firms (see Epstein, 1981), we also included a second-wave measure (works own cases) of whether respondents described their primary responsibility as "clients you bring in" or "clients of the firm": about 50 percent of the men, compared to less than a third of the women, indicated the "client-bringing" role. A further measure of work with more lucrative corporate clients is discussed below.

The next set of variables in various ways measure positions of responsibility and power of respondents in their work during waves 1 and 2 of the panel. Several of these measures (i.e., of autonomy, involvement in decision making, and hierarchical position) were used to create the hierarchical typology of positions in the profession used in chapter 2. This allows us to consider the effects of specific dimensions of power and responsibility apart from the larger typology (cf. Halaby and Weakliem, 1993).

The first of these is a measure of autonomy that asks respondents to indicate by one of four responses if they design no, a few, some, all, or most important aspects of their work. Second is a measure of participation in decision making that indicates on a five-point scale neither direct nor indirect participation in decision making, an advisory role, or direct participation in one area, some areas, or in all or most policy decisions. Third is a measure of hierarchical position that indicates whether there is no, one, or two or more levels of individuals below the respondent.

Two further measures of resources and status involve corporate clients and specialization status. The former measure ranks in quartiles the proportion of the respondent's work that is with corporate clients. The latter measure derives from respondents' ratings of fields on a scale from one to ten, with results that, for example, rank corporate/commercial work (6.99) and civil litigation (6.84) higher than family (5.37) and criminal (5.35) law (see Hagan, 1988).

It is of interest to note that at the time of the wave 1 survey men and women lawyers in Toronto were very similar in the proportion of corporate clients they served and in their average levels of specialization status, and there was little change in these measures between waves. On the other hand, women lawyers were lower in autonomy, participation in decision making, and hierarchical position than men lawyers at wave 1, but they gained considerably on all of these measures and became quite similar to men on these dimensions by wave 2.

Our final measures involve hours worked, docketed, and billed. All three of these measures were included in wave 2, while only docketed hours were included in wave 1. In wave 2 we asked respondents to answer nine questions about how many hours they worked on weekdays and weekends, during the day and at night, at home and in the office. The only significant gender difference involved the lesser willingness of women to work weekends in the office. When the hours were summed overall, there was no significant gender difference. However, some more notable differences were found in hours docketed and billed. This is reflected in the bottom part of table 6.1, where we find that men docketed about 30 hours more than women in wave 1, and this difference increased to about 100 hours in wave 2. On average in wave 2, men billed about 1,627 and women about 1,500 hours, well over a 100-hour difference. The latter difference in billed hours is a focus of analysis below.

Earnings, Billings, and Commitment

We begin our analysis of gender differences in income with the first wave of data that includes reports of earnings for the 1984 tax year. The entry in the first column of table 6.2 reflects the $44,000 difference in male and female lawyers' earnings previously reported in table 6.1. This difference is cut by more than half, to about $19,000, by introducing the linear and quadratic

Table 6.2
Determinants of 1984 Income of Toronto Lawyers (Standard error in parentheses)

Variables [a]	Eq. 1 Unstandardized Coefficient	Eq. 2 Unstandardized Coefficient	Eq. 3 Unstandardized Coefficient	Eq. 4 Unstandardized Coefficient
Gender	44.25(6.04)***	18.63(5.38)***	13.11(5.13)**	12.84(5.13)*
Age		22.89(2.09)***	20.99(2.37)***	20.79(2.37)***
Age Squared		−0.24(0.02)***	−0.21(0.03)***	−0.21(0.03)***
Elite Law Degree			−1.20(5.04)	−1.26(5.03)
Law School Grades			8.97(4.53)*	7.95(4.58)*
WASP			−6.75(5.16)	−6.05(5.17)
Married			1.60(5.62)	1.76(5.61)
Child 0–5			−10.08(5.54)*	−9.96(5.53)*
Child 6–12			12.64(7.09)*	12.09(7.09)*
Child 13+			−12.71(7.95)	−12.08(7.95)
Parental Leave			−6.50(12.39)	−7.09(12.38)
Child Care Hours			−0.11(0.12)	−0.11(0.12)
Work Commitment			0.88(0.90)	0.67(0.91)
Internal Market [b]			18.09(6.17)**	17.20(6.19)**
Internal to External Market			30.22(7.81)***	30.55(7.80)***
External to Internal Market			9.69(9.44)	9.24(9.42)
Partner			11.70(6.99)*	13.37(7.07)*
Autonomy			1.10(3.04)	0.64(3.05)
Decision Making			−0.74(2.42)	−1.10(2.43)
Corporate Clients			4.58(2.20)*	4.61(2.20)*
Hierarchical Position			9.91(2.96)***	9.86(2.30)***
Specialization			9.41(2.67)***	9.26(2.66)***
Docketed Hours				0.01(0.00)
Constant	50.88	−420.90	−545.46	−540.28
R^2	0.13	0.42	0.57	0.58

* $p < 0.05$; ** $p < 0.01$; *** $p < 0.001$, one-tailed.
Note: The unstandardized coefficients in this table can be interpreted as thousands of dollars of change in 1984 income associated with a unit change in the independent variable.
[a] See text for description and discussion of variables.
[b] Market variables refer to job location within and movements between firms with 20 or more lawyers.

effects of age to control for differences in experience between men and women lawyers in the second column of table 6.2.

When a number of other factors that influence lawyers' incomes are taken into account in table 6.2, the gender gap in earnings is further reduced to $13,000. These influences include familiar effects of variables we have previously associated with human capital theory (e.g., law school grades and corporate clientele) and gender stratification theory (e.g., hierarchical position). However, when a wide range of these variables and, in addition, docketed hours in column 4 are taken into account, male lawyers still earn about $13,000 more than female lawyers in 1984. This is a substantial and statistically significant difference.

We turn next to 1990 earnings in table 6.3. The entry in column 1 of this table reflects the overall $41,000 difference in women and men lawyers' earnings that endures six years after the first survey. Controlling alone for the effects of age reduces this difference to about $30,000. In column 2 we introduce the same collection of human capital, gender stratification, docketed hours, and other variables introduced in the previous analysis of 1984 earnings, plus several new variables (e.g., hours of housework) included for the first time in the wave 2 survey. A number of these variables again have significant effects, including the human capital (e.g., law school grades) and gender stratification (e.g., hierarchical position) variables; and now docketed hours also has a significant effect. However, after all these variables are brought into the analysis, the gender gap in income is still over $22,000.

The major difference in the analysis of 1984 and 1990 incomes occurs in column 3, when we replace docketed hours with hours billed. The effect of hours billed is highly significant, indicating that net of all the other variables in the equation, each hour billed returns about $60 of earned income. When the effect of this central human capital variable is introduced in column 3, the gender gap between men and women lawyers is reduced to about $13,000 a year. However, even with differences in hourly billings taken into account, the gap between men and women lawyers is still statistically significant and about the same as that observed in 1984.

Recall that human capital theory further predicts that hours worked will also yield higher rewards for men because men are presumed to invest more specialized effort in their work than women. This prediction is given a preliminary test in column 4 of table 6.3 by adding an interaction term that reflects the return on mens' hourly billings compared to women's, with all other effects in the model held constant. This effect is statistically significant and indicates that in 1990 male lawyers receive a return on each hour billed that is larger than that received by female lawyers. This difference is further confirmed in columns 5 and 6 where we separate men and women lawyers and rerun the earnings equations. Here we find that net of all other influences, men earn about $70 for each hour of billed income, while women earn about $40. Although there are other significant differences reported in this table, it is particularly striking that as human capital theory predicts, men gain nearly double the return on each hour billed than women. So men lawyers do not simply make more money because they bill more hours than women, they also are rewarded more per hour for each hour of work they do. Of course, the argument of the chosen spheres version of human capital theory is that it is productivity-based differences in investments in family and other work by women and men that operate through billable hours to produce indirect and interaction effects on earnings.

Thus it is of considerable interest to know how the difference that exists in hours billed by gender emerges. Recall that Becker argues that a small difference in such measures of productivity can initiate quite disparate human capital investments by women and men, and that this initial small difference is linked to intrinsic variation in the comparative advantage of women for bearing and caring for children. In contrast, gender stratification theory links differences in productivity to the more immediate social context of work, or more specifically, to "differences in workplace constraints and opportunities" (Bielby, 1992:290). Kanter (1977a) notes that in large part, "organizations make their workers who they are" (263).

To assess these alternative possibilities we present an analysis of the determinants of 1990 hourly billings in table 6.4. The first entry in column 1 of this table reflects the average difference of about 127 more hours in annual billings by men compared to women. To best model the effects of age on hourly billings it is necessary to add a cubic age term to the linear and quadratic age effects in column 2; doing so actually increases the gender difference in billings to about 200 hours. Controlling for a wide range of variables in column 3 only reduces this difference slightly to about 194 hours. Nonetheless, the influences in column 3 are substantively interesting. As human capital theory would predict, law school grades lead to higher numbers of billed hours, as does also partnership, while corporate clients reduce hourly billings. However, as we will see, this latter finding is unique to women in the sample.

Meanwhile, the most important finding in table 6.4 is reported in column 4. Recall that the central argument of the gender stratification position developed above is that men lawyers more often than women lawyers use their hierarchical positions to enhance their hourly billings. The interaction

Table 6.3

Determinants of 1990 Income of Toronto Lawyers (Standard error in parentheses)

Variables [a]	Eq. 1 Unstandardized Coefficient	Eq. 2 Unstandardized Coefficient	Eq. 3 Unstandardized Coefficient	Eq. 4 Unstandardized Coefficient	Eq. 5 (Men) Unstandardized Coefficient	Eq. 6 (Women) Unstandardized Coefficient
				Equations (Eqs.)		
Gender	41.16(8.13)***	22.48(8.20)**	12.84(7.80)*	−38.60(29.28)		
Age		25.50(3.76)***	28.85(3.61)***	29.13(3.61)***	31.77(5.51)***	28.61(9.07)***
Age Squared		−0.25(0.04)***	−0.28(0.04)***	−0.28(0.04)***	−0.31(0.05)***	−0.29(0.11)**
Elite Law Degree		0.80(7.49)	2.51(7.15)	2.66(7.13)	12.81(13.11)	−6.03(7.43)
Law School Grades		16.42(6.33)**	15.60(6.32)**	15.61(6.33)**	16.79(10.34)*	10.80(7.22)
WASP		−7.39(7.71)	−5.44(7.36)	−5.16(7.34)	−17.46(12.36)	8.05(8.03)
Married		4.80(9.26)	4.40(8.84)	5.13(8.82)	−19.25(15.85)	23.23(9.21)**
Child 0–5		−4.57(9.02)	−2.41(8.61)	−1.75(8.59)	10.74(14.74)	−10.58(9.21)
Child 6–12		3.28(8.42)	−0.23(8.06)	−0.76(8.03)	1.78(12.96)	4.06(9.46)
Child 13–18		9.62(10.71)	7.53(10.21)	7.37(10.18)	9.75(16.54)	−1.60(11.89)
Child 19+		−29.71(12.09)**	−28.22(11.54)**	−27.75(11.51)**	−20.57(16.79)	−48.62(16.01)***
Housework Hours		−0.74(0.41)*	−0.64(0.39)*	−0.66(.39)*	−0.95(0.93)	−0.39(0.35)
Parental Leave		−11.55(16.70)	−11.25(15.94)	−11.82(15.89)		−14.17(12.69)
Child Care Hours		−0.11(0.19)	−0.15(0.19)	−0.17(0.18)	−0.06(0.45)	−0.26(0.17)
Work Commitment		0.18(0.90)	−0.43(0.86)	−0.28(0.86)	−1.15(1.56)	0.39(0.92)

	(1)	(2)	(3)	(4)	(5)	(6)
Internal Market [b]		34.23(11.13)***	29.66(10.65)**	32.81(10.76)***	44.42(18.09)**	30.15(12.25)**
Internal to External Market		-14.56(18.36)	-13.68(17.46)	-13.68(17.46)	-20.87(32.02)	-4.58(17.48)
External to Internal Market		22.24(11.80)*	25.65(11.90)*	25.66(11.90)*	25.66(19.78)	26.05(13.45)*
Partner		15.73(11.68)	7.22(11.16)	7.19(11.13)	5.07(19.86)	7.09(11.61)
Works Own Cases		-4.47(8.07)	-3.66(7.68)	-3.07(7.66)	-6.46(12.66)	0.49(9.15)
Autonomy		2.17(4.39)	1.36(4.19)	0.96(4.18)	-2.47(6.75)	4.44(4.92)
Decision Making		2.30(3.09)	2.98(2.93)	2.57(2.92)	5.80(5.26)	1.16(3.16)
Corporate Clients		3.85(3.33)	3.44(3.32)		-2.29(6.05)	9.10(3.44)**
Hierarchical Position		17.60(3.68)***	16.20(3.52)***	15.71(3.52)***	17.69(6.37)**	14.03(3.64)***
Specialization		11.09(3.78)**	11.74(3.60)***	11.49(3.59)***	17.08(5.99)**	5.84(4.04)
Docketed Hours		0.02(0.01)**				
Billed Hours			0.06(0.01)***	0.04(0.01)**	0.07(0.01)***	0.04(0.011)**
Gender x Hours Billed				0.03(0.01)*		
Constant	116.00	-715.08	-82.81	-802.01	-884.99	-776.440
R^2	0.06	0.44	0.49	0.50	0.473	0.553

*$p < 0.05$; **$p < 0.01$; ***$p < 0.001$, onetailed.

Note: The unstandardized coefficients in this table can be interpreted as thousands of dollars of change in 1990 income associated with a unit change in the independent variable.

[a] See text for description and discussion of variables.

[b] Market variables refer to job location with in and movement between firms with 30 or more lawyers.

Table 6.4
Determinants of 1990 Hourly Billings of Toronto Lawyers (Standard error in parentheses)

Variables [a]	Eq. 1 Unstandardized Coefficients	Eq. 2 Unstandardized Coefficients	Eq. 3 Unstandardized Coefficients	Eq. 4 Unstandardized Coefficients	Eq. 5 (Men) Unstandardized Coefficients	Eq. 6 (Women) Unstandardized Coefficients
Gender	127.25(38.46)***	200.86(41.07)***	193.99(47.02)***	-21.95(122.91)		
Age		149.29(91.30)*	11.92(102.83)	5.50(102.50)	32.48(135.38)	892.41(595.40)
Age Squared		-3.57(1.93)*	-0.82(2.09)	-0.71(2.08)	-1.35(2.67)	-20.61(13.96)
Age Cubed		0.03(0.01)**	0.01(0.01)	0.01(0.01)	0.01(0.02)	0.15(0.11)
Elite Law Degree			-32.62(42.80)	-34.21(42.65)	-53.24(67.72)	-25.24(55.77)
Law School Grades			75.54(37.74)*	73.07(37.63)*	88.93(53.72)*	5.96(53.94)
WASP			-56.79(44.14)	-56.05(43.98)	-78.21(63.54)	-42.71(60.38)
Married			2.20(52.96)	1.86(52.76)	-14.15(82.35)	-14.41(68.99)
Child 0–5			-31.58(51.72)	-26.51(51.60)	-86.71(76.35)	10.88(69.27)
Child 6–12			60.55(48.80)	59.74(48.62)	67.77(67.57)	27.44(72.44)
Child 13–18			69.73(61.29)	63.10(61.16)	58.78(86.56)	116.02(89.72)
Child 19+			-35.86(69.76)	-35.08(69.50)	-63.35(87.64)	65.89(119.57)
Housework Hours			-1.94(2.33)	-1.70(2.33)	-0.12(4.77)	-0.531(2.60)
Parental Leave			-19.79(95.42)	-11.73(95.16)		-25.05(94.97)
Child Care Hours			0.95(1.11)	0.89(1.11)	4.53(2.29)*	-0.69(1.27)
Work Commitment			6.80(5.18)	7.36(5.17)	1.58(8.26)	16.66(6.27)**

	Model 1	Model 2	Model 3	Model 4	Model 5
Internal Market [b]		96.26(63.57)	89.04(63.44)	-31.59(93.29)	335.65(88.30)***
Internal to External		34.73(104.82)	27.13(104.51)	-26.18(164.84)	120.29(130.30)
External to Internal		45.96(70.59)	35.57(70.54)	-158.66(101.63)	300.59(97.77)**
Partner		106.71(66.63)*	112.09(66.44)*	113.19(102.47)	59.16(87.01)
Works Own Cases		-52.36(45.93)	-68.03(46.50)	-102.11(65.16)	-39.16(68.80)
Autonomy		2.09(25.13)	0.51(25.05)	20.87(34.71)	0.80(37.03)
Decision Making		8.02(17.52)	8.38(17.45)	52.17(27.24)*	-27.25(23.64)
Corporate Clients		-40.27(19.89)*	-40.95(19.82)*	-13.05(31.40)	-53.29(25.35)*
Hierarchical Position		32.62(21.06)	-3.75(28.40)		
Hierarchical Position in 1985				98.65(41.13)**	-8.28(45.52)
Change in Hierarchical Position				44.567(33.75)	-11.49(27.73)
Specialization		-0.49(21.53)	1.51(21.48)	27.43(30.76)	-34.64(30.14)
Gender x Hierarchical Position			73.04(38.44)*		
Constant	-421.50	1227.37	1422.53	785.11	-11303.10
R^2	0.08	0.16	0.17	0.25	0.22

* $p < 0.05$; ** $p < 0.01$; *** $p < 0.001$.
Note: The unstandardized coefficients in this table can be interpreted as thousands of dollars of change in 1990 income associated with a unit change in the independent variable.

[a] See text for description and discussion of variables.
[b] Market variables refer to job location within and movements between firms with 20 or more lawyers.

term added in the fourth column of this table operationalizes the tendency of men relative to women to use hierarchical positions to accumulate hourly billings. This interaction is statistically significant.

To further explore the meaning of this interaction effect we estimate hourly billing equations separately for men and women lawyers in the final columns of table 6.4. The analysis presented in this table uses the two waves of Toronto data to further assess the assumption of gender stratification theory that the higher hierarchical positions of men are the cause rather than the consequence of their higher hourly billings. To assess this assumption we now use more specific measures of hierarchical position in 1985 and change in hierarchical position between waves, with the equations estimated separately for men and women lawyers. The results are revealing.

The effect of hierarchical position is only apparent for men, and the effect is as measured in 1985 rather than as it has changed between waves. So the causal sequence is apparently from hierarchical position to hourly billings: with each step on this measured hierarchy, hourly billings increase by an average of nearly one hundred hours. Meanwhile, women obtain no significant benefit from their hierarchical positions or changes in them. These findings are consistent with the gender stratification position.

The findings in the final columns of table 6.4 also indicate that men receive an increase of about fifty hours in annual billings with each increase of level of involvement in firm decision making, while women again experience no significant benefit. Law school grades are also of unique benefit to men, as also, oddly, are hours of child care. The latter effect may actually be a proxy for the benefit men receive from having a spouse at home who specializes in child care and other forms of household support. Meanwhile, women lose hours from their involvement with corporate clients, while men do not.

However, women gain substantially by staying or moving into the internal sector of the profession and from commitment to work. The first of these findings is consistent with the gender stratification argument that women have better access to billable work in larger firms where they are freed from dependencies on men and more restricted referral networks. Women also increase their billable hours with increased work commitment. The latter finding suggests that when it comes to women gaining billable hours, "they earn it" through increased commitment. This is an important finding that is a focus of the final analysis in this chapter.

It is likely that work commitment is not only involved in increasing billable hours but also in determining who decides to work in full-time private practice as well. This is the process of sample selection discussed earlier in this chapter. To analyze this process we returned to a consideration of all 815 respondents in our panel. Since private practice is commonly regarded as the most competitive sector of the profession, it makes sense to expect that persons employed full-time in this sector would be somewhat different from others, especially in terms of commitment to work. To confirm this expectation we used gender-specific models to predict the likelihood in 1991 of being employed full-time in private practice of law. These models considered the influence of work commitment measured in wave 1, change in work commitment between waves, and having a pre-school-age child born between waves. As expected, initial and changed work commitment significantly influenced the likelihood of full-time employment in private practice, indicating that more highly committed lawyers were more likely to engage in this type of practice. In addition, having a pre-school-age child significantly reduced the likelihood of full-time private practice for women, but not men. Recall that about one-third of the women in private practice in 1990 have children of pre-school-age. So it is only in relative terms that these women are less likely to practice privately. However, human capital theory assumes that women with children more generally will not only be less likely to compete in the private sector, but also that if they do, they will do so with less commitment than men. To assess the possibility that this pattern is a source of bias in our analysis, we incorporated correction terms based on the preceding analysis to all the earnings and billable hours equations estimated in this chapter (see Berk, 1983). The only equations in which the resulting correction term produced a significant effect involved women lawyers' hourly billings, and even in these equations the effects of other variables were little changed. When we removed the correction term from the equations for women lawyers' hourly billings and instead included the measure of prior work commitment and change in work commitment, the former was statistically significant. So overall, it appears that sample selection is not a source of bias in our analysis, but that it is nonetheless important to directly observe how work commitment influences the accumulation of hourly billings.

We come, then, to a final and crucial test of the human capital position, namely that women's commitment is undermined by their involvement in familial roles, most prominently parenting. To examine this possibility in the wider range of contexts that is available to us, we analyze in table 6.5 the effects of having children on 1991 commitment to work and on changes between waves in work commitment among women and men who are in and out of full-time private practice. This is done in the first column of table 6.5 by regressing 1991 work commitment on having children of different ages, and by then adding 1985 work commitment to the equation

Table 6.5

Children and Work Commitment among Women and Men Toronto Lawyers, 1985–1991

	1991 Commitment	Change in Commitment
Women in Private Practice (N = 184)		
Child 0–5	1.51(0.60)**	1.08(0.56)*
Child 6–11	2.46(0.67)***	2.18(0.62)***
Child 12–17	–0.51(0.99)	–0.72(0.92)
Child 18+	1.97(1.22)*	1.45(1.13)
Work Commitment 1985		0.60(0.11)***
Constant	34.17	11.86
R^2	0.12	0.26
Men in Private Practice (N = 191)		
Child 0–5	1.45(0.62)**	1.01(0.58)*
Child 6–11	0.49(0.61)	0.32(0.57)
Child 12–17	1.14(0.80)	0.49(0.74)
Child 18+	–0.23(0.78)	–0.31(0.72)
Work Commitment 1985		15.29
Constant	35.76	15.29
R^2	0.05	0.19
Women out of Private Practice (N = 278)		
Child 0–5	0.75(0.67)	0.48(0.64)
Child 6–11	1.75(0.76)*	1.89(0.72)**
Child 12–17	4.52(1.42)**	4.17(1.35)**
Child 18+	–0.71(1.42)	–0.21(1.35)
Work Commitment 1985		0.47(0.08)***
Constant	32.41	15.56
R^2	0.06	0.16
Men out of Private Practice (N = 164)		
Child 0–5	4.44(1.00)***	3.26(0.85)***
Child 6–11	1.86(1.09)*	1.03(0.92)
Child 12–17	3.56(1.42)**	2.70(1.19)*
Child 18+	1.35(1.35)	3.68(1.16)**
Work Commitment 1985		0.86(0.10)***
Constant	32.41	1.21(3.79)
R^2	0.18	0.43

* $p < 0.05$; ** $p < 0.01$; *** $p < 0.001$; one-tailed.

estimated in the second column. This table presents the effects of having pre-school-age, primary-school-age, and older children. Recall that the split in the ages of the preschool and primary-school children coincides with the timing of the two waves of this panel study, so that each measures a change in age that can be assumed to have causal precedence in changing commitment.

The effects on work commitment for women in full-time private practice of having pre- and primary-school-age children are, from the human capital perspective, unexpectedly positive and statistically significant, with the effect of primary school children being more positive than preschool children. For full-time privately practicing men, the effect of having pre-school-age children is also positive and significant, although the effect of primary school children is negligible and nonsignificant. For women outside of full-time private practice, having preschool children has no significant effect on work commitment, while the effects of having children in primary and secondary school are positive and significant. Finally, for men outside of full-time private practice, the effects of having children of a variety of ages are significant and positive.

These findings indicate that in sharp contrast with the assumptions of human capital theory, the effects of having children are favorable for the work commitment of women in full-time private practice. This is true for pre-school-age children, and even truer as these children come of school age. Even for women outside of full-time private practice, the effect of school-age children is to increase commitment to work. Men are also generally favorably affected by having children, although the effects are restricted more to the early years of parenthood. Women who continue to work full-time outside the home seem more similar to men in the experience of having children than is commonly assumed. In particular, "intrinsic differences" that are central to Becker's chosen spheres theory of human capital theory do not undermine the commitment of women in full-time private law practice to work outside the family, and in fact the opposite is more likely to be the case.

Rethinking Choice and Commitment

Human capital theory offers a general explanation of differences in earnings within and across occupations, and this reasoning is applied extensively in court decisions and in the study of lawyers. As in previous chapters of this book, we have found some support for human capital theory in our analyses of lawyers' earnings. For example, law school grades have durable, favorable effects on earnings, and there are apparent effects of corporate clientele as well. With regard to gender, although women and men lawyers report working about the same number of hours overall, men report docketing and billing larger numbers of hours than women; and when differences in docketing and billing are taken into account in the second wave of our panel, they reduce the difference between the earnings of men and women working full-time in private law practice. Yet remaining gender differences in earnings after these controls also provide continuing support for gender stratification theory.

Meanwhile, further analyses revealed that the gender difference in earnings that results from the number of hours billed is augmented by a striking difference that results from the rate of return on these billings per hour worked. Men gain nearly twice the return in earnings as women for each hour they work. The chosen spheres version of human capital theory attributes this disparity to intrinsic differences in commitment to work and investment in human capital that result from the comparative advantage of women in bearing and rearing children. Yet differences in direct measures of family involvements, for example, hours spent on child care, do not mediate effects of gender on earnings or hours billed in ways expected by human capital theory. But perhaps most importantly, the results of our analysis of hourly billings support the expectations of gender stratification theory, namely, that men gain billable hours through the use of hierarchical positions in firms, as well as from greater involvement in decision making. Women, on the other hand, gain from location and movement within and into larger firms, where they may have greater access to work referral networks and a reduced dependency on male colleagues. These findings seem to have more to do with the social context and embeddedness of productivity (Granovetter, 1992) than with competitive demands or comparative advantages that involve investment in family.

However, the chosen spheres version of human capital theory is perhaps most obviously problematic with regard to its most fundamental assumption, namely that decisions by women lawyers in the full-time practice of law to have children result in reduced commitments to their careers. We found no support for this assumption, and instead we found evidence to the contrary. In particular, women lawyers who continue to practice full-time in the private sector *increase* their commitment to work after having children, and women outside of this sector also increase their work commitment as their children progress into and through school. The failure of human capital theory to anticipate this outcome may derive from its fundamental misconception of the role of choice about children and work in the careers of professional women.

It may be precisely because professional women often do exercise some choice in having children and deciding to continue careers, immediately after giving birth or later on, that they sustain and renew commitment to their professional work. To the extent that women are "intrinsically different" in this regard, it may derive from the process of consciously making the choice to work outside the home. For many working mothers, this choice may be socially embedded in the shared decisions of peers who have confronted similar choices and increasingly have decided to continue full-time professional work. In any case, there is no evidence here for Becker's argument that an intrinsic difference in the comparative advantage of women for the care of children in the family is the source of differences in commitment that lead to alternative strategies of investment in human capital among men and women engaged in the full-time private law practice.

Stratification research has long observed the tendency of employers to prefer male employees who are married and have children as a sign of stability (see Rosenfeld, 1980:588). The findings of this chapter discourage the tendency of employers and human capital theory to make the opposite assumption for women. In particular, we have found evidence that challenges the assumption that bearing and rearing children reduces the commitment of women who continue to pursue full-time private practice; and given their lower economic rewards compared to men, these women lawyers actually seem to have a stronger claim of professional commitment to their work than do men. Recall that net of other variables that favorably influence earnings in law, men earn a marginal return in income that is much higher than that received by women per hour of billable work. The question that most reasonably follows from these findings, then, is not why women in the private practice of law sometimes bill fewer hours than do men, but why they bill as many hours as they do. Given our findings, a plausible answer is a high commitment of women to work in the profession, over and above the earnings it produces.

7

The Pleasures and Perils of Practice

*Leaving the practice of law turned out to be the best career decision
I could have made. But I didn't know it at the time. At the time that I
left, the profession had a veneer of welcoming women, but its structures made it a very inhospitable environment. Although I 'made it'
and became a partner in a distinguished downtown law firm, I never
felt entirely comfortable in that role. I never felt I really belonged,
or that any success was due to my own accomplishments. When I
left, I thought it was because I needed a job that allowed more time
for family, personal, and social activities. I work as many hours at
my present job, but I am happier in my work. I think it is because the
daily stress of accommodating to a foreign (male) environment is
gone.*

Studying Satisfaction

The practice of law is a pleasure to some and a source of dissatisfaction for
others. Long work hours and problem drinking are two perils long noted
among men who practice law. When lawyers were predominantly male, these
problems often were ignored or treated with stoic acceptance. However,
with the large-scale entry of women into law, and with the increased over-
lapping of work and family roles, the stressful nature of legal practice has
become a more widely recognized issue for both men and women. An awareness of the stresses and strains of legal practice has generated much concern, and some research.

Yet this research suggests that many if not most lawyers enjoy their
work and take considerable pleasure in it. Lawyers are not unique in this
regard. Studies indicate that most employed persons like their work, and

many women may be surprisingly similar to men in this regard. Campbell, Converse, and Rodgers (1976) report from a broad-ranging survey of life satisfaction among Americans that "there is practically no difference between women and men in average job satisfaction" (300-301). Indeed, there are a number of studies that indicate that women's attitudes toward their jobs are more favorable than those of men (Glenn et al., 1977; Penley and Hawkins, 1980; Quinn et al., 1974). This has led some to wonder why women aren't more dissatisfied with their work conditions. The previous chapters of this book certainly give grounds for feelings of dissatisfaction.

Several explanations are offered for these counterintuitive findings. First, women may differ from men in the characteristics of work that they value (Kanter, 1977a). Second, women may gain satisfaction from family involvements that positively influence their evaluations of work (Veroff et al., 1981). Third, women may for reasons of socialization and/or acquiesence resist expressing true feelings about their work (Glenn and Feldberg, 1977). Fourth, women may use different comparison groups and standards of evaluation than men, comparing themselves only to other women who work in and outside the home (Glenn et al., 1977). It is the last of these explanations that is most widely endorsed. Abbott (1994) expresses a common view when he concludes that "gender's influence on job satisfaction seems peculiar. Women are more satisfied than 'objective' criteria suggest they ought to be. . . . The difference seems to lie in choice of reference groups, women often comparing themselves only to other women." However, while this view is highly plausible, there is as yet little or no empirical research to demonstrate its validity (see Hodson, 1990).

Nonetheless, further reason to doubt the meaning of results from job satisfaction studies is found in research that focuses on signs of distress and depression among men and women. This research includes references to "the chronic fatigue, the anxiety, the sense of always being behind, or the near panic that working mothers often feel" (cited in Stanford Law Project, 1988:1229). Gore and Mangione (1986) report that one of the more consistent research findings is that the mental health of employed married women is poorer than that of employed married men. They conclude that this finding is not surprising from a sex role perspective, because while work is compatible with the family role expectations of men, it is less compatible with the family roles of most women. A result may be role stress and poorer mental health for women. This is essentially the role conflict thesis introduced in chapter 5.

There is also much journalistic and interview material to support the view that women are dissatisfied with their job situations (e.g., Abramson and Franklin, 1974; Repa, 1988; Tucker et al., 1989; Galanter and Palay,

1991:58n). Biographical accounts like the following from our own research are distressingly common.

> I have been practicing law in a law firm for five years and I am 36 years old. I waited to have children until I was 34 years old. I now have two little girls, ages 2 and 4 months. I have very recently handed in my resignation from the firm for which I have worked for the past three and a half years. Although I kept office hours from 7:45 a.m. to 5:00 p.m. five days a week and was back at work 4 days after my youngest child was born, I was told by the management of the firm that I was expected to work past 5:00 and that 'I was a good lawyer and an asset to the firm but that the practice of law was not a 9 to 5 job.' I felt so much pressure to be in the office late in the day and on the weekend that I could no longer enjoy any time away from the office.

As media accounts of this kind of work dissatisfaction among men and women lawyers have accumulated, the profession at large has become more concerned.

A *Barrister* magazine survey was conducted in 1980 and found that 40 percent of surveyed attorneys were dissatisfied with their work. However, magazine surveys are notoriously unreliable, and the American Bar Association (A.B.A.) subsequently conducted several national surveys that found lower levels of job dissatisfaction (cited in Hirsch, 1985). Nonetheless, these more systematic surveys also found that women lawyers were more dissatisfied than men, a departure from the research literature cited above.

The differences in the A.B.A. survey varied considerably across settings and stages of practice. For example, in a 1986 survey 18 percent of the men and 21 percent of the women in solo practice reported dissatisfaction. Among junior associates in firms, 19 percent of the men and 40 percent of the women were dissatisfied; among senior associates the respective figures were 13 and 25 percent; and among partners, 9 percent of the men and 15 percent of the women (cited in Hirsch, 1989). Although these findings of dissatisfaction follow tendencies in other occupations to diminish with age (Hodson, 1990; Menkel-Meadow, 1989a), they nonetheless also provide some quantitative support for the disturbing anecdotal accounts from lawyers noted above.

Two recent studies of elite law school graduates at Stanford and the University of Michigan speak further to these issues. Approximately equal numbers of male and female lawyers were surveyed from graduating classes up to 1986 in the Stanford study (Stanford Law Project, 1988). Results suggest that both female and male graduates of the 892 surveyed are very satisfied with their present jobs, with average scores of 5.31 and 5.12 respectively on a seven-point scale coded to indicate increasing levels of satisfaction. However, female graduates were more likely than their male counterparts also to report that they overeat, cry, have nightmares, and experience loneliness or depression. The authors of the Stanford study conclude that "[the] findings suggest female legal professionals . . . may experience higher levels of stress than do male legal professionals. This finding is consistent with the literature that reveals that the strain of balancing career and family roles causes women to experience substantial psychological distress, and perhaps even psychological disorder" (1209).

The Michigan study by David Chambers (1989) considers over 1,000 graduates of the 1976 to 1979 classes. Answers to an open-ended question about balancing work and family reflect the exhaustion frequently noted by working women, with accounts like the following: "I 'balance' by losing myself — my free time. I have no hobbies, little time to assess who I am and where I want to go. I 'balance' by forgoing social opportunities and chit-chat with peers." And, "I value my marriage and my friends. I have a two-year-old and am expecting another. I am half crazy because I put in fewer hours at work than my colleagues and I feel I am falling behind" (266). However, Chambers also found that women in his sample varied from regarding their private lives as their salvation to reports of finding themselves in constant crises of conflicting demands.

As in the Stanford study and in much other research on job satisfaction, when Chambers turned to the quantitative survey measures he found that most of the respondents were satisfied with their careers overall. About half of all women and men described themselves as "quite satisfied." Chambers also found some further evidence that women lawyers working full-time who had children were somewhat more satisfied with their work than women without children as well as men with and without children. However, Chambers concluded that "for our purposes, the most important point about the women with children is probably not that they seem somewhat more satisfied than others but that, despite all the reasons why it might be otherwise, they are fully *as* satisfied as the others" (278). Is it possible that these women are both beleaguered and satisfied?

Chambers carefully weighs the possibilities in answering this question. He notes that professional working women may feel a strong need to believe that they are managing their lives successfully, and that in indicating satisfaction they may therefore be engaging in a form of reaction formation or denial. Or, in a variation on the comparison thesis, he notes that these women may have accepted a tension between private and professional life and adjusted their standards accordingly. One mother who reported herself quite satisfied commented, "I get so tired of being tired and doing my career and home both more half-assed than I am used to doing. It's hard to stop doing one's very best, but I have come to accept my lowered expectations of myself" (281).

However, in the end Chambers discounts these explanations and instead adopts a version of the hypothesis that women find satisfaction in their diversity of roles. He suggests that women enjoy their families and their jobs, and that while the two may sometimes conflict, each also provides respite from the other. "Some people," Chambers writes, "enjoy the triathlon. Some people like scaling mountains carrying babies on their backs" (287). In any case, he suggests that "it seems a bit odd to doubt people who are so rich when they say they are contented" (284).

Chambers' study is by far the most thorough and thoughtful analysis available of gender differences in satisfaction in lawyering. Yet this is an unfinished story. Chambers is careful to note that his data are from the graduates of an elite law school, which leaves most lawyers out of the picture. He also notes that less-satisfied lawyers may not be working full-time and may not even have responded to the survey. He is also sensitive to the fact that asking about job satisfaction in different ways can produce different responses. Finally, Chambers notes that feelings of job satisfaction may change over time, and that they may currently be declining for most women as well as men.

All of these points are relevant to the analysis undertaken next. Our analysis differs from previous work in that it includes nonelite as well as elite lawyers, it considers those who have left practice as well as those who have stayed, it includes a new measure of job satisfaction, and it is, of course, based on more recent data. We also consider the link between job satisfaction and feelings of depression and despondency that is suggested by some of the research reviewed above. Finally, we explore some of the efforts women are making to change the conditions in which they must work. The picture that emerges is somewhat different from that provided in previous studies.

Our Respondents Speak for Themselves

Before undertaking a quantitative analysis of the survey responses from our Toronto sample, it is instructive to consider some of their comments. The issue of career and job satisfaction generated more of these comments than any other topic in our surveys, and some of these responses were quite positive. Perhaps the most positive comment came from a senior male lawyer who pursued public service:

> Law provides almost limitless possibilities for personal growth, and the freedom to pursue dreams. As a student I specialized in a few areas, but took enough general courses that I could and did completely change my specialization after five years at bar. Thereafter the law and a warped sense of service took me from one end of the country to the other, and from Texas to the high Arctic. It allowed me to be creative and unconventional while being assessed as socially worthwhile. . . . But there is a caveat: I lost sight of the big picture for a while and put too much of myself into my work. While my physical defenses were down I developed a life-threatening disease which I am now obliged to dispose of. But for that, my love affair with the profession of law has brought me nothing but happiness.

Some senior women lawyers also described their experiences in positive terms. One writes,

> I have had opportunities because I was a woman, both professionally and managerially. The former involved situations where a woman was preferred, for example, in high-profile cases involving women's issues. The latter involved male-dominated environments, where a woman could be less threatening, more accessible, easier to confide in about sensitive issues. There have also been fewer stereotypical rules for me, for example, allowing more flexible hours while I was raising children, which male colleagues couldn't or didn't attempt because of the "image" problems unorthodoxy created. As you can see, I am delighted to be a woman in this profession and I hope that others will find opportunity for satisfying personal and professional lives without either trying to emulate men or taking politically radical positions. Neither is necessary for happiness as a lawyer.

Another respondent observes, "Since graduating from law school in 1960, I have never felt discrimination because I was a woman. I stayed home to raise my children from 1967 to 1984, although I worked part-time during that period. I consider myself very fortunate and enjoy my job." A third respondent recalls, "I was called to the bar forty-two years ago and only once or twice did I experience any bias because I was a woman. I really believe that many women professionals have a thin skin. They chose the profession — dominated by men — live with it or leave it. There is a much better way than complaining and that is hard work and a sense of humour. You'll then earn respect from clients, fellow lawyers and friends. It is not a right."

However, while the above comments represent a distinct point of view among our respondents, another view was more common, and the transition to it is reflected in the following opinion: "I have found older lawyers, typically men, but also some of the more senior women, very difficult to work with and for. There is little flexibility for changing ideas as to a balance of work and family and the idea that 'it was done this way when I went through, therefore you will have to do it that way too' flourishes." Often general concerns like the following were expressed by men as well as women: "My concern about career satisfaction reflects an impression of change in the practice of law from professionalism and sound ethics to greed and sharp practice. The pressure to compete and get ahead are robbing the law of some of its touchstones and converting it to a big business. This probably echoes the experience of the whole community but the result is no less disturbing."

A frequent theme in lawyers' expressions of dissatisfaction is that "the fun is gone" from their practice of law. One respondent writes, "The trend toward mega-firms and the fixation on the almighty bottom line are destructive and dehumanizing. In my short time as a lawyer (thirteen years) I see fewer and fewer people having fun and more and more willing to do anything (ethics be damned) to get ahead." Another comments, "Most of my colleagues agree much of the 'fun' of practicing law has disappeared and that we are becoming slaves to the work. I regret this terribly and I believe that we, as professionals, are doing ourselves a great disservice by creating a working environment that reduces us to clock punches." A third respondent remarks, "I am not a junior or a young lawyer anymore. I have an extremely busy practice and now cannot service everyone who calls me. I work every Sunday and several nights a week. This is not fun." One more member of the sample notes, "I feel I've become much more obsessive in both my personal and professional life. I am beginning to wonder if I've lost all sense of fun and play."

By far the most frequent expressions of dissatisfaction come from women lawyers and involve general feelings of malaise and frustration in trying to meet the demands of what often is perceived as a male lawyering culture. For example, a respondent comments on the general experience of being a woman in a male-dominated profession: "Throughout my sixteen years of law, I feel being a woman has created many difficult and unpleasant hurdles. No matter how much you achieve, it is discredited." Another respondent in a firm setting observes, "The most difficult aspect of being a female lawyer and partner is the conflicting feelings I get about my own position in the firm. Objectively my work assignments and opportunities may seem fair, but the firm is still a very male-dominated place, often inhospitable to myself and my female colleagues."

A third respondent who left a Toronto firm to practice in a smaller setting offers perhaps the most critical assessment:

> I found a lot of lawyers in Toronto to be smarmy, ass-kissing, backstabbing hypocrites. I was often disgusted by the convenient 'ethics' of the older lawyers in bigger firms, who could miraculously justify all kinds of unprofessional behaviour, not the least of which was sexual harassment of young women lawyers. I saw younger lawyers buying into those rationalizations wholesale, and it made me ill. I still put up my guard when dealing with Toronto lawyers, and I still catch them lying and backstabbing from time to time. They have lost touch with basic human values like integrity and honesty, and I'm glad I'm no longer a member of that club.

However, the most common source of dissatisfaction for women, and some men, is the difficulty of matching work and family demands. For example, a woman lawyer observes, "The greatest frustration of my career to date has been the constant struggle to maintain a 'normal' lifestyle. Discussion with female or male colleagues suggests they share the same concerns. Full-time employment often means not getting home before ten or eleven at night and working many weekends. For those who value family life, private practice, though rewarding in terms of quality of life and challenge, may not be a perfect fit." Another respondent writes, "It seems to me that employers are saying 'It's all or nothing, and I want it all' rather than allowing me to say my career can wait a bit while I have kids or my career can develop at a slower pace than it otherwise might." A third respondent, a woman partner and mother, adds this dissatisfied account: "Being a lawyer and a mother, I have simply had to give up my personal life. I have virtually no time for myself. I would like to add that it is very lonely being a female partner in a large Toronto law firm. Despite being friends with many of my colleagues, it is the men who lunch together, socialize together. It is a terrible feeling of isolation."

Nonetheless, some women in our research seem to have adjusted to their feelings of dissatisfaction by adopting an attitude of resignation. For example, a respondent suggests, "If I won a lottery, I would quit tomorrow and never look at another statute again. However, because I am practical, single, earning a good income and have job security, I am staying. Whoever said one was supposed to love one's job? I guess that's why it's called work." Some women also take solace in the difficult conditions of other women they encounter in the profession: "I like where I work, the people I work with, and most of my clients. When I feel dissatisfied it is because of stress and overwork. . . . I feel that after fifteen years I have a higher level of job satisfaction than most of the other women I know."

Many women may therefore feel ambivalent about their work situation. One respondent writes,

> I was struck by how my high job satisfaction contrasted sharply with stress created by my home life situation. . . . I use an institutional daycare, so hours are rigid. I must shoehorn my practice into 8:30 to 5:30, with almost no exception. This means work is not allowed to encroach on home life, but it means I am always "working" either in child care or law. I am only "off duty" on the fifteen minute drive twice a day. No wonder I drive at the speed limit — to prolong the time. I intend to consider this and try to redesign things a little.

Another comments,

> Although I am far from being thrilled, stimulated, and enthralled with my job, the remuneration is very good. I can't think of another job at which I would earn more money. . . . Unfortunately, I don't feel that I am furthering any "social good" or ensuring justice is done with my job. I am a hired gun fighting for and about money. Community service is not encouraged at my firm, and given that I am expected to docket about 1,900 hours a year, that doesn't leave much time for extracurricular activities. What I hate most about my job is the stress — pressure from clients, opponents, and superiors.

Another respondent observes, "My answers may seem somewhat contradictory — showing my current state of mind! While I enjoy the work I do, I would like to have more time for my family." A fourth woman lawyer concludes, "Though I'm basically satisfied that my current position offers good opportunities (though not outstanding ones), I would be happier if I could cut back to focus more on raising my family. I'm a walking social stereotype, but there it is. With so many like me, and the reasons so good, law firm expectations have to give sometime!"

Finally, and perhaps most significantly, there are the women who have left legal practice. Joan Brockman (1992) recently has enumerated reasons why women seem to be leaving the profession of law in growing numbers, including the nature of legal work, long hours, low pay, child care commitments, loss of employment, poor prospects for advancement, spouse's career, stress, and sometimes alternative opportunities. A number of our respondents echoed these themes in their comments. One respondent writes, "I left practice because my own firm was more misogynist than my clients. . . . Issues of systemic discrimination are repeatedly ignored so that the legal environment is inhospitable to those women who want power but are not prepared to play by the 'boys' rules.' " Another indicates,

> I recently decided to leave my firm. . . . While practice does have several things to commend it, I have felt the focus of the work to be somewhat empty (e.g., making wealthy people wealthier), and the pressures are absurd and often unnecessarily oppressive. I have spoken with many other lawyers about my decision and our respective feelings about our jobs, and I believe there is a fairly pervasive element of dissatisfaction and unhappiness, largely related to hours of work and degree of pressure. I think there is a real need to broaden our ideas of what makes a good lawyer and allow people to select different levels or intensities of practice. So much of our definition of an outstanding lawyer seems to focus on the ability to endure a staggering workload and constant demands for faster turnover without flinching, and without responding to the deprivation which occurs in other areas of our lives which for many of us are just as crucial as career to our sense of worth and well-being.

A third respondent concludes, "It's a total grind. It is intellectually dead and highly competitive in the worst way — money is all that matters to most lawyers I know. I'm leaving at the end of the summer. Goodbye."

However, it is perhaps the following account by a woman lawyer who has left practice that best illustrates the kind of stereotypes and structurally imposed working conditions that drive many women from the profession.

> In my experience, female solicitors are particularly encouraged to use computers, probably based on the assumption that all women can type. In my case, I was the only solicitor who used the computers extensively and on a daily basis. When my secretary resigned, no replacement was engaged on the grounds that it was not cost-effective. Promises made by the partners and other associates to "share" staff were not kept. As a result, I became responsible for all of my own typing, document preparation, municipal searches, and other tasks formerly performed by my secretary. In a predominantly real estate practice, the preparation of documents can be very time-consuming. I worked six-day, seventy-hour weeks for months at a time, with adverse effects on my health and job satisfaction. I do not believe that a male lawyer in the firm would have been required to work under those conditions. Needless to say, my typing skills improved immensely — useful perhaps, but hardly a career goal.

A more general and common feeling of women lawyers who commented about the culture of firms in our survey is captured in the thoughts of a final respondent: "I have hated my experience as a lawyer so far. Women in my Bay Street firm never get to attend closings, lunch with clients, etc. A majority of corporate lawyers are male and take young male lawyers under their wing. I don't feel the above is done intentionally. Nonetheless, it makes firm life very lonely. If my next job isn't better, I will leave the practice of law."

Analyzing Satisfaction

We move next to a quantitative effort to assess expressions of job satisfaction in response to survey questions. Measuring and analyzing job satisfaction through surveys is at once both easy and difficult. It is easy in the sense that there are well-developed scales that have been used in past research and that can be applied in the study of lawyers. Below we introduce items from such a scale, used in both waves of our Toronto lawyer study. However, it is also clear from the above accounts that job satisfaction has many facets or dimensions. Mueller (1992) makes this point by citing the example of a person who is satisfied with her pay but dissatisfied with feedback about her job performance. If scores involving these two dimensions of job satisfaction are combined, the person will be shown to be neither satisfied nor dissatisfied in the composite.

One implication of this kind of complication in measuring job satisfaction is that we should be open to considering alternative measurement approaches (see also Hodson, 1990). One of our respondents noted, "It is my impression that there is a very high level of disappointment with the reality of lawyering, but that this is only revealed in confidence and to peers or immediate family." It may be important to find alternative ways of discerning these dissatisfactions, for example, by focusing on movement in and out of the profession and between jobs. Above we cited examples of women who abandoned the practice of law. The following example, though not from our research, is useful because it combines many of the elements we have considered in this book to explain the decision of a women to move from one private practice setting to another. This example also provides insights on how thoughts about job satisfaction can change over time and across situations.

> Given my previous experiences within the legal profession, my current professional arrangement is terrific. I am given my *choice* of work to do, authority over all support staff, input on all major office decisions and enormous support of my decision to have a child. This is particularly remarkable in light of my inauguration into the legal world, which was extremely distressing. I articled at a prestigious firm and was surprised to find myself the only woman lawyer. Women had worked there before but all had left within a few years and no woman had ever been a partner in the firm's history. It wasn't

until I finally left the firm that I realized I had been treated unfairly. I was very young and unwilling to recognize sexual discrimination within this noble profession. Upon reflection, I see that I was assigned almost exclusively to collection and family law files. My court appearances were always pursuant to mundane foreclosures or agricultural implement repossessions. All the while, other members of the firm including men only one year senior to me at the bar were involved in very high-profile litigation and lucrative corporate/commercial work. My salary was markedly lower than the male lawyer's one year "ahead" of me and the reason given was that his billings were larger. I was given all the nonpaying or low-paying work! Nevertheless, I was consistently able to bill at least five times my salary. I was disregarded when office policy was set, yet "paraded" at public functions as the female lawyer at this 'modern' firm. Although I had been sexually harassed by an important bank executive the year before (and had made my displeasure known to the partners), I was again required to sit next to this man at the annual Christmas dinner! Periodically, I was reminded that I should appear at work every evening and on weekends while other married male employed lawyers consistently left the office promptly at 5:00 and did not return at night. Ultimately, I was told I was not investing enough time and effort into my work. I was told I was never going to be made a partner, so I could look for another job — I could take as long as I wanted so no one would realize I had been 'asked' to leave and simply depart when other employment was secured. I refused to comply with this request and left immediately. (Robertson, 1992:55)

This example raises the possibility that movements between professional positions as well as in and out of the profession may be more revealing than expressions of generalized job satisfaction. We have given some attention to such movements in previous chapters and will do so again below. However, it is also possible to inquire about thoughts of moving as a more specific way of measuring job satisfaction. In the American Bar Association survey discussed above, it was found that the proportion of women who planned to change their jobs within the next few years was three times that of men (28.5 percent compared to 9.4 percent) (Nelson and Trubek, 1988). This is a more substantial gender difference than is indicated with other satisfaction measures. We emphasize the importance of this reflection of job dissatisfaction below.

First we consider the eighty women and forty-five men in our Toronto sample who have left the practice of law. As these numbers alone indicate, women are more likely to leave than men. This and following results parallel those reported for the cross-sectional Ontario sample considered in chapter

5. The Toronto respondents who had left law since the initial survey were asked in the follow-up survey to indicate their reasons for doing so.

More than half of the women (57.6 percent) and about a third of the men (33.2 percent) indicated they left law for reasons of dissatisfaction. The sources of dissatisfaction were articulated in various ways, but the answers clearly seem to cluster around issues of hours, conditions of practice, and more general concerns about quality of life. It is interesting that both men and women express these sources of dissatisfaction, but also that women do so more than men. Meanwhile, about two-thirds of the men compared to fewer than half of the women (43 percent) cited other responsibilities, limitations, and most notably other opportunities to explain their departures from law. More specifically, nearly a third of the men (31.1 percent) cited other opportunities as their reason for leaving law, compared to only 10 percent of the women. Most of the men in a residual "other" category left for retirement.

So overall while women usually leave legal employment for reasons of dissatisfaction, men usually leave because of other opportunities or limitations that do not involve their dissatisfaction with practicing law. The women who leave legal practice are easy to miss in studies of lawyer satisfaction, because such studies are usually cross-sectional and focused on currently employed lawyers. These women have appeared in our research because we have made them a focus of our work, through systematic stratified sampling in the Ontario research, and by following individuals over time in the Toronto panel. Since these individuals may not fully come to terms with the nature of their dissatisfactions while they are at a particular work location, it is especially important to include them in sampling designs.

As suggested above, it may also be possible to pick up on the development of dissatisfaction by focusing on thoughts of looking for alternative employment among those who are currently working in law. We wanted to consider items that would reflect situations like the following of a respondent who reported, "I am dissatisfied with the practice because it does not leave room for the individual. I am single and because of the long hours, I expect I will always be single. Secondly, I find that the emphasis is on dockets and billings and there is less and less concern about employees and clients. The environment is soul-destroying. I am currently looking for a new position to give practice another chance. If it fails to bring me personal satisfaction, I will be leaving the profession entirely." Such reports were common in our research. For example, another woman lawyer commented, "I feel that the amount of stress placed upon lawyers as a result of billing pressure is enormous. It means that junior lawyers like myself do not have the time to learn or understand what it is we are producing and creates an enormous amount of stress when trying to balance a home life with a career. If the billing pressure is not relieved for me, either by way of part-time opportunities or more 'realistic' expectations, I do not think that I will be in the practice of law two years from now." Another respondent lamented,

> Many of my friends and colleagues state the concern that a recent emphasis on the business of the practice of law has diminished their enjoyment and commitment to practice. The ridiculous emphasis on 2,000 billable hours a year distorts young lawyers' training and doesn't help their clients get sound, considered advice. I am strongly considering leaving law, or at least the traditional firm-based practice. There is more to life than grinding out mindless documents day and night for a partnership that appears to be ungrateful for the effort and insatiable for the dollars. My complaint, you will note, is a lack of satisfaction with the work. . . . I have little interest in my work . . . and I get minimal satisfaction from my contributions to my clients and society. . . . And since the mega firms in Toronto are unlikely to make any significant changes in the short term, it is time for me to explore other options.

A fourth woman lawyer simply concluded, "The world doesn't need another real estate lawyer. I don't 'love the law' enough to want to stand on my head trying to juggle family commitments and outside interests. I am looking to leave."

We included in the 1985 and 1991 waves of the Toronto panel five items that are commonly used in job satisfaction scales, and one of these items asked, "Do you plan to look for a new job in the next year?" In the 1991 follow-up survey we also asked, "Have you considered looking for a new job that would allow you to better balance your personal life and work?" The remaining items in both waves of the survey asked how satisfied respondents were with their jobs, whether they would recommend their jobs to a friend, whether they would take their jobs again if given a choice, and how their jobs compared to what they wanted when they first took them.

As in previous work, the answers given by men and women lawyers to these questions in our surveys were predominantly positive. We therefore present percentaged results in table 7.1 coded to indicate the proportion who express such satisfaction; all Toronto lawyers working in law in 1991 are included in this table. The predominant pattern is that about three-quarters of the women and men indicate satisfaction on the five measures that appear in both surveys. This pattern is also fairly stable across the two waves of the study, with women and men seeming rather satisfied in the

Table 7.1
Job Satisfaction of Women and Men Toronto Lawyers, 1985 and 1991 (*N* = 692)

Measure of Job Satisfaction	1985		1991	
	Women	Men	Women	Men
How satisfied are you with your job? [a]	78.2	81.3	78.3	79.4
Would you recommend your job to a friend? [b]	70.6	67.4	65.2	65.8
Given a choice, would you take the same job again? [c]	78.7	77.7	74.4	75.8
How does your current job measure up to the sort of job you wanted when you took it? [d]	71.1	74.5	73.3	74.5
Do you plan to look for a new job in the next year? [e]	62.5	69.7	67.0	76.1
Have you considered looking for a new job that would allow you to better balance your personal life and work? [e]			39.0	54.1

[a] Percentage answering satisfied or very satisfied.

[b] Percentage answering recommend or recommend highly.

[c] Percentage answering probably or definitely.

[d] Percentage answering pretty much or exactly.

[e] Percentage answering no or definitely not.

aggregate with their jobs. Indeed, on the first four items in the table, women and men seem remarkably similar, with reported levels of satisfaction differing by about an average of 1 percentage point, and seldom by more than 3 percentage points.

However, the last two items in the table involving thoughts about changing jobs are a distinct departure from the overall trend. Responses to these items are coded to indicate certainty of staying in a present job, with respondents answering that they are not or have not thought of looking for alternative employment. The majority of the respondents indicated that they were planning to "stay put" in both waves of the panel, and this sentiment increased over time, as much past research on job changes indicates it should (e.g., Felmlee, 1982). However, in both waves of the panel women indicated they were less certain of staying, and the difference between women and men increased over time, with the difference growing from about 7 to 9 percent. An apparent source of this difference is reflected in the larger disparity in certainty when women and men were asked in the follow-up survey whether they had considered looking for a new job to achieve a better balance between their personal life and work. Only 39 percent of the women indicated they had not done so, compared to 54 percent of the men. These job search measures of work satisfaction clearly seem to reveal a dimension along which men and women differ, a difference that is consistent with findings about job changes in the A.B.A. survey noted previously.

We combine the two measures of thoughts about changing jobs as a measure of work satisfaction in the next part of our analysis. Responses to the two items are added, with each coded in its original categories from one to five as probably, perhaps, uncertain, not, and definitely not planning or having considered looking for another job. This scaled measure of not contemplating a job change can be interpreted as reflecting work satisfaction and was compared with the more common and generalized measure of job satisfaction for women and men across practice settings in 1985 and 1991. The results are interesting.

As earlier results would predict, the generalized measure in 1985 revealed no distinct pattern of difference by gender. The same measure in 1991 produced a uniformly small but consistent tendency across settings for men to indicate greater satisfaction than women. However, the search measure in 1991 indicated a larger difference in favor of the satisfaction of men across all practice settings. For example, in firms with more than twenty lawyers, men on average scored 7.15 on this satisfaction measure, compared to 6.43 with women. In corporate settings, the respective scores were 7.19 and 6.42. Because this difference occurs across all settings, and because some of the explanatory variables we have introduced in earlier chapters are most meaningful in the private practice sector, the remaining analyses in this chapter are focused on full-time privately practicing lawyers.

The correlation between being male and the job search measure of work satisfaction for all full-time privately practicing lawyers is substantial and significant, as indicated in table 7.2. The remainder of this table uses standardized regression coefficients (discussed in the Appendix to this volume) to identify determinants of job satisfaction in tables 7.2 and 7.3. The second column of table 7.2 introduces age. It is important to take age into account because men in the Toronto sample are older than women, and

Table 7.2
Decomposition of Effect of Gender on Job Satisfaction among Toronto Lawyers in Full-Time Private Practice, 1991 ($N = 375$)

Variables [a]	Equations (Eqs.)				
	Eq.1 Standardized Coefficient	Eq.2 Standardized Coefficient	Eq.3 Standardized Coefficient	Eq.4 Standardized Coefficient	Eq.5 Standardized Coefficient
Gender	0.192***	0.151**	0.140**	0.106*	0.088
Age		0.105*	0.093	0.099	0.088
Elite Law School			0.032	0.031	0.033
Law School Grades			0.067	0.069	0.056
WASP			−0.072	−0.071	−0.066
Marital Status			−0.010	−0.002	−0.003
Child 0–5			0.030	0.081	0.090
Child 6–12			−0.029	−0.017	−0.024
Child 13–18			0.028	0.027	0.015
Child 19+			0.035	0.034	0.042
Hours of Housework			−0.023	−0.024	−0.015
Parental Leave			−0.001	0.001	0.006
Work Commitment			0.047	0.057	0.055
Internal Market[b]			0.013	0.019	−0.005
Internal to External Market			0.083	0.077	0.061
External to Internal Market			0.078	0.087	0.072
Partner			0.057	0.047	0.070
Works Own Cases			−0.027	−0.032	−0.027
Autonomy			0.010	0.008	0.006
Decision Making			0.149**	0.154**	0.137**
Corporate Clients			−0.133**	−0.130**	−0.144**
Hierarchical Position			0.094*	0.096*	0.068
Specialization Status			0.027	0.024	0.008
Hours of Child Care				−0.111*	−0.111*
Income					0.115*
Constant		5.661	3.111	2.969	3.402
R^2		0.046	0.123	0.131	0.139

* $p < 0.05$; ** $p < 0.01$; *** $p < 0.001$; one-tailed.

[a] See text of this and prior chapter for description of variables.

[b] Market variables refer to job location within and movements between firms with 20 or more lawyers.

because in prior research it is apparent that job satisfaction increases with age and that individuals become less inclined to change jobs. The results in column 2 of table 7.2 correspondingly indicate that the job satisfaction of lawyers increases with age and that younger lawyers are more likely to consider moving. Controlling for differences in age reduces the effect of gender by about one-fifth. However, the effect of being male nonetheless remains notable.

The third column of results reveals that lawyers who are more involved in firm decision making and who are in more powerful hierarchical positions are more satisfied with their current jobs. Alternatively, having a larger corporate practice reduces job satisfaction. This may reflect the changing fortunes of corporate law during the recent recession indicated in the earlier discussion in chapter 1. Meanwhile, controlling for the large number of variables added in column 3 does little to reduce the effect of gender, which remains substantial and significant.

The final two columns of table 7.2 introduce the measures of hours of child care and 1990 income. Recall that women lawyers spend more time on child care than men and receive lower earnings. The introduction of hours of child care into the equation estimated in column 4 reduces the effect of gender on job satisfaction by about one-quarter. This indicates that in significant part women are less satisfied than men with their current jobs because of the demands that are also placed on them to care for their children. However, the effect of gender on job satisfaction still remains significant until in the last column of table 7.2 we control for income. With both hours of child care and income in the equation, the effect of gender finally becomes nonsignificant. Overall, women lawyers seem less satisfied with their jobs than men because they are younger, more burdened with child care, and earning less.

The subjective consequences of this situation deepen when we consider the feelings of depression and despondency that may follow. The 1991 survey of Toronto lawyers included seven items commonly used to measure depression (e.g., Ross, 1985). These items asked the number of days during the past week that the respondent "felt you just couldn't get going, felt sad, had trouble getting to sleep or staying asleep, felt that everything was an effort, felt lonely, felt you couldn't shake the blues, had trouble keeping your mind on what you were doing." Scores are added to form a scale, with an average score of 3.534 for men and 6.337 for women.

Thus, as in earlier studies we find that women are more likely to be depressed than men. These studies provide evidence that job problems are a source of this difference in depression, and to explore this possibility more directly among lawyers, in table 7.3 we analyze the effects on depression of gender and job satisfaction measured with the search scale. The gender co-efficient reported in the first column of table 7.3 indicates that overall women lawyers are more depressed than men lawyers. The coefficients reported in the second column indicate that as in the case of job satisfaction, age plays a part in this gender difference. Younger lawyers are more depressed, so that when the age difference between women and men lawyers is controlled, the gender difference is reduced by about one-fifth, but still remains significant. The variables included in column three of table 7.3 include marital status and having children. Being married and having older children reduce feelings of depression and account for the tendency of older lawyers to be less depressed (i.e., the effect of age is reduced to nonsignificance). The effect of gender is again also reduced by controlling these age-related variables, but remains statistically significant.

The final columns in table 7.3 introduce the measures of income and job satisfaction. Having a lower income increases feelings of depression, and controlling for the gender gap in incomes in column 4 further reduces the effect of gender on depression by about 15 percent. In turn, introducing the search measure of job satisfaction in column 5 of table 7.3 reduces to nonsignificance the effects of both income and gender. Overall, these findings indicate that men lawyers report being less depressed than women lawyers because they are older, have older children, make more money and are more satisfied with their jobs. The effects we have observed of gender differences in incomes on job satisfaction and feelings of depression are consistent with gender stratification theory, while the favorable effects of older children are consistent with the role enhancement or diversity thesis also associated with this theory.

To assure that these results were not obscuring gender-specific effects of having children on women and men, we also regressed the search measure of job satisfaction and depression on the measures of having children of different ages. These measures were not significantly related to job satisfaction, but there were again significant effects for depression, among both women and men. All of the effects on depression were negative, indicating that having children of primary-school age and beyond high-school age significantly reduced feelings of depression among women, and the latter also did so among men. Again, these findings are consistent with the role diversity thesis favored by gender stratification theory, and inconsistent with the role overload thesis associated with human capital theory.

This brings us to the final issue to be addressed in this chapter: the efforts that women are making to change work conditions that can cause dissatisfaction. There are a number of reasons why we might expect that women would make little effort to change their job situations. We have seen

Table 7.3

Decomposition of Effect of Gender on Feelings of Depression among Toronto Lawyers in Full-Time Private Practice, 1991 ($N = 375$)

Variables [a]	Equations (Eqs.)				
	Eq.1 Standardized Coefficient	Eq.2 Standardized Coefficient	Eq.3 Standardized Coefficient	Eq.4 Standardized Coefficient	Eq.5 Standardized Coefficient
Gender	−0.177***	−0.137**	−0.119*	−0.101*	−0.079
Age		−0.101*	−0.063	−0.053	−0.031
Elite Law School			−0.035	−0.038	−0.029
Law School Grades			−0.045	−0.032	−0.018
WASP			−0.023	−0.028	−0.044
Marital Status			−0.093*	−0.093*	−0.093*
Child 0–5 years			−0.095	−0.103	−0.081
Child 6–12 years			−0.092*	−0.090*	−0.091*
Child 13–18 years			−0.067	−0.056	−0.052
Child 19+			−0.122*	−0.131*	−0.120*
Hours of Housework			−0.011	−0.021	−0.024
Parental Leave			−0.040	−0.047	−0.046
Work Commitment			−0.001	0.002	0.016
Internal Market [b]			−0.047	−0.023	−0.024
Internal to External Market			−0.007	0.009	0.024
External to Internal Market			0.030	0.044	0.063
Partner			−0.008	−0.031	−0.013
Works Own Cases			0.054	0.050	0.043
Autonomy			0.004	0.007	0.008
Decision Making			−0.038	−0.022	0.013
Corporate Client			0.046	0.061	0.025
Hierarchical Position			−0.016	0.012	0.029
Specialization Status			0.005	0.021	0.023
Hours of Child Care			0.052	0.052	0.024
Income				−0.115*	−0.086
Job Satisfaction					−0.250***
Constant	6.337	9.820	13.013	11.297	14.689
R^2	0.031	0.040	0.106	0.114	0.168

* $p < 0.05$; ** $p < 0.01$; *** $p < 0.001$; one-tailed.
[a] See text of this and prior chapter for description of variables.
[b] Market variables refer to job location within and movements between firms with 20 or more lawyers.

that they have less power in the profession than men lawyers, and feelings of unhappiness and depression might be expected to further reduce efforts to reform an inhospitable occupational environment. As we have seen, many dissatisfied women may leave legal practice, and this raises the question of whether those who stay simply take as given the conditions in which they work, or whether they are making efforts to change the legal profession.

We addressed this question in our follow-up survey of Toronto lawyers by asking respondents to indicate whether they had tried to influence areas of their work, and if so, whether they perceived their efforts as successful. Our analysis of these questions is focused on the lawyers in our panel who were working full-time in private practice. Three areas of practice were considered: maternity leave, partnership, and range of clients. We assumed that women lawyers might be particularly concerned with widening maternity leave provisions, diversifying partnership arrangements, and expanding the range of clients served.

The results reveal considerable effort and some success in each of these areas. More than half of the women had tried to influence maternity leave policies, and nearly 40 percent of the women reported some success in doing so. So about 80 percent of those women who made efforts in this area had some success. Only about a quarter of the men made efforts in this area, but about the same proportion indicated success. This indicates that men almost always succeeded when they tried in this area, which suggests the importance of enlisting male support in reform efforts.

About the same proportions of men and women lawyers, in the area of 40 percent, tried to influence partnership policy. However, men were nearly twice as likely to be successful in these efforts as women, with nearly 29 percent of the men succeeding, compared to just less than 15 percent of the women. This suggests that partnership is a more contentious issue than maternity leave within law firms, and that women are having only limited success in changing the terms of these arrangements that are so central to the organization of firm life.

Finally, about half the men and about 40 percent of the women tried to influence the range of clients served by their firms, and about 30 percent of both groups perceived that they achieved some success. This implies that women were actually somewhat more successful in accomplishing change in this area than were men. Although we do not know from the measure used what the specific nature of changes attempted were, it is nonetheless interesting that women's efforts in this area achieved some success. Overall there is considerable evidence in this analysis of the influence of women in firms, albeit less so in an area of perhaps greatest concern —

partnership. However, our data suggest that this is not due to a lack of effort on the part of women who continue to practice in firms (see also Menkel-Meadow, 1985, 1987; Williams, 1990; Barnett, 1990; O'Connor, 1991; Cahn, 1991).

Demanding Practices

Past research comparing the job satisfaction of men and women in law and other occupations reports only scattered evidence that women are less pleased with their work than men. However, we have suggested that a more revealing approach to this issue may involve a measure of satisfaction that places greater emphasis on thoughts about changing jobs and the desire to find work that is better balanced with family responsibilities. When we apply such a measure in our research a more likely picture emerges in which women are shown to be less content with their work situations than men. This dissatisfaction may in part result from women more often being at earlier stages of their careers than men, but it is also produced by the different opportunities of men and women to engage in rewarding work. In turn, the greater job dissatisfaction of women results in more frequent feelings of despondency and despair.

One of the most interesting findings in this chapter is the suggestion that both the problems of balancing work and family life *and* poorer work opportunities and rewards for women are involved in their job dissatisfaction, abandonment of the profession, and feelings of despondency and depression. Having children while working full-time in and of itself does not produce feelings of depression among women, as the role overload hypothesis suggests. Indeed, having older children has psychological benefits for both women and men, as the role diversity hypothesis predicts. Nonetheless, there are indications in our search measure of satisfaction that being underrewarded does lead to a questioning of the sacrifices that many jobs demand of women. The following account of one woman's plans to abandon law articulates the form this dissatisfaction may often take.

> I fear I am going to join the ranks of female ex-lawyers. This profession is too demanding to justify continuing in it, without the financial remuneration and intangible rewards my male colleagues receive. I may be dreaming, but it is my impression that, for example, business and government are more interested in obtaining intelligent, hardworking people than the legal profession. I regret that I have to make this kind of decision, because I obviously feel it is vital that women are equally represented in the profession, as they are equally represented in society as a whole. It is unfortunate the older

women lawyers can't stay in the profession to assist the younger women entering the profession, to break the ground for them and to become role models and mentors. As long as the majority of women lawyers are junior lawyers, the problems will probably never be solved. And as long as senior women lawyers are not allowed the career fulfillment that keeps the senior male lawyers at their desks, they will continue to opt out in favour of other pursuits, whether they are family, other careers or alternate legal jobs. . . . The "mentoring" may be part of it but I don't think a lot of people will identify getting a good job in a firm that has held its own or gotten bigger as "mentoring." Getting to work on good files at a firm that has them has a lot to do with present success and I know my male classmates essentially became "big billers" because they simply were given the work. (Robertson, 1992:62)

This comment raises the question of whether the conditions of firm life will change. Law has long been a brutally demanding profession, as noted at the outset of this chapter, and the problems resulting from this commonly have been ignored. It is an open question whether new concerns expressed about working conditions and raised more explicitly by the entry of larger numbers of women into the profession will result in changes in firm practices. Will women change law, or will law change women? Menkel-Meadow (1989b) poses this issue by suggesting that "whether a feminist critique of the legal profession will emerge and transform the profession or social structural obstacles will silence feminist concerns or force assimilation is a question that must be answered empirically and theoretically" (239). Chambers (1989:287) addresses a similar concern when he suggests that "a question with which we are left is whether there will ever come a point, as more women reach positions of power in the profession, when women and then men will seek in large numbers to achieve other, more fully satisfying balances" (287).

We have found some evidence that women and men are making efforts to influence various aspects of legal practice, including provisions for maternity leave, partnership arrangements, and the range of clientele served. These efforts seem least successful on core issues such as partnership, and more successful when undertaken by men than by women. Nonetheless, the women in our Toronto panel indicate that they feel they are making some progress. In the chapter that follows we argue that if greater advances are to be achieved, it will be necessary to shift the ground rules under which some of these efforts are undertaken.

8

A Contested Profession

*While it seemed that in the late 1980s it was fashionable, and pro-
fessionally correct, to work as much as possible and to always ensure that everybody knew about it, young lawyers are starting to
think, and say, "This is ridiculous!" . . . It will be interesting to see
if the tension between law firm management's desire to grind out the
dollars and the growing desire for fundamental change on the part
of younger lawyers and women will be resolved in a way that enhances the professional lives of lawyers. People are no longer satisfied with sacrificing their families and their personal lives for the
good of organizations who do not understand that professional
fulfillment is not found in twelve-hour, six-day work weeks. However, a recession will limit opportunities for change. . . . And, in the
end . . . you have to pay your mortgage.*

Two Theories in Practice

The profession of law, long known for its stability and resistance to change,
is today a contested domain. The changes that have altered the contours of
this profession — the shift from individual practice to firm partnerships
with large numbers of associates and growing numbers of women — could
hardly have made it otherwise: the same developments that have transformed
the shape of legal practice have stimulated demands for reform. Some aspects of the transformation — especially changes in its hierarchical organization and gender composition — are more contentious and productive of
demands for reform than others, and the transformation is ongoing.

This book began by highlighting changes in the overall structure of
the profession during recent decades. We then analyzed the careers of individual women and men lawyers. In this chapter, we offer conclusions about

where these changes and accompanying reforms might lead. First, however, we review our empirical findings in relation to the human capital and gender stratification theories often used to analyze developments in the legal profession and other occupations.

The premises of these theories are distinct and have differing policy implications. We noted at the outset of this book that a common version of human capital theory replaces old assumptions about a preordained separation of work and domestic spheres with assumptions about chosen spheres of specialization, which are used to justify differences in career experiences and outcomes. The emphasis of this theory is on efficient and choice-driven investment in human resources, which is assumed to be maximized through the specialization of men in careers outside the home and of women in childbearing and rearing within the home. According to this theory, small intrinsic differences between the genders encourage specialization of investments in efforts that over time create large gender differences in accumulated human capital and resulting occupational rewards. Gender stratification theory counters that such conceptions help create separate strata that operate to the disadvantage of women in occupations and professions, for example, leading to discrimination against women in their efforts for career advancement. An alternative restricted spheres version of human capital theory acknowledges constraints on career opportunities of women, opening possibilities for an integration of perspectives, but this prospect is undeveloped and deemphasized in the human capital tradition.

This leads human capital theory to have a greater implicit if not explicit following in managing circles of law firms, as well as among economists who have elaborated and articulated this theory, while gender stratification theory has a stronger following among sociologists, feminist legal scholars, and women lawyers. In this context, it can be argued that human capital theory provides a more male-oriented view of the profession, while gender stratification theory is more sympathetic to the concerns of women. There is a further tendency for gender stratification theory to focus on structural and group-linked determinants of the professional experience, in contrast with human capital theory's voluntaristic focus on individual choice.

Both theories see the profession as undergoing important changes, but their reactions to these changes differ. Because human capital theory tends to see the profession as appropriately focused on the role of individual choice in guiding efficient investment in human resources, it encourages a minimalist response to the changes. This is consistent with the profession's reliance on self-regulation in response to complaints by and about individual practitioners, with minimally constrained market forces otherwise allocating outcomes. There is relatively little concern about broader issues of discrimination in human capital theory, or among the human capitalists who run law firms. In contrast, gender stratification theory sees the structural transformation of the profession as imposing limitations of choice and constraints that unjustly and inefficiently jeopardize the careers of women lawyers.

Individually focused efforts at self-regulation offer some hope of remedy for problematic aspects of the professional transformation of legal practice. However, gender stratification theory emphasizes problems, including issues of gender discrimination, that encourage a shifting of the burden from individual-employee-initiated complaint mechanisms of self-regulation to more proactively organized efforts directed at firms and other bureaucratized employers.

Interestingly, a revised restricted spheres version of human capital theory, which acknowledges a tendency of men to exploit stereotyped conceptions of women's roles, provides some basis and support for an employer-based approach oriented to achieving organizational compliance in reforming the profession, while gender stratification theory alone may not provide a sufficient theoretical base to demonstrate effectively the need or means for reforms in the legal profession. To make these points most effectively, it is necessary to begin with an overview of the findings of our research.

The Changing Profession

There are a number of reasons why the structure of the legal profession has changed. The opening of educational and occupational opportunities and the changing roles of women more generally provided a context in which the legal profession at first reluctantly and then more willingly accepted women into its ranks. This occurred during the first half of this century through family practices and government work and in more recent decades through the larger firms that dominate the profession. This more recent phase is crucial not only because it has so markedly changed the involvement of women in the profession, but also because it is changing the shape of the profession itself.

The practice of law became much more highly centralized and concentrated in large firms during the 1970s and 1980s. After nearly half a century in which the population of lawyers grew at about the same rate as the population of the United States and Canada, through the 1970s and 1980s the growth rate of lawyers multiplied several times over that of the general population. This growth also occurred in government and business settings, but it was led by the expansion of large firms that could not have developed as they did without admitting large numbers of new women as well as men. Our analysis in the second chapter of this book demonstrated that this period of growth involved, in relative terms, a shrinking pool of centralized and concentrated partnerships in large firms, with increasing numbers of lawyers in intermediate and lower positions. In short, this was a period of growth with a ceiling on upward outcomes that is not likely to have improved in the early recessionary period of the 1990s.

The concentration of partnerships in large firms involves a centralization of human and cultural capital, consisting most importantly of the client-producing reputations and relationships of the partners. The point of firm formation is to distribute and control the investment of the partnership's client-producing capital by enlisting legal labor in ways that maximize firm profits. A modified version of human capital theory that emphasizes the cultural dimensions of reputations and client relations argues that women were recruited during this period of firm formation and growth because they were perceived as being at least as likely as men to assist in the profit-enhancing use of partnership capital without "shirking" or "grabbing" firm clients. That is, women were recruited into the profession during a period when they were needed to fill entry- and intermediate-level positions and were perceived to be compliant employees who would not threaten the accumulation of partnership capital, either by neglecting or stealing clients, or ultimately by demanding full shares of the benefits of partnership. It is possible that in these early years of firm growth many partners in law firms were encouraged by the belief that as in the teaching profession of an earlier era, women would assume entry-level positions in the profession, work diligently for a number of years, and then abandon their early years of invested work to bear children and raise families, leaving partnership positions to men assumed to be more committed to their occupational careers.

Such assumptions foreshadowed a glass ceiling on law firm mobility prospects for women. Our analysis in chapter 2 confirmed that this ceiling became an increasing reality in the Toronto legal profession during the 1980s, especially for women but also for men. Although the actual numbers of women and men lawyers at partnership levels of these firms increased in absolute terms during this period, their relative shares of partnership positions declined, and this ceiling effect was more pronounced for women than men. During this period, men and women were developing careers in a legal profession whose parameters were changing in ways that traditional conceptions of professional autonomy would not predict.

Much of this book has traced the impact of these aggregate-level trends in the changing structure of the profession on the career experiences of individual women and men lawyers. For example, in chapter 3 we considered the process by which women and men lawyers in Toronto found apprentice and entry positions into legal practice. Canada is one among a number of Western industrial nations that retains a formal apprenticeship period for lawyers, often used by firms to try out students, some of whom are hired back into entry-level associate positions. Our analysis of the changing structure of the legal profession in the 1980s implied that this process of apprenticeship would be relatively open and meritocratic, oriented in human capital terms to selecting the best and the brightest new sources of legal talent (i.e., as measured, for example, by law school grades) for firm employment, thereby overcoming past tendencies, for example, to discriminate against women. There is, however, a further interest in how personal contacts emphasized in network elaborations of stratification theories might also influence this process. Personal contacts can be thought of as a further form of human or social capital.

Our findings revealed that by the mid-1980s in Toronto, women were not significantly different from men in their success in finding the articling and initial employment positions they wanted, and that as human capital theory predicts, law school grades were the strongest and most consistent determinants of finding desired positions. Nonetheless, we also found that a quarter to a third of all articling positions were obtained with help through personal contacts, and that private school contacts that were more common among men also were used more successfully by men to find first jobs in large firms. Men who changed employers between articling and first jobs cited better opportunities as the reasons more often than women did, while women were more likely than men to indicate dissatisfaction in not being hired back from articling positions into first jobs. The latter findings, combined with the kinds of questions and comments often heard in articling interviews, lend some support to gender stratification theory and foreshadow problems to follow.

Our attention shifted next to entry into partnership, a critical juncture in the lives of privately practicing lawyers. It often is argued that partnerships are analogous to marriages in that choices are made on the basis of intangible qualities that defy quantitative assessment or charges of discrimination. The ironic argument from a human capital perspective is that partnership choices are most efficiently made in an impressionistic fashion. Major U.S. court decisions, such as *Hishon v. Spalding*, have both recognized and restricted such arguments, at least establishing that explicit considerations of gender are unacceptable bases for partnership decisions. Yet as gender stratification theory argues, gender is still involved.

This is not to say that human capital variables are irrelevant. For example, the successful development of corporate clients has consistently strong effects throughout our partnership analysis, and having these clients is clearly an important source of capital in establishing claims to partnership. However, it is also the case that apart from the influence of other variables, such as experience and the development of corporate clients, women who have taken parental leaves are less likely to be made partners. In contrast, men who have children are more likely to achieve partnership. These findings at the level of individual practicing lawyers parallel the aggregate trends observed earlier, namely that women are losing ground relative to men in the changing structure of the legal profession. So that while both men and women are assuming a smaller relative share of the partnership core in the centralization and concentration of the ownership capital of this profession, women are losing more ground than men. After adjusting for differences between Toronto men and women lawyers in their experience in practice, development of corporate clients, and other variables, we estimated that about half the men who start on the partnership ladder can expect to become partners, compared to about one-third of the women. In the "tournament of lawyers" that Galanter and Palay (1991) so provocatively describe, women are losing the battle for partnerships to men.

The further strains and conflicts that this professional environment produces for women were made apparent when our analysis turned to efforts to balance work and family. For example, we found that women lawyers in large firms were especially likely to delay parenting, and that women with children worked the equivalent of another full-time job in child care, averaging forty-eight hours per week with their children, compared to twenty-one hours for men. This finding is paralleled along a number of dimensions, including primary responsibility for dealing with unscheduled needs of children and other more prosaic aspects of maintaining a family life, including housework.

Further effects of these demands became apparent when we examined the decisions of lawyers in our Ontario sample to change areas of practice or leave law. Women were more likely to change jobs than men, and in doing so they were about twice as likely as men to move to government or leave the practice of law entirely. An event history analysis revealed that hours spent on child care accounted for much of the tendency of women to leave law, with the majority of these departures by women being from private practice, most often from large firms. As well, the reasons for women and men leaving law were quite different, with nearly two-thirds of the women expressing dissatisfaction with conditions of practice as a reason for leaving law, compared to about one-half of the men; meanwhile, about a quarter of the men who left law in Ontario cited better opportunities as a reason, compared to only about 12 percent of the women. These findings parallel those reported by lawyers immediately after articling. The patterning of these dissatisfactions and opportunities help to dispel the common assumption of human capital theory that the decisions of some women to leave law for the family are by choice.

Meanwhile, most women do not leave law, and more often continue to work full-time in firm settings than anywhere else. Many of these women experience role overload and conflicts of work and family, but their work roles may in other respects be rewarding, so that the diversity of their role involvements may enhance more than diminish their life experiences. The chosen spheres version of human capital theory implicitly accepts the premise of role overload and conflict as contributing to a tendency of women to specialize in work at home. In contrast, gender stratification theory suggests that women invest more time than men in family and child care while maintaining high levels of work commitment, despite being underrewarded for doing so. In this sense it can be argued that women lawyers are more committed to the legal profession than men.

Our analysis addressed aspects of these issues by first considering patterns of billings and earnings. This analysis found some support for human capital theory. Law school grades and corporate clientele were associated with increased earnings. But perhaps most importantly, men billed more hours than women, and these billings returned nearly twice the earnings per hour for men than women. The chosen spheres version of human capital theory attributes this difference to the greater work commitment and specialized investment of men in their careers.

However, the pattern of results fits the assumptions of gender stratification theory better than the chosen spheres version of human capital theory. First, when differences emphasized in human capital theory are taken into account, including differences in hours billed, men still earn more than women, the disparities observed being much greater than in other occupations. Second, direct measures of family involvement do not account for gender differences in earnings or billings in the ways that human capital theory predicts. Third, we found that men accumulated more hourly billings than women through the use of hierarchical positions in firms, not because women gave up hours as a result of competitive demands or comparative specializations that involved investments in the family. Fourth, much like men lawyers, women lawyers who continued full-time private practice increased rather than decreased their commitment to work after having children, while women who were outside of this sector increased their work commitment as their children began and continued through school.

The chosen spheres version of human capital theory would seem to misjudge the role that choice can play in the careers of professional women.

Alternatively, the restricted spheres version of this theory and gender stratification theory point to the role of constraints in shaping choices made by women. Our final data-based chapter explores subjective reflections of these constraints in gender differences in Toronto lawyers' reports of job satisfaction and expressions of personal despondency and depression.

Like members of other occupations, lawyers generally indicate favorable levels of job satisfaction, and some past studies of lawyers perhaps surprisingly report that women are as satisfied as men with their jobs. However, we proposed a different approach to this issue that reflects the tendency of women to change jobs and leave the practice of law in larger numbers than men. Recall that we reported from our cross-sectional analysis of Ontario lawyers that women were about twice as likely as men to move to jobs in government and leave law entirely. In our longitudinal analysis of Toronto lawyers we found similar patterns. Furthermore, the Toronto panel data replicated the pattern of reasons for leaving law noted above, with more than half the women citing dissatisfaction compared to about one-third of the men, and with about a third of the men citing better opportunities compared to about 10 percent of the women. One way to assess the development of this kind of dissatisfaction among those who are still working in law is to measure job satisfaction in terms of thoughts about looking for alternative employment.

When we applied the latter kind of measure of work satisfaction among women still working, we found that women were significantly less satisfied than men. We found that this was so in part because women in the sample were younger than men. However, when this age difference was taken into account, women were also found less satisfied with their jobs because they were more burdened with child care and earned less money. We then turned to an analysis of a measure of despondency and depression. Here we again found that women were more despondent and depressed than men lawyers, and that this was again in part because they were younger in age and had younger children. However, when these age differences were held constant, we found further evidence that women were less content because they were making less money than men, and because more generally they were less satisfied with their jobs.

Further study of the effects of children on the unhappiness of women and men lawyers produced findings parallel to those found earlier for work commitment. That is, for women lawyers, as for men, having children, especially of school age, is associated with greater happiness. These results are consistent with the role diversity and enhancement thesis associated with gender stratification theory, and inconsistent with the role overload and strain thesis emphasized in the chosen spheres version of human capital theory.

In general, our findings tend to support aspects of human capital theory that are generic to the theory and unlinked with the chosen spheres version of this perspective. That is, we find support for aspects of lawyering that are underemphasized in gender stratification theory and that are consistent with the emphasis of human capital theory on the role of human resource development — as indicated by the influence of law school grades, cultivation of corporate clients, age-linked experience, and the accumulation of billable hours. However, these findings are consistent with the undeveloped restricted spheres version of a human capital theory that also provides an opening for the insights of gender stratification theory. The restrictions and constraints emphasized in these perspectives are reflected most notably in the pervasive influence of gender in partnership decisions and on earnings and billings. The influence of gender on these outcomes documents a stratification of opportunities that especially disadvantages women, during a period in the profession when prospects for upward mobility are restricted more generally. These constraints on women lawyers are further reflected in their expressions of job dissatisfaction and feelings of despondency and depression.

Women in the profession are caught in a series of cross-pressures that constrain their opportunities for occupational success and personal happiness. On the one hand, we have seen that they are penalized in partnership decisions if they take maternity leaves. Partnership is crucial to upward mobility in firms and to attaining higher levels of income and power in a profession that is centralizing and concentrating its ownership capital. Women who choose to have children and play a prominent role in their parenting risk losing their footing on a mobility ladder that leads to increasingly precarious and inaccessible places of power and influence in this profession.

Yet women who have children and continue to work full-time in private practice do not lose their commitment to work, and they are often more satisfied with their work and happier with their personal lives, especially as their children enter school; in these respects, working women lawyers are rather similar to men lawyers. Further, women who do not practice in this full-time private sector of the profession, as we have noted, also increase their commitment to work as their children enter school. These findings encourage stripping human capital theory of its chosen spheres assumptions and reforming the legal profession in ways that will reduce its discriminatory treatment of women and better accommodate demands of work and family. Work and family have long been regarded as compatible roles for men, and with accommodations, our findings suggest that these roles can be similarly compatible for women.

Yet the profession resists reform, often based on premises like those of a chosen spheres version of human capital theory. And, when proposals for professional reform are entertained, the proposals, though important and well-intended, often do not go far enough. Both the restricted spheres version of human capital theory and gender stratification theory have something to tell us about the challenges that confront us in more effectively pursuing professional reform.

Rights and Duties of Nondiscrimination

Efforts to reduce the discriminatory treatment of women in the legal profession have involved court-enforced legislation of civil and human rights and the creation and enforcement of rights and duties of nondiscrimination through self-imposed professional codes and rules of conduct enforced through disciplinary proceedings. Canada has relied more heavily than the United States on professional self-regulation and less on court enforcement. In fact, Glenn (1990:437) reports that the Canadian professions annually produce about the same number of disciplinary proceedings as in the entire United States. These proceedings extend to ethical violations in which no harm is caused to the client.

At the same time, however, the Canadian professions have not uniformly followed the pattern in some parts of the United States of developing detailed, black letter rules of professional conduct. The tendency instead is to articulate general standards. So, for example, the preface to the Code of Professional Conduct adopted in 1987 by the Canadian Bar Association indicates that "the Code does not attempt to define professional misconduct or conduct unbecoming, nor does it try to evaluate the relative importance of the various rules or the gravity of a breach of any of them. Those are the responsibility of the various governing bodies" (cited in Glenn, 1990:438). However, some provincial governing bodies have been slow to respond, and pressure is building for a more uniform approach to this issue. As Smith (1992:9) notes, "treating women as equals is not just a matter of good manners, good taste, or being nice, but indeed is a matter of professional responsibility and ethics."

Tennant (1992) reports that a comprehensive nondiscrimination provision is contained in proposed revisions to the Michigan *Rules of Professional Conduct*. These revisions were ordered by the Michigan supreme court on the basis of state task force reports and include the explicit provision that "[a] lawyer shall not engage in invidious discrimination on the basis of gender, race, religion, disability, age, sexual orientation, or ethnic origin, and shall prohibit staff and agents subject to the lawyer's direction and control from doing so" (cited in Tennant, 1992:57). These provisions are intended for general use, but they also have specific relevance in relation to discrimination in employment.

The Law Society of Upper Canada has had a related version of such a rule since 1974, which directs that "[t]he lawyer not discriminate on the grounds of race, creed, colour, national origin, sex, marital status or age in the employment of other lawyers or articled students, or in dealings with other members of the profession." But Wilson (1993) reports that no cases have been brought to the attention of the Law Society on the issue of discrimination in access to the profession, or advancement within the profession, for example, through admission to partnership. In 1972 the Benchers of the Law Society of British Columbia refused to pass a narrower provision dealing with refusals to hire women students into articling positions, reasoning that, "[w]hile the Benchers are unanimously of the opinion that no member or firm of members should refuse articles to an applicant on the grounds of race, religion or sex, the majority were of the opinion that such a rule would be difficult if not impossible to enforce and were opposed to promulgating a rule which could not be enforced." This proposed rule arose from an incident in which a firm explicitly refused articles to a woman applicant on the basis of her gender. The Law Society expressed regret, but declined to intercede (see Smith et al., 1973). The Law Society of British Columbia did not pass an antidiscrimination rule until 1992.

The enactment of nondiscrimination rules can sometimes have important symbolic and educational as well as regulatory and enforcement functions, and these combined purposes are perhaps best served through highly publicized court cases. Examples include several cases pursued in the United States courts under the Civil Rights Act of 1964. We noted in chapters 4 and 6 that this act was used in the partnership denial cases of *Hishon* in Atlanta and *Ezold* in Philadelphia. Gupta (1993) suggests that the same reasoning should be applicable under the Canadian Human Rights Code, which states that it is illegal "in the course of employment, to discriminate adversely in relation to an employee on a prohibited ground of discrimination."

The significance of the U.S. partnership cases should be emphasized. They establish the applicability of general statutes to the employment of lawyers in firms, the illegality of grounding employment decisions on considerations of gender, the importance of performance reviews in the defense or rejection of promotion decisions, and the severity of the sanctions that can be imposed on firms that are found in violation of these statutes. The latter sanctions can have a notable impact.

For example, the American courts awarded substantial damages in the Ezold case and in the related case of *Hopkins v. Price Waterhouse* (1990), which involved a denial of partnership in a large U.S. accounting firm. The plaintiff in *Hopkins* was awarded back pay of over $370,000, to the date seven years earlier when partnership should have been granted. A similar award was imposed in *Ezold*, although this outcome was subsequently reversed. Nonetheless, the possibility of awards of this size may encourage firms to move more carefully in decisions to delay or deny partnership.

It is also likely that women in the professions, including law, will slowly expand the range of remedies pursued through the courts to address a wider spectrum of employment practices. A key part of this process will involve challenging excessive demands that restrict many women with children from pursuing firm partnerships. Schellenberg (1993) appropriately notes that to require such things as a twelve-hour work day, or evening, weekend, or last-minute availability, to demonstrate commitment to a law firm or to one's own career, is to effectively exclude many women from being able to successfully demonstrate that commitment. A series of court decisions, including most notably the Canadian case of *Brooks v. Canada Safeway* (1989), have challenged the notion that it is fair to place all the burden of bearing children on women when procreation is a benefit to all of society. *Brooks* makes the point that raising children is a contribution as much or more than a choice. *Brooks* further asserts that businesses, and by implication law firms, have a responsibility to assume some of the costs experienced by women in bearing children. It would seem inconsistent with *Brooks* to insist, for example, that mothers of young children meet the same level of billings as men as a condition of attaining and maintaining partnership. In the Canadian Bar Association's (1993) Gender Equality Task Force Report on *Touchstones for Change*, it is argued that insistence on high levels of billings for mothers of young children is a form of "adverse effects" discrimination.

Nonetheless, women in our research were not optimistic in gauging the prospects for change. One respondent observed,

> Every women lawyer with children with whom I have discussed the matter has advised that it is very difficult to cope with child-rearing responsibilities with the demands of full-time practice. Quality of

life seems to be more and more of an issue for men and women, and sometimes members of a firm who have made sacrifices in giving up family and recreational time and other activities to meet the heavy demands of a practice are reluctant to allow others the flexibility of part-time, at-home, or other alternative work style, even if compensation is adjusted accordingly. This places a strain on working relationships. I think that it is vital that firms be prepared to try new approaches and flexible working arrangements.

Another woman lawyer argued,

The greatest strain on women in the workplace is not so much the hours of additional work at home but the responsibility: if women don't do it themselves, it won't get done. Similarly, with respect to children, they must make the choices (or they are the most directly affected by the choices). As a lawyer, you ask to be treated equally and are lucky to get that without discrimination. But this is the trap. Women are different, and have different needs and responsibilities. To be treated equally is to discriminate against those special needs, similar to treatment of the disabled. Yet those differences are not disabilities. They offer their own advantages. It does not yet appear to be possible to accommodate these differences.

It is proving a major struggle for women to gain significant exemptions from excessive work demands as conditions of employment and partnership. At the same time, women are also shown frequently to exceed standards of work performance often assumed by men to be associated with pregnancy and maternity, as findings in our earlier chapter on billings and earnings suggest. Somewhere between performance and need there should be room for accommodation and compromise.

Nonetheless, to date cases challenging employment and promotion practices in law firms have been relatively infrequent in the United States and nonexistent in Canada. This cannot be, as a chosen spheres version of human capital theory might suggest, because women are unconcerned about these issues and have freely chosen their fates. Nor can it be because these problems do not arise in law firms. We have found that women often are dissatisfied with their jobs and are active within firm settings in seeking reforms of various kinds, including efforts to change conditions of partnership. Yet the question will still be asked: Why do legally trained women not use available remedies more often to protest job discrimination?

Human capital theory implies an answer to this question in its explanation of why law firms form in the first place. Recall that this theory argues that firms are formed when partners employ associates to work on client files, as a means of assuring that associates will do so with a reduced likelihood of shirking their responsibilities, grabbing the clients, or leaving prematurely. If the work was simply contracted out, it is argued that shirking, grabbing, and leaving would be more common. The core of this argument is that trust relationships established in firms act as an efficient check on the impulse of associates and partners to shirk, grab, or leave.

Human capital theory may be partly correct in the importance it attaches to the role of trust in the formation of firms, although it may also characteristically neglect the full role of monitoring within firms, for example, through hierarchical structures of supervision, the mechanism of billable hours, and the threat of loss of partnership and employment prospects that are more naturally noticed from the perspective of gender stratification theory. When viewed in the context of the latter constraints, considerations of trust can be seen as significant. The importance assigned to trust in firm relationships makes it difficult if not impossible for women to question the treatment they receive leading up to the partnership decision, as well as, for example, the earnings they receive afterward. Wilson (1993:11) notes, "It is obviously not easy for an aspiring woman lawyer in a large firm to start off her career with a complaint to the Law Society against those in control of her future." Challenges to mistreatment likely will be seen as groundless questioning of the relationships of trust that underwrite firm life, and victims of mistreatment will risk prospects for continued and future employment by complaining officially or unofficially about their experiences. So in this context, it is probably more accurate to note that trust is actually constraint misconceived as choice.

This situation is doubly demeaning to women who experience discrimination in firms, because to sustain such relationships of trust without challenge is to implicitly acquiesce to the premise that the treatment received is a fair evaluation of variable investments of human capital, which in turn are presumed to reflect differing levels of commitment. This is alienating and demeaning. Yet this is a situation common to victims who might otherwise rely on rights-based remedies, and it is a source of concern about the effects of the provision of unenforceable rights.

Bumiller (1988) makes these points in her insightful account of *The Civil Rights Society*, drawing first on the warning of Tocqueville that democratic freedoms can silence the claiming of rights. She cites the more general relevance of Tocqueville's "master," who warns, "You are free to think differently from me, and to retain your life, your property, and all that you possess; but you are henceforth a stranger among your people. You may retain you civil rights, but they will be useless to you, for you will never be chosen by your fellow citizens. . . . You will remain among men, but you will be deprived of the rights of mankind" (cited in Bumiller, 1988:102). Tocqueville makes an apt if unreflective use of male pronouns in this context.

Bumiller locates much of the inadequacy of civil rights remedies in the placement of the burden for initiating actions and proving their validity on individual victims. She notes that there is a cultural predisposition to place responsibility for success and failure on individuals, and that this combines with narrow definitions of legally recognizable claims to encourage individuals to abide by the warning of Tocqueville and common sense: that is, to accept their fates rather than undertake the risks of legal recourse. The consequences of this situation are especially disturbing in the context of a profession of law, because, as Bumiller notes, "the inability of civil rights strategies to fulfill their promise appears to have left many who experience discrimination on uncertain ground . . . where they are without faith in themselves or the law" (1988:117).

However, it may be that this assessment is in fact overly pessimistic in the context of the legal profession. We have noted a limited symbolic and educational value to the legal profession of recent partnership cases, based on claims under U.S. civil rights statutes, as rare as these cases may be. Further and greater value could be derived from self-regulatory efforts within the profession, based on specifically formulated duties of nondiscrimination. And these cases might increase in number and significance in the future. However, if these duties are to be most effectively enforced, they will also need to benefit from an approach that better recognizes the structural conditions from which individual problems of discrimination derive in the profession. Bumiller urges more generally that "we need to begin the search for a restatement of rights that abandons the objectivity and individuality of current doctrine and that recognizes the interests of social groups and individuals. People who possess salient group identities need to find in the law reinforcement for the expression of their individual selves and positive referents for the qualities they share as a collectivity" (1988:116). This is a call to shift the burden of enforcement from individual complainants to a collective level that is more consistent with changes in contemporary society. This call may have particular significance in the legal profession.

Reconstructing the Legal Profession

Current approaches to the self-regulation of the legal profession represent what Coleman (1993) has called a primordial form of social organization. As we have seen, their common form consists of procedures that are reactively and coercively mobilized in response to complaints by individual victims. However, when we come to such issues as partnership and remuneration in modern law firms, we are no longer dealing with atomized individuals or unorganized interests. The lone practitioner and the family firm are today atypical.

More generally, we no longer live in a society primarily organized around kinship ties and families or related premordial institutions, such as religious bodies. Contemporary society is organized more around positions than persons, with occupants of these positions located in relation to other positions in organizations, that are in turn positioned in relation to other organizations. Similarly, the modern law firm is a formal, hierarchically structured organization, and lawyers, more than most citizens, occupy positions in an interlocking world of organized interests.

Yet the legal profession still primarily relies on forms of self-regulation that involve individuals filing complaints against other individuals. Most of this regulation involves complaints by clients about the activities of sole practitioners (for example, see Arnold and Hagan, 1992). Some of this regulation must continue, but meanwhile larger issues are neglected, such as the inclusion of women as a fully enfranchised group within the profession. These are issues involving organized collectivities, such as the National Association of Women and the Law in Canada and the American Bar Association Commission on Women in the United States.

These groups lobby as collectivities for reforms in the profession. In doing so, these groups expose the dangers and the opportunities of our modern condition. Much has already been said about the dangers. They involve the tendency to interpret the patterns of women's careers in the profession as expressions of choice and specialization, and to regulate the profession almost exclusively through reactive complainant-based mechanisms of coercive enforcement. These are primordial tendencies.

But alongside the dangers of such tendencies there may also be some opportunities. Coleman (1993:14) urges that in a rationally reconstructed society, social control need not depend so exclusively on coercion, constraint and negative sanctions, and instead can also make use of strategically devised incentives and rewards for performance. Both the restricted spheres version of human capital theory and gender stratification theory point to the need to restructure occupations and professions along lines that accommodate women more effectively as well as efficiently. The promise of Coleman's approach, which we pursue below, is that there are ways in which incentives can be proactively and collectively organized to increase the likelihood of organizations changing their norms and modes of operation.

However, to date much of the popular literature aimed at professional and business women has focused on ways of altering the norms and expectations of women rather than those of the organizations in which they work (Rhode, 1988:1203). For example, widely marketed books and magazines typically emphasize strategies women can use to more effectively assimilate into work organizations. Deborah Rhode summarizes some of these tactics: "[W]ork longer and later than male colleagues; avoid confrontation with male superiors and 'personal' relationships with female subordinates; defer to higher authority but cultivate assertiveness with lower-level employees; pay careful attention to objective measures of occupational status (salary, power, location of office, number of windows); and remember that 'nice girls finish last'" (Harragan, 1977; see also Ferguson, 1984; Rhode, 1988:1203). Similarly, an article in the *American Bar Association Journal* offers the following suggestions to women about how to succeed in a "man's world" of law:

> Don't 'shirk' late hours or weekend projects. Don't cook and tell, i.e., avoid going home to cook dinner — or if you do, don't let anyone know.
>
> Keep your 'personal life' in the background. . . . Never make excuses based on the needs of your spouse or children!'
>
> Don't 'think of yourself, or allow anyone to think of you, as anything but a hard-driving, capable lawyer.' (Strachan, 1984:94–5)

The point is that the entry of women in sizeable numbers into the profession has involved more accommodations on the part of women than on the part of the firms in which they work. As one woman lawyer from our study who entered law at mid-life observes:

> I would have been happy to earn less money and put in a good eight-to nine-hour day. I know I would have made a valuable contribution to any firm. Unfortunately, my opinion remains that if one is not willing or able to work ten to twelve hours a day as well as at least one day on the weekend, on a regular basis, then there is no place for you in the legal profession. I was told by one of the senior partners at my articling firm that I was a fool for entering the profession at my age with my other responsibilities and the sooner I quit wasting their time and mine, the better off everyone would be. In my opinion, it is the profession's loss that there is no place for a mature entry-level lawyer, with their "life experience," simply because other responsibilities preclude working the hours many lawyers work.

A rational reconstruction of the legal profession to include a more enlightened working environment for women as well as men will involve a shift in attention away from employees in order to focus on employers who are the source many of their problems. Of course, gender stratification theory encourages this more structural approach. The challenge is to more rationally construct responses to problematic employers by creating incentives for the adoption of enlightened policies. Human capital theory and Coleman's incentive approach (1993:13) to the rational reconstruction of organizations urge us to reconsider the role of market-based incentives in creating such policies.

In doing so, it is possible to benefit from an increased awareness of employer responsibilities that is reflected in some reform programs. For example, an important reform program recently was initiated under the direction of a Committee to Enhance Professional Opportunities for Minorities, chaired by Cyrus Vance for the New York City Bar Association (1991). Vance is a former U.S. Secretary of State and a member of the prominent New York firm of Simpson, Thacher, and Bartlett. The Vance Committee was especially concerned about the underrepresentation of Hispanic and African American men as well as women in the legal profession. The Committee initially enlisted thirty-five leading New York law firms in signing a preliminary statement of goals, one of whose objectives was that during the period from 1992 to 1997 10 percent of all lawyers hired should be of minority background. The signatories to the program were extended thereafter to include 172 law firms and corporations, with a further commitment to improve retention and promotion prospects for minority lawyers. As well, a position was created for an assistant to the president for "improving promotion and retention of minorities in the profession," with funding provided by contributing firms.

This program makes the point that while women currently are focused on breaking through the glass ceiling, many ethinic minorities are still confronted with the more basic problem of getting through the front door and onto the ground floor. Indeed, so few minorities were represented in our samples that we were unable to analyze their experiences in this book. The New York program is important in acknowledging that these problems of discrimination against minorities, and by implication against women as well, are employer-based. This is a beginning step in shifting the burden of responsibility to employers.

However, neither women nor other minorities will benefit from "revolving door" employment practices that offer poor prospects for retention and promotion. Although problems of retention and promotion are acknowledged through the appointment of a staff employee in the New York program, this program is still likely to have effects that are largely limited to hiring, unless it can more directly and effectively address structural problems of retention and promotion. If the staff employee in the New York program operated more in the role of an autonomous safe counsel or ombudsperson to receive and address complaints about retention and promotion problems, the likelihood of progress on the latter kinds of issues might be advanced somewhat. However, a staff employee still will have difficulty addressing entrenched structural barriers, especially in a position voluntarily funded by contributing firms.

The changing structure of the profession and the centralization and concentration of partnerships that we have emphasized makes it more likely that the New York program will add to entry-level competition in the profession without affecting the glass ceiling. If so, problems of blocked mobility may be pluralized without being changed. We need an approach that targets the glass ceiling more directly, ideally through strategic incentives focused on the employer practices to be changed.

One way of creating incentives to alter the glass ceiling involves systematically tracking employers' hiring decisions through their decisions about retention and promotion, as we have partly done with the panel research design applied in this study. Periodicals like the *Canadian Lawyer* currently conduct surveys of associates that provide subjective measures of partnership prospects and practice experiences. However, with the participation of only about 20 percent of Canadian law firms, and an average response rate of about 40 percent of associates surveyed within those firms, the results of this effort must be treated with considerable caution. Better and more objective information is required. Bar association and law society membership files can be used to calculate more revealing rates of retention and promotion by cohort, gender, and other attributes within specific firms and across years. Using such records for firms that annually hire men and women into articling and entry positions, it is possible to compute annual and cumulative rates of admission into partnership. Armed with such information, potential recruits can estimate their longer-term prospects based on the past track record of firms in question. To the extent that firms compete for the best and the brightest articling students and new associates, as they clearly and increasingly do, publication of these rates could create some incentive among firms to see that these rates improve, and especially to see that the notably lower success rates of women and minorities improve. This may be a significant way of making the market for legal talent more responsive to the longer-term interests of new lawyers, men as well as women, including minorities.

Still, the strategy we propose may seem a too simple and minor step, and it is certainly true that this approach alone will not solve all the problems of women and minorities in the profession. It is important to encourage further efforts. Particularly important are concrete strategies that better accommodate work and family demands among both men and women. Such strategies include greater support for child care and related support services by both employers and policymakers, improved assistance for single-parent families, enhanced leave and part-time policies, and more flexible schedules for full-time practitioners, as well as creative solutions such as "telecommuting" or "flexiplace" legal practice (Rhode, 1988:1206; see also Mossman, 1992). These options need to be made available without "professional risk." As Rhode (1988) argues, "Individuals should not have to leave promotional tracks to meet family commitments. Nor should they labor under suspicion as shirkers as a result of caretaking choices. Policies responsive to such strategies need not impair workplace performance. What rather may be required is additional staffing, less categorical in-or-out policies, less rigid status distinctions, and greater governmental involvement" (1206).

The more complicated question, of course, is how to secure such changes. Tax incentives and governmental involvement would be helpful catalysts in some areas (Rhode, 1988:1206). Collective efforts by formal professional associations and informal workplace organizations may also prove critical. Such efforts can include appeals to employer self-interest and incentives, as noted above. As women constitute a growing percentage of law school graduates, it becomes increasingly costly to discount their needs and devalue their talents. In the long run, failure to mitigate work-family conflicts will prove expensive to firms, other legal employers, and individual lawyers. It will increase employee absenteeism and turnover, impair recruitment success, compromise job performance, as well as jeopardize the well-being of valued employees (Rhode, 1988:1206).

However, some costs are less apparent to employers than others. For example, managing partners generally have been more attentive to the immediate losses that follow from reduced work hours or the absence of a key lawyer at an inconvenient moment (Rhode, 1988:1206).

How, then, can employers be encouraged to expand their employees' work options? Employers need to be convinced that the options can be cost-effective and provide other benefits to the firm as well (Marks, 1990:367). The main reasons why an employer will offer part-time work or flexible scheduling is to retain a valued employee. Employers allocate substantial resources in recruiting, hiring, and training lawyers, and they should want to cultivate rather than squander the results of these investments. The American Bar Association (1990) estimates that it costs $100,000 to replace an associate. However, as Marks (1990) notes, there are many cases where lawyers will leave firms after three or four years, just when they are becoming of value to the firm, to join another firm that has more flexible personnel policies (366). The further argument for a law firm to encourage work options is to gain in recruitment (Marks, 1990:366–67). Firms that respond to the changing needs of the labor force will be in superior positions to attract, retain, and motivate the best legal talent. As an American Bar Association report observes,

> Attracting and retaining the best legal talent in the 1990s will require accommodating management policies to the new demographics of the legal profession: female and male lawyers in roughly equal numbers, many of them balancing the demands of dual careers and new families, others struggling with single parenthood or ailing parents, still others needing windows of flexibility to accomplish a variety of important life goals. These lawyers are committed to the profession, but have competing demands in their life which must be balanced. (1990:5)

Therefore, the American National Association for Law Placement now asks participating firms such questions as "What is your parental leave policy? What is your part-time policy?" Law students consume this information with great interest.

The American Bar Association provides advice and sample policies for law firms with respect to parental leave, alternative work schedules, and sexual harassment (1990; see also Boston Bar Association, 1991; Marks, 1990; Nielson, 1990; Simms, 1990). Similar model policies have been issued by numerous Canadian provincial law societies (for example, British Columbia and Ontario) and the Canadian Bar Association's Gender Equality Task Force. One set of model employment policies will be discussed in greater detail.

Beyond this, law societies could usefully sponsor education programs for firms and other legal employers about the nature and consequences of sexual and gender harassment (Law Society of British Columbia, 1992:3–9). Prevention efforts could include the dissemination of policy statements to employees, education through seminars, meetings or workshops, and special training sessions provided for supervisory and managerial staff to recognize potential problems and how to deal with them effectively (Aggarwal, 1987:194–98). Firms and other legal employers should be encouraged to adopt workplace harassment policies, and law societies should advise employers with regard to the implementation of such policies.

For many lawyers, men and women, a confusion exists about what behaviors are truly appropriate and supportive of unbiased professionalism. Recognition of this dilemma prompted the Women Lawyers Association of Michigan to commission a practical guide to cross-gender professionalism (see Weber, 1990). This publication outlines inappropriate conduct, including inappropriate forms of address; comments about personal appearance, patronizing or overly solicitous behavior; sexual innuendos, jokes, and harassment; inappropriate nonverbal behaviors; verbal and physical actions that exclude women or ignore their presence, or question their ability to be competent. Such guidelines, distributed through the law societies and bar associations and through continuing legal education programs, are likely to be effective means of eliminating sexual and gender harassment.

Finally, there is a further leadership role to be played by law societies and bar associations in encouraging innovative employment policies and maternity and parental leave policies. Law societies might encourage part-time work and job sharing by providing lower fees and lower insurance premiums for such members. And membership fees might be reduced or eliminated for members in periods of temporary absence from the practice of law, such as parental responsibility or other leaves. A study of the Law Society of British Columbia (1992) recommends that law societies conduct periodic surveys of parental leave policies of law firms and other legal employers and publish the information for members and students. Law societies might also assist firms in obtaining temporary replacement of employees for parental leaves by maintaining a register of members seeking temporary or part-time work (Law Society of British Columbia, 1992). The consequences of failing to respond and innovate in such ways is suggested by the following comment of a lawyer in our study:

> In my view, the emerging role for lawyers is to assist in this process of self-determination. What this means for the profession internally is a re-examination of who we are — by race, gender, and class — and how we treat each other as colleagues. The ethnocultural and class heritage of lawyers, as a whole, is not representative of the general Canadian population. The profession continues to discriminate on the basis of gender: it is more difficult for female lawyers to obtain partnerships, and often the only way a female lawyer who is a parent can maintain her status in a firm is by denying the importance of her parenting responsibilities. Yes, these things will change over time, but we need to be proactive and progressive about assisting the process of change now; otherwise, again, we will be left behind — and rightly so — as a profession out of step with the times.

It is also important to continue encouraging cases like *Hishon* and *Ezold* and the development of professional code statements about rights and duties of nondiscrimination. Even when such cases are lost or settled out of court, they can help establish basic principles. Model programs also need to be encouraged. An important model program for reconstructing law firm partnership arrangements was recently developed by the Boston Bar Association (B.B.A.) Task Force on Parenting and the Legal Profession (1991).

The B.B.A. Task Force begins by asserting the kind of position articulated in *Brooks v. Canada Safeway*, namely that employer policies providing for parental leave and part-time or flexible work schedules are a matter of right, and "the most visible and important signs of the commitment of legal employers to supportive benefits for parent employees" (1). The task force argues that there are notable long-term economic benefits to be derived from such policies in reducing turnover costs associated with losing women employees. It then seeks a balance between the benefits and obligations of employers to support families and the near-term costs of doing so, which it assumes must be borne both by employers and employees. Clearly, women employees always have borne such costs, and what is novel in this program is an expanded recognition of employer obligations.

These obligations begin with parental leave benefits of up to one year in duration. The program is explicit in mandating that if parental leave does not exceed this duration during the firm's usual six- to ten-year period preceding partnership, then eligibility for advancement should be unaffected. More generally, "firms should focus on an assessment of professional development and should not delay eligibility for partnership solely as a result of the length or number of an individual's parental leaves" (8). In return, the program urges that the employee advise the employer as early and with as much certainty as possible of parental leave plans.

The B.B.A. program also provides for part-time work "as a benefit 'must,'" noting that "the availability of part-time work increasingly will be the measure by which firms will be judged as hospitable or inhospitable to those employees" (10). It does so while clearly acknowledging that law firm work is time-intensive and that part-time work therefore represents a major departure from firm culture. Nonetheless, the program asserts that lawyers who work part-time should be given work of the same quality as full-timers and that there should be no second-class citizens.

The terms under which these goals are pursued are significant. First, it is suggested that lawyers who wish to take 20 percent time away from work (to work 80 percent time) should be able to do so with the expectation that eligibility for partnership and advancement will be unaffected, and with compensation therefore proportionately adjusted to the amount of the expected full-time salary. The reasoning is that a reduction of up to 20 percent in an attorney's hours of work is a reasonable accommodation for a firm to make in light of an attorney's family obligations, and that this adjustment can often be the difference between a tenable and untenable balance between work and family life. It could be argued that this provision represents "the thin edge of a wedge" that opens up the issue of parental rights in the context of partnerships.

However, the B.B.A. program goes on to provide for further optional reductions in work time. It proposes that employees who wish to work between 60 and 80 percent of full time for up to one year also be entitled to do so without prejudice to promotion or advancement. Again, remuneration should be proportional to time worked, with advancement based on professional development and with the firm "avoiding reductions in the rate of advancement that are attributable to part-time status *per se*" (11). Provisions are also suggested for considering part-time arrangements of longer durations.

The Boston program is, of course, only one of many possible variations, but the principles on which it is premised are important. Such programs in Canadian firms would effectively represent efforts to bring the private practice of law into compliance with principles articulated for employers in *Brooks*. Obvious problems would nonetheless remain. For example, the Boston program assumes that the distribution of firm profits through calculations of billable hours and by other means is in itself gender-neutral; we have seen in Chapter 6 that it is not. Nonetheless, the Boston program is a useful starting point for much work that remains to be done. One of our respondents offers an articulate final appeal for a program of this kind.

> I feel that one issue which is not addressed at all by the legal profession is providing flexibility for parents of young children, especially female parents, who end up with most of the responsibility. Maternity leave policies at most firms are ridiculous and draconian. Leaves based on number of years of service discriminate against the very people who are most likely to require leave — women of child-bearing years. Women should not be forced to postpone child-bearing in order to qualify for a reasonable length of maternity leave (six months). If law firms would begin to support their employees in this area, they would find that they had grateful and loyal employees in the years after child-bearing. After all, a woman's productive years of lawyering number far more than her productive years of child-bearing.

Finally, is important to consider reasons why no bar association or law society in North America yet has used its membership records to monitor retention and promotion in the ways we have proposed. This probably partly reflects a discomfort about making firms accountable in such ways, as well as an uncertainty about the grounds for doing so. The primordial legal inclination is to approach such issues on a case-by-case basis, looking for the "smoking gun" that proves discrimination and compels a legal remedy for the individual involved.

Yet North American employment law long has held that a specific intention to discriminate need not be demonstrated to establish a pattern of employment discrimination: aggregate disparities unexplained by skill and productivity requirements are sufficient to prove discrimination. These disparities are apparent across law firms, for example, as demonstrated in this book. By reasoning analogous to that in individual cases, these patterns compel a collective response from the profession. It is incumbent on the profession to initiate programs to address issues of gender and other forms of discrimination.

We have argued that cases like *Hishon* and *Ezold* have instrumental, symbolic, and educational value, even when they are settled out of court or result in a negative judgment. However, these cases are painfully few and far between, and the reliance on finding "the smoking gun," which even then may not be sufficient, is a meager response in an era in which women effectively have been used as cannon fodder for professional growth and retrenchment. The patterns demonstrated in this book and elsewhere compel a more rational effort to reconstruct the profession in ways that better accommodate the needs of women as well as men. There is an empirically and jurisprudentially demonstrated need for programs that encourage the inclusion, retention, and promotion of women as well as other minorities in the profession, and that use socially organized incentives as well as case-based coercion in doing so.

Appendix

No advanced mathematical skills are required to follow any of the analyses presented in this book. Discussions of sampling and measurement issues are framed in substantive terms, and mathematical notation and references are purposefully kept to a minimum. In this Appendix we provide some further detail and discussion of the methods and techniques used in this study, so that the interested reader can better understand the results of our work.

Sampling

Although the sampling decisions that guided this research are discussed briefly in the opening chapter of this book, some further information is added here. The research designs for both the Toronto and Ontario studies involved disproportionate stratified sampling. This sampling strategy assures that sufficient numbers of cases are drawn from a range of identified strata of interest, including smaller ones, while also allowing the use of weighting to obtain estimates of parameters for the total population. Weightings are used where indicated in the various chapters to restore the unequally sampled strata by giving greater or lesser importance to the specified sample elements. Weights are assigned to disproportionately sampled elements by simply taking the inverse of their inclusion probabilities.

The sampling frames for the Toronto and Ontario studies were generated from the membership records of the Law Society of Upper Canada, and both studies were organized as mail-back surveys. Three main strata were sampled in the Toronto study, and four in the provincial study, with each main stratum divided and sampled in equal numbers by gender to produce six and eight strata respectively. The three main strata in the Toronto study consisted of (1) large firm lawyers (twenty-six or more lawyers), (2) smaller-firm lawyers (up to twenty-five lawyers), and (3) nonfirm lawyers (in all other settings). The four main strata in the Ontario study included (1) members of agencies, boards, commissions, or tribunals; (2) temporarily absent members; (3) all other employed members; and (4) members suspended for discontinued payment of fees.

As indicated in chapter 1 and in this chapter, the Toronto and Ontario studies can be made comparable by careful selection of cases and use of weights. However, each of the studies also has its unique features. The Toronto study developed into a panel design with the addition of a follow-up survey in 1991 to the original survey in 1985. The response rate to the original Toronto survey was 65.3 percent (1,051 responses from 1,609 sampled respondents), and with 23 known retired and deceased members removed, the response rate to the follow-up survey was 79.3 percent (815 responses from 1028 available respondents). The panel design of this study allowed us not only to observe changes in the continuing careers of lawyers but to give attention as well to lawyers who left law completely during the six year interval between surveys. During this period, 125 lawyers left the profession.

The Ontario survey was restricted to members who were called to the Ontario Bar between 1975 and 1990. The two strata of temporarily absent and suspended (for nonpayment) members were included to represent in a cross-sectional fashion members who had departed from the practice of law on either a temporary or longer-term basis. Although there is some underrepresentation of longer-term departed members of the profession, largely resulting from difficulties in establishing current addresses, the recency of this survey and its attention to absent and departed members are unique. The response rate to the Ontario survey was 67.7 percent, with 1,597 questionnaires returned from 2,358 sampled respondents, including completed questionnaires from 177 lawyers who had departed from the practice of law.

Access to data collected at two points in time in Toronto and more recently across the province of Ontario provided us the opportunity to assess the representativeness of our sampling in a variety of ways, as well as the opportunity to make some comparisons of the structure of legal practice in and outside Toronto. Only a portion of this material can be reported here to make the essential points that attrition of respondents through nonresponse does not appear to be a significant problem in the Toronto panel design, and that there are very notable structural changes in the profession that can be revealed by comparing information gathered in the Toronto and Ontario surveys.

For example, the first two columns in table A.1 present the distribution of Toronto lawyers in 1985 across positions of employment outlined in chapter 2, as reflected by the samples in the wave 1 and wave 2 surveys of lawyers in 1985 and 1991 in Toronto. The purpose of this comparison is to determine if loss of lawyer respondents in the second wave of the survey impaired the representativeness of the Toronto panel design. This and following comparisons are based on samples that are weighted as described above to represent respectively the populations of Toronto and Ontario lawyers.

It appears that the attrition in the second wave of the Toronto study is relatively random. The distributions of respondents in the first two columns of table A.1 are quite similar, varying by less than 1.5 percent across categories, indicating that selective attrition did not reduce the representativeness of the panel design.

Some further substantive comparisons can also be made between the Toronto panel, begun in 1985, and the Ontario survey undertaken in 1990. To make comparisons meaningful between surveys, the 1990 Ontario survey had to be divided into those lawyers working inside and outside Toronto. In addition, because the Ontario survey included only entrants into the profession for the previous fifteen years (1975–1990), it was necessary to restrict the 1985 Toronto survey to a comparable fifteen-year period (1970–1985). Note that the latter restriction of the Toronto survey again shows no evidence of problems of panel attrition. In columns 3 and 4, when only Toronto entrants to the profession from 1970 to 1985 are considered, the distributions of lawyers across categories still look quite similar.

The Ontario survey was divided in columns 6 and 7 into those working inside and outside of Toronto, allowing us to compare distributions of lawyers in these locations in 1990. Managing partners and nonautonomous lawyers are located disproportionately in Toronto compared to other places in the province, while solo practitioners are disproportionately located outside of Toronto, relative to the remainder of the province. This reflects the presence of the larger firms in Toronto and the tradition of solo practice outside the metropolitan center. The top and bottom positions of firm practice are well represented among Toronto lawyers in 1990, but solo practitioners, who make up only about 15 percent of Toronto lawyers, constitute more than a third of all practicing lawyers outside of Toronto. These distributional differences between Toronto and the remaining smaller cities and towns of Ontario are consistent with comparisons between Heinz and Laumann's (1982) study of the urban Chicago Bar and Landon's (1988) study of smaller town and rural lawyers in Missouri.

We can further use the distributions presented in columns 3 and 6 of this table to make some general comparisons of the structure of the Toronto legal profession in 1985 and 1990. This comparison reflects a growth dis-

Table A.1

Distributions of Sampled Toronto and Ontario Lawyers, 1985–1990

	1985 All Toronto Wave 1 Lawyers, Weighted to Lawyer Population (N = 1,055)	1985 All Toronto Wave 2 Lawyers, Weighted to Lawyer Population (N = 774)	1985 Toronto Wave 1 Lawyers: 1970–85 Entrants, Weighted (N = 778)	1985 Toronto Wave 2 Lawyers: 1970–85 Entrants, Weighted (N = 587)	1990 Ontario Lawyers: 1975–90 Entrants, Weighted (N = 1,540)	1990 Ontario Lawyers: 1975–90 Toronto Entrants, Weighted (N = 839)	1990 Ontario Lawyers: 1975–90 Outside Toronto Entrants, Weighted (N = 687)
Managing Partners	16.0	15.1	12.0	11.9	4.9	6.8	2.5
Supervising Partners	11.2	11.1	9.9	10.6	5.9	9.3	1.9
Partners in Small Firms	15.3	14.9	12.0	10.7	3.1	2.9	3.5
Solo Practitioners	8.5	8.3	8.7	7.9	24.7	15.3	35.9
Managing/Supervising Lawyers	11.4	11.3	12.3	12.1	9.5	10.0	9.0
Semiautonomous Lawyers	24.2	25.1	30.4	30.7	34.0	35.6	32.3
Nonautonomous Lawyers	8.3	9.7	11.0	12.5	13.3	16.1	9.8
Part-time or Unemployed Lawyers	5.1	4.5	3.8	3.6	4.5	3.9	5.1

Note: Wave 1 and 2 in this table refer to the 1985 and 1991 Toronto panel survey.

cussed in greater detail in chapter 2 by gender and in relation to the lower levels of the profession that include nonautonomous and semiautonomous lawyers, the largest segments of the profession. Semiautonomous lawyers increased from about 30 to 36 percent of Toronto lawyers, while nonautonomous lawyers increased from about 11 to 16 percent. Meanwhile, there was a drop in managing partners from about 12 to 7 percent, and a decline in partners in small firms from about 12 to 3 percent. Solo practice increased from about nine percent to over 15 percent. Overall, our samples reflect a considerable amount of restructuring that occurred in the Toronto legal profession during the late 1980s, which we discuss in greater detail and in relation to gender in chapter 2.

Significance Tests

Frequent references are made in discussions in this book to the statistical significance or nonsignificance of results. These references also involve concerns about sampling, addressing the question of whether relationships observed in our analysis could have occurred as a result of chance fluctuations in the selection of the samples or as a result of random measurement error.

For example, the first two tables presented in chapter 3 involve cross-tabulating or classifying respondent characteristics (e.g., gender) with responses to survey items (e.g., about practice settings desired and attained and about help in acquiring these positions). Often in such tables it is useful to know whether the differences observed (for example, by gender) are greater than could be expected by chance fluctuations in sampling or measurement rather than as a result of an underlying relationship. Chi-square tests of statistical significance are used in these tables to estimate the probability of such differences occurring by chance.

Chi-square statistics are calculated from the numbers of cases appearing in the cells of tables that present cross-tabulations of variables. The expected numbers of cases in the cells of such tables are the numbers that would appear if the variables were unrelated, or in other words, the numbers that would appear if the cases were perfectly random and independent in their distribution across cells. Chi-squares (χ^2) are calculated by a formula whose result increases with the difference between the numbers actually observed in cells compared to the numbers expected at random. Chi-squares of zero can result when observed and expected frequencies are identical, but this almost never happens because of variations introduced by random sampling and measurement error. Probabilities (p) are reported along with chi-squares to estimate how likely it is that the differences between observed and expected values have occurred by chance.

Social scientists sometimes fetishize significance tests by insisting that some exact probability level, such as five times out of one hundred ($p = .05$), not be exceeded before a relationship is considered to be nonrandom or statistically significant. This is what is meant by a "test of significance." While we report significance levels in the analyses presented and discussed in this book, we do not adhere slavishly to them in our interpretations. For example, in discussing the percentaged tables presented in chapters 2 and 3 our main emphasis is on the more intuitive and substantive (e.g., percentage) differences and not on significance levels as such.

Multiple Regression Analysis

Although where possible we have used percentaged tables and other simple descriptive statistics to present results of our work in this book, it often is necessary to consider simultaneously a number of variables thought to influence outcomes of interest. Multiple regression analysis is an intuitively straightforward and easily explained method to consider the influence of a number of variables on an outcome of interest. Some brief comments about this technique may be helpful in understanding analyses presented in this book.

The coefficients estimated in ordinary least squares regression equations take two forms. The first form is a "raw" or unstandardized coefficient which measures influence on an outcome variable in the actual untransformed metric units of the independent variable involved. This is advantageous when, as in chapter 6, we have an independent variable, billable hours, that can be assessed in terms of its per unit influence on an outcome such as income. We are able to speak in this instance of the average dollar return for each hour billed.

The second form of coefficient is standardized through a conversion into units (of standard deviation) that are defined relative to the distributions of each variable. The latter coefficients are often useful because they make it possible to compare on a common scale the strength of the effects of independent variables measured in different units. This is advantageous when, as in chapter 7, we are able to assess the relative influences of having children and job satisfaction on feelings of depression among men and women lawyers.

It is important to emphasize that the effects of both unstandardized and standardized coefficients are "net" of all others included in a multiple regression analysis, in the sense that the effects of all the other variables are statistically held constant. This feature of multiple regression and other techniques introduced below makes them useful in reaching conclusions that go beyond mere association or correlation and facilitates inferences about net predictive influences and causation. As indicated above, the size of unstandardized and standardized regression coefficients is a guide to their strength, in a way that is analogous to the size of percentage differences observed in cross-tabulations. Significance levels associated through *t*-tests with these coefficients also indicate how likely the relationships observed are to have occurred by chance. This is analogous to the chi-square tests of significance we discussed previously.

Logistic Regression Analysis

Ordinary least squares techniques can be used to undertake the kind of multiple regression analysis just described, when the outcome variable is measured in continuous units such as income or billable hours. However, these techniques are less appropriate when the outcome variable of interest consists of discontinuous unranked or ranked categories, such as partnership. In these circumstances, ordinary least squares regression techniques often are replaced with an approach called logistic regression. The latter technique is well suited, as in chapter 4, as a method for analyzing the odds or probability of one outcome occurring (e.g., the attainment of partnership) relative to another (e.g., the failure to attain partnership). Logistic and ordinary least squares regression share some features in common, but there are important differences as well (Aldrich and Nelson, 1984).

For example, the interpretation of logistic regression coefficients differs from the interpretation of least squares and is in some ways cumbersome. These coefficients are expressed in a logarithmic form, and although they are quite useful for exploring the significance and direction of relationships, they do not have the straightforward probabilistic interpretation we ultimately want from this approach. Logit coefficients can be exponentiated and expressed as antilogs, as they are in the tables of chapter 3, 4, and 5, and these transformed parameters are sometimes interpreted in terms of probabilities (see Alba, 1987; but also Roncek, 1991). However, a better-accepted strategy for establishing probabilities is used later in chapter 4. This involves estimating probabilities of outcomes such as partnership that are associated with values of relevant variables such as gender, when the other variables in the model (e.g., experience) are held at their mean levels. The latter aspect of this procedure simulates the effect of respondents being made equal on all characteristics other than the variables considered. This procedure is used to advantage at the end of chapter 4 to assess the partnership prospects of men and women in the profession.

Event History Analysis

A final technique used in chapter 5 of this book is called event history analysis (see Tuma and Hannan, 1984). This technique is often used in situations in which there is information on the timing of an event, such as a departure from legal practice. Event history models involve the estimation of an outcome that is often called a hazard rate: the instantaneous probability of experiencing a particular event at some exact time. This rate combines an emphasis on issues on timing and risk, making it particularly relevant to decisions about leaving law.

In the event history analysis that we present toward the close of chapter 5, we model the effects of a number of variables on the rate of transition or movement from the first professional position in a firm setting to a departure from the practice of law. That is, we model the timing of decisions of women and men lawyers to leave firm practices and the practice of law entirely. The antilogs of estimated parameters are presented for this analysis because of their ease of interpretation. Antilogs can be interpereted as multipliers of rates. Values greater than 1.0 reflect increases in these rates, and values less than 1.0 reflect decreases. The percentage change in the rate for one group relative to another is just $100 (e - 1)$, where e represents the antilog.

All of the techniques used in this book are widely applied in the social sciences and are reviewed in greater detail in the referenced sources indicated in the above discussion. Our emphasis, of course, is less on the explication of these methods than on the articulation of their implications as applied in the context of studying lawyers' lives.

References

Abbott, Andrew. 1993. "The Sociology of Work and Occupations." *Annual Review of Sociology* 19:187–209.

Abel, Richard. 1979. "The Rise of Professionalism." *British Journal of Law & Society* 6:82–98.

———. 1986. "The Transformation of the American Legal Profession." *Law & Society Review* 20:7–17.

———. 1988a. "Lawyers in the Civil Law World." In R. L. Abel and P. S. C. Lewis, eds., *Lawyers in Society,* vol. 2, *The Civil Law World. Berkeley*: University of California Press.

———. 1988b. "United States: The Contradictions of Professionalism." In R. L. Abel and P. S.C. Lewis, eds., *Lawyers in Society*, vol. 2, *The Civil Law World.* Berkeley: University of California Press.

———. 1989. "Comparative Sociology of Legal Professions." In R. Abel and P. S. C. Lewis, eds., *Lawyers in Society*, vol. 3, *Comparative Theories.* Berkeley: University of California Press.

Abramson, J., and B. Franklin. 1986. *Where Are They Now? The Story of the Women of Harvard Law 1974.* New York: Doubleday.

Adam, Barry, and Douglas Baer. 1984. "The Social Mobility of Women and Men in the Ontario Legal Profession." *Canadian Review of Sociology and Anthropology* 21:21–45.

Aggarwal, Arjun P. 1987. *Sexual Harassment in the Workplace.* Toronto: Butterworths.

Alba, Richard. 1987. "Interpreting the Parameters of Log-Linear Models." *Sociological Methods and Research* 16:45–77.

Aldrich, John A., and Forrest D. Nelson. 1984. *Linear Probability, Logit and Probit Models.* Beverly Hills: Sage Publications.

American Bar Association. 1990. Lawyers and Balanced Lives: A Guide to Drafting and Implementing Workplace Policies for Lawyers. New York: American Bar Association. Commission on Women in the Profession.

Arnold, Bruce, and John Hagan. 1992. "Careers of Misconduct: The Structure of Prosecuted Professional Deviance among Lawyers." *American Sociological Review* 57:771–80.

Arthurs, H. W., R. Weisman, and F. H. Zemans. 1986. "The Canadian Legal Profession." *American Bar Foundation Research Journal* 447–520.

———. 1988. "Canadian Lawyers: A Peculiar Professionalism." In R. L. Abel and P. S. C. Lewis, eds., *Lawyers in Society*, vol. 1, *The Common Law World*. Berkeley: University of California Press.

Arthurs, H. W., J. Willms, and L. Taman. 1971. "The Toronto Legal Profession: An Exploratory Survey." *University of Toronto Law Journal* 21:498–528.

Auerback, Jerold. 1976. *Unequal Justice*. New York: Oxford University Press.

Backhouse, C. 1985. "To Open the Way for Others of my Sex: Clara Brett Martin's Career as Canada's First Woman Lawyer." *Canadian Journal of Women and Law* 1:1–41.

Balbus, Isaac D. 1977. "Commodity Form and Legal Form: An Essay on the 'Relative Autonomy' of the Law." *Law & Society Review* 11:571–588.

Barnett, Martha W. 1990. "Women Practicing Law: Changes in Attitudes, Changes in Platitudes." *Florida Law Review* 42:209–27.

Barnett, Rosalind C., and Grace K. Baruch. 1985. "Women's Involvement in Multiple Roles and Psychological Distress." *Journal of Personality and Social Psychology* 49:135–45.

Barnett, R. C., G. K. Baruch, and Rosalind C. Rivers. 1982. *Lifespring: New Patterns of Love and Work for Today's Women*. New York: McGraw-Hill.

Baruch, Grace K., L. Bierner, and Rosalind C. Barnett. 1985. "Women and Gender in Research on Stress." Working Paper no. 152. Wellesley, Mass.: Wellesley College, Center for Research on Women.

Becker, Gary. 1964. *Human Capital*. New York: Columbia University Press.

———. 1985. "Human Capital, Effort, and the Sexual Division of Labor." *Journal of Labor Economics* 3(Suppl.): S33–S58.

———. 1991. *A Treatise on Family*. Cambridge, Mass.: Harvard University Press.

Berk, Richard. 1983. "An Introduction to Sample Selection Bias." *American Sociological Review* 48:386–97.

Bernstein, Peter. 1978. "The Wall Street Lawyers Are Thriving on Change." *Fortune* 97 (5): 104–12.

Bielby, Denise. 1992. "Commitment to Work and Family." *Annual Review of Sociology* 18:281–302.

Bielby, Denise D., and William T. Bielby. 1984. "Work Commitment, Sex Role Attitudes, and Women's Employment." *American Sociological Review* 49:234–47.

———. 1988. "She Works Hard for the Money: Household Responsibilities and the Allocation of Effort." *American Journal of Sociology* 93:1031–1059.

_____. 1989. "Family Ties: Balancing Commitments to Work and Family in Dual Earner Households." *American Sociological Review* 54:776–89.

Blau, Francine D., and Marianne A. Ferber. 1985. "Women in the Labor Market: The Last Twenty Years." *Women and Work: An Annual Review* 1:19–49.

Boston Bar Association. 1991. *Parenting and the Legal Profession: A Model for the Nineties.* Boston, Mass.: Boston Bar Association Task Force on Parenting and the Legal Profession.

_____. 1991. Report. Boston, Mass.: Boston Bar Association, Task Force on Parenting and the Legal Profession.

Bourdieu, Pierre. 1977. *Outline of a Theory of Practice.* Cambridge: Cambridge University Press.

_____. 1984. *Distinction: A Social Critique of the Judgment of Taste.* Cambridge, Mass.: Harvard University Press.

Boyd, Monica. 1982. "Sex Differences in the Canadian Occupational Attainment Process." *Canadian Review of Sociology and Anthropology* 19(1): 1–28.

Boyd, Monica, John Goyder, Frank E. Jones, Hugh A. McRoberts, Peter C. Pinco, and John Porter, eds. 1985. *Ascriptions and Achievement: Studies in Mobility and Status Attainment in Canada.* Ottawa: Carleton University Press.

_____. 1988. "Changing Canadian Family Forms: Issues For Women." In N. Mandell and A. Duffy, eds.. *Reconstructing the Canadian Family: Feminist Perspectives.* Toronto: Butterworths.

Brockman, Joan. 1992. "'Resistance by the Club' to the Feminization of the Legal Profession." *Canadian Journal of Law & Society* 7:47–92.

Buckley, Melina. 1993. "Review of Canadian Law Society Provincial Surveys." Unpublished report. Ottawa: Canadian Bar Association.

Bumiller, Kristen. 1988. *The Civil Rights Society: The Social Construction of Victims.* Baltimore, Md.: Johns Hopkins University Press.

Cahn, Naomi R. 1991. "Defining Feminist Litigation." *Harvard Women's Law Journal* 14:1–20.

Campbell, Thomas J. 1984. "Regression Analysis in Title VII Cases: Minimum Standards, Comparable Worth, and Other Issues Where Law and Statistics Meet." *Stanford Law Review* 36:1299.

Campbell, Angus, Phillip E. Converse, and Willard L. Rodgers. 1976. *The Quality of American Life: Perceptions, Evaluations and Satisfactions.* New York: Russell Sage Foundation. Cahn, Naomi R. 1991. "Defining Feminist Litigation." *Harvard Women's Law Journal* 14:1–20.

Canadian Bar Association. 1993. *Touchstones For Change: Equality, Diversity and Accountability.* Ottawa: A Canadian Bar Association Task Force Report.

Carlin, Jerome. 1962. *Lawyers on Their Own: A Study of Individual Practitioners in Chicago.* New Brunswick, N. J.: Rutgers University Press.

_____. 1966. *Lawyers' Ethics: A Survey of the New York City Bar*. New York: Russell Sage Foundation.

Chambers, David. 1989. "Accommodation and Satisfaction: Women and Men Lawyers and the Balance of Work and Family." *Law & Social Inquiry* 14:251–87.

Chester, Ronald. 1985. *Unequal Access: Women Lawyers in a Changing America*. South Hadley, Mass.: Bergin & Garvey.

Clark, S. O. 1942. *The Social Development of Canada*. Toronto: University of Toronto Press.

_____. 1976. *Canadian Society in Historical Perspective*. Toronto: McGraw-Hill Ryerson.

Clement, Wallace. 1975. *The Canadian Corporate Elite: An Analysis of Economic Power*. Toronto: McClelland and Stewart.

Coleman, James S. 1990. *Foundations of Social Theory*. Cambridge, Mass.: Harvard University Press.

_____. 1993. "The Rational Reconstruction of Society." 1992. Presidential Address. *American Sociological Review*. 58:1–15.

Cooney, Teresa M., and Peter Uhlenberg. 1989. "Family-Building Patters of Professional Women: A Comparison of Lawyers, Physicians, and Postsecondary Teachers." *Journal of Marriage and the Family* 51:749–758.

Coverman, Shelley. 1989. "Role Overload, Role Conflict, and Stress: Addressing Consequences of Multiple Role Demands." *Social Forces* 67:4:965–82.

Cronbach, L. J. 1951. "Coefficient Alpha and the Internal Structure of Tests." *Psychometrika* 16:297–334.

Crossing the Bar. 1993. Exhibition on a Century of Women's Experience "Upon the Rough and Troubled Seas of Legal Practice in Ontario." Toronto: Law Society of Upper Canada Archives.

Curran, Barbara A. 1986. "American Lawyers in the 1980s: A Profession in Transition." *Law & Society Review* 20:19–51.

Curran, Barbara A., Katherine J. Roskh, Clara N. Carson and Mark C. Puccetti. 1985. *The Lawyer Statistical Report: A Statistical Profile of the U.S. Legal Profession in the 1980s*. Chicago: American Bar Foundation.

Daniels, Ronald. 1993. "Growing Pains: The Why and How of Law Firm Expansion." *University of Toronto Law Journal* 43:147–206.

Davis, Arthur K. 1971. "Canadian Society as Hinterland Versus Metropolis." In Richard J. Ossenberg, ed., *Canadian Society: Pluralism, Change and Conflict*. Scarborough, Ontario: Prentice-Hall.

Derber, Charles. 1982. *Professionals as Workers: Mental Labor in Advanced Capitalism*. Boston: G. K. Hall.

DiMaggio, P., and J. Mohr. 1985. "Cultural Capital, Educational Attainment, and Marital Selection." *American Journal of Sociology* 90:1231.

Dranoff, Linda Silver. 1972. "Women as Lawyers in Toronto." *Osgoode Hall Law Journal* 10:177–190.

Earle, Walter, and Charles Perlin. 1973. *Sherman & Sterling, 1873–1973.* New York.

Elder, Glen. 1985. *Life Course Dynamics: Trajectories and Transitions.* Ithaca, N.Y.: Cornell University Press.

England, Paula. 1981. "Assessing Trends in Occupational Sex Segregation, 1900–1976." In I. Berg, ed., *Sociological Perspectives on Labor Markets.* New York: Academic Press.

——. 1982. "The Failure of Human Capital Theory to Explain Occupational Sex Segregation." *Journal of Human Resources* 17:358–70.

England, P., and G. Farkas. 1986. *Households, Employment, and Gender.* New York: Aldine.

Epstein, Cynthia Fuchs. 1970. *Women's Place: Options and Limits in Professional Careers.* Berkeley: University of California Press.

——. 1981. *Women in Law.* New York: Basic Books.

Epstein, Richard. 1992. *Forbidden Grounds: The Case against Employment Discrimination Laws.* Cambridge, Mass.: Harvard University Press.

Erlanger, Howard. 1980. "The Allocation of Status within Occupations: The Case of the Legal Profession." *Social Forces* 58:882–97.

Felmlee, Diane. 1982. "Women's Job Mobility Processes within and between Employers." *American Sociological Review* 47:142–51.

Fenning, Lisa Hill. 1984. "Los Angeles Perspective on *Hishon*: The Slowly Eroding Partnership Barrier." In *Women in Law Firms: Planning for the Future.* Chicago: American Bar Association Press.

——. 1985. "Parenting and the Big Firm Career." Speech delivered to the National Association for Law Placement. August 22, 1985.

——. 1987. "Report from the Front: Progress in the Battle Against Gender Bias in the Legal Profession." Paper presented at the Conference on Women in the Legal Profession. Madison, Wisc., August.

Fenning, Lisa Hill, and Patricia M. Schnegg. 1983. "The Status of Women in L. A.'s Biggest Firms." *Los Angeles Lawyers* 6:27.

Ferguson, Kathy E. 1984. *The Feminist Case against Bureaucracy.* Philadelphia: Temple University Press.

Finkelstein, Michael. 1980. "The Judicial Reception of Multiple Regression Studies in Race and Sex Discrimination Cases." *Columbia Law Review* 80:737–54.

Fisher, Franklin. 1980. "Multiple Regression in Legal Proceedings." *Columbia Law Review* 80:702–36.

Fligstein, Neil. 1992. *State and Markets: The Transformation of the Large Corporation, 1880–1895.* Cambridge, Mass.: Harvard University Press.

Fligstein, Neil, and Wendy Wolf. 1978. "Sex Similarities in Occupational Status Attainment: Are the Results Due to the Restriction of the Sample to Employed Women?" *Social Science Research* 7:197–212.

Fossum, Donna. 1981. "Women in the Legal Profession: A Progress Report." *American Bar Association Journal* 67:578–82.

Fox, Mary Frank and Sharlene Hesse-Biber. 1984. *Women at Work.* Boston: Mayfield Publishing.

Galanter, Marc. 1983. "Mega-Law and Mega-Lawyering in the Contemporary United States." In R. Dingwall and P. Lewis, eds., *The Sociology of the Professions: Lawyers, Doctors and Others.* London: Macmillan.

Galanter, Marc, and Thomas Palay. 1991. *Tournament of Lawyers: The Transformation of the Big Law Firm.* Chicago: University of Chicago Press.

Gilson, Ronald J., and Robert H. Mnookin. 1985. "Sharing among the Human Capitalists: An Economic Inquiry into the Corporate Law Firm and How Partners Split Profits." *Stanford Law Review* 41:567–95.

Glancy, D. 1970. "Women in Law: The Dependable Ones." *Harvard Law School Bulletin* 5.

Glazer, Nathan. 1979. "Lawyers and the New Class." In B. B. Briggs, ed., *The New Class?* New Brunswick, N. J.: Transaction Books.

Glenn, E. N., and R. L. Feldberg. 1977. "Degraded and Deskilled: The Proletarianization of Clerical Work." *Social Problems* 25:52–64.

Glenn, H. Patrick. 1990. "Professional Structures and Professional Ethics." *McGill Law Journal* 35:425–38.

Glenn, Norval, Patricia Taylor, and Charles Weaver. 1977. "Age and Job Satisfaction among Males and Females: A Multivariate, Multisurvey Study." *Journal of Applied Psychology* 62:189–93.

Goode, William. 1960. "A Theory of Role Strain." *American Sociological Review* 25:483–96.

Goffman, Erving. 1971. *Relations in Public.* New York: Harper & Row.

Gore, Susan, and Thomas Mangione. 1986. "Social Roles, Sex Roles and Psychological Distress: Additive and Interactive Models of Sex Differences." *Journal of Health & Social Behavior* 24:300–312.

Granovetter, Mark. 1973. "The Strength of Weak Ties." *American Journal of Sociology* 78:1360–80.

———. 1974. *Getting a Job: A Study of Contacts and Careers.* Cambridge, Mass.: Harvard University Press.

———. 1983. "The Strength of Weak Ties: A Network Theory Revisited." *Sociological Theory* 1:201–33.

———. 1992. "The Sociological and Economic Approaches to Labor Market Analysis: A Social Structural View." In Mark Granovetter and Richard Swedberg, eds., *The Sociology of Economic Life.* Boulder, Colo.: Westview Press.

Gupta, Neena. 1993. "Shattering the Glass Ceiling? A Review of the American Experience in Challenging Discriminatory Partnership Practices under Title VII of the U.S. Civil Rights Act." Unpublished paper, University of Toronto Faculty of Law.

Hagan, John. 1988. "Feminist Scholarship, Relational and Instrumental Control, and a Power-Control Theory of Gender and Delinquency." *British Journal of Sociology* 34 (3) :301–36.

———. 1990. "The Gender Stratification of Income Inequality Among Lawyers." *Social Forces* 68:835–55.

———. 1991. "Gender and the Structural Transformation of the Legal Profession in the United States and Canada." In M. Hallinan, D. M. Klein, and J. Glass, eds., *Changes in Societal Institutions*. New York: Plenum Press.

Hagan, John, Marie Huxter, and Patricia Parker. 1988. "Class Structure and Legal Practice: Inequality and Mobility Among Toronto Lawyers." *Law & Society Review* 22:9–55.

Hagan, John, and Marjorie Zatz. 1989. "Paths to Power: The Large Firm Mobility Route and the Gender Stratification of Lawyers." Unpublished manuscript. Toronto: Faculty of Law.

Hagan, John, Marjorie Zatz, Bruce Arnold, and Fiona Kay. 1991. "Cultural Capital, Gender, and the Structural Transformation of Legal Practice." *Law & Society Review* 25:239–62.

Halaby, Charles, and David Weakliem. 1993. "Ownership and Authority in the Earnings Function: Nonnested Tests of Alternative Specifications." *American Sociological Review* 58:16–30.

Hall, D. T. 1972. "A Model of Coping with Role Conflict: The Role Behavior of College Education Women." *Administrative Science Quarterly* 1:319–33.

Halliday, Terrence. 1986. "Six Score Years and Ten: Demographic Transitions in the American Legal Profession, 1850–1980." *Law & Society Review* 20:53–78.

Harragan, Betty Lehan. 1977. *Games Mother Never Taught You: Corporate Gamesmanship for Women*. New York: Warner Books.

Harvey, C. 1970. "Women in Law in Canada." *Manitoba Law Journal* 4:9–38.

Heinz, John P., and Edward O. Laumann. 1982. *Chicago Lawyers: The Social Structure of the Bar*. New York: Russell Sage Foundation; Chicago: American Bar Foundation.

Hiller, Harry. 1976. *Canadian Society: A Sociological Analysis*. Scarborough, Ontario: Prentice-Hall.

Hirsch, Ronald Leslie. 1985. "Are You on Target?" *Barrister* 12:17–20.

———. 1989. "Will Women Leave Law?" *Barrister* (Spring): 16:22–26.

Hodson, Randy. 1990. "Gender Differences in Job Satisfaction: Why Aren't Women More Dissatisfied?" *Sociological Quarterly* 30:385–99.

Hoffman, Paul. 1973. *Lions in the Street: The Inside Story of the Great Wall Street Firms*. New York: Saturday Review Press.

Horowitz, Irving L. 1973. "The Hemispheric Connection: A Critique and Corrective to the Entrepreneurial Thesis of Development with Special Emphasis on the Canadian Case." *Queen's Quarterly* 80:327–59.

Houseknecht, Sharon K., Suzanne Vaughan, and Anne S. Macke. 1984. "Marital Disruption among Professional Women: The Timing of Career and Family Events." *Social Problems* 31:273–84.

Houseknecht, Sharon K., Suzanne Vaughan, and Anne Statham. 1987. "The Impact of Singlehood on the Career Patterns of Professional Women." *Journal of Marriage and the Family* 49:353–66.

Hughes, Everett. 1945. "Dilemmas and Contradictions of Status." *American Journal of Sociology* 50:353–9.

Huxter, Marie. 1981. "Survey of Employment Opportunities for Articling Students and Graduates of the Bar Admission Course in Ontario." *Law Society Gazette* 15:169–213.

Jones, Charles, Lorna Marsden, and Lorne Tepperman. 1990. *Lives of Their Own: The Individualization of Women's Lives.* Toronto: Oxford University Press.

Kalleberg, Arne, and Ivar Berg. 1987. *Work and Industry: Structures, Markets and Processes.* New York: Plenum.

Kanarck, Carol M. 1986. "Can Part-time Lawyers Break the Barriers?" *Barrister* 13:51–3.

Kanter, Rosabeth Moss. 1977a. *Men and Women of the Corporation.* New York: Basic Books.

———. 1977b. "Some Effects of Proportions on Group Life: Skewed Sex Ratios and Responses to Token Women." *American Journal of Sociology* 82:965.

Klaw, Spencer. 1958. "The Wall Street Lawyers." *Fortune* 98 (8): 112–20.

Kingston, Jennifer. 1988. "Women in Law Say Path is Limited by Mommy Track." *New York Times,* August 8, 1.

Kopelman, R. E., J. H. Greehaus, and T. F. Connolly. 1983. "A Model of Work, Family, and Interrole Conflict: A Construct Validation Study." *Organizational Behavior and Human Performance* 32:198–215.

Kulig, Paula. 1990. "Study Shows Firms Lack Women Partners." *Law Times* (February 19–25): 1–2.

Ladinsky, Jack. 1963. "Career Lawyers, Law Practice and Legal Institutions." *American Sociological Review* 28:47–54.

Landon, Donald. 1988. "LaSalle Street and Main Street: The Role of Context in Structuring Law Practice." *Law & Society Review* 22:213–36.

Larson, Magali. 1977. *The Rise of Professionalism.* Berkeley: University of California Press.

Law Society of British Columbia. 1991. *Women in the Legal Profession: A Report of the Women in the Legal Profession Subcommittee.* Vancouver: Law Society of British Columbia.

———. 1992. *Gender Quality in the Justice System: A Report of the Law Society of British Columbia Gender Bias Committee.* Vancouver: Law Society of British Columbia.

Lehrer, Evelyn L., and Marc L. Nerlove. 1986. "Female Labor Force Behavior and Fertility in the United States." *Annual Review of Sociology* 12:181–204.

Leibowitz, Arleen and Robert Tollison. 1980. "Free Riding, Shirking and Team Production in Legal Partnerships." *Economic Inquiry* 18:380.

Lezin, Valerie, and Sherrill Kushner. 1986. "Yours, Mine, and Hours: How Part-time Lawyers are Challenging Traditional Notions of Work Time." *Barrister* 13:4–7.

Liefland, Linda. 1986. "Career Patterns of Male and Female Lawyers." *Buffalo Law Review* 35(2): 601–19.

Lipset, S. M. 1968. *Revolution and Counterrevolution: Change and Persistence in Social Structures.* New York: Basic Books.

———. 1986. "Historical Traditions and National Characteristics: A Comparative Analysis of Canada and the U.S." *Canadian Journal of Sociology* 11:113–55.

Lopato, Helena Znaniecka, Cheryl Allyn Miller, and Debra Barnewolt, eds. 1984. *City Women: Work, Jobs, Occupations, Careers,* vol. 1. New York: Praeger.

Lortie, Dan. 1959. "Laymen to Lawmen: Law Schools, Careers and Professional Socialization." *Harvard Education Review* 29:352–69.

Macaulay, Stewart. 1963. "Non-contractual Relations in Business: A Preliminary Study." *American Sociological Review* 28:55–67.

———. 1982. "Law Schools and the World Outside Their Doors. II: Some Notes on Two Recent Studies of the Chicago Bar." *Journal of Legal Education* 32:506–47.

———. 1987. "Images of Law in Everyday Life: The Lessons of School, Entertainment, and Spectator Sports." *Law & Society Review* 21:185–218.

McChesney, Fred. 1982. "Team Production, Monitoring, and Profit Sharing in Law Firms: An Alternative Hypothesis." *Journal of Legal Studies* 11:379–93.

Macke, Anne S. 1984. "The Ordering of Significant Life Events among Professional Women as a Determination of Involvement in Career." Paper presented at the Women and Work Symposium, University of Texas, Arlington, Texas.

MacKinnon, Catharine A. 1986. "Women Lawyers — on Exceptions." In *Feminism Unmodified.* Cambridge, Mass.: Harvard University Press.

———. 1989. *Toward a Feminist Theory of the State.* Cambridge, Mass.: Harvard University Press.

Marks, Linda. 1990. "Alternative Work Schedules in Law: It's About Time!" *New York Law School Review* 35:361–7.

Marks, Steven R. 1977. "Multiple Roles and Role Strain: Some Notes on Human Energy, Time, and Commitment." *American Sociological Review* 42:921–36.

Martin, Sheilah. 1992. "The Dynamics of Exclusion: Women in the Legal Profession." Paper presented at Conference on Gender Equality for the Legal Profession. Toronto, Ontario, October 29.

Mayer, Martin. 1966. *The Lawyers.* New York: Harper & Row.

Menkel-Meadow, Carrie. 1985. "Portia in a Different Voice: Speculations on a Women's Lawyering Process." *Berkeley Women's Law Journal* 1:39–63.

_____. 1986. "The Comparative Sociology of Women Lawyers: The 'Feminization' of the Legal Profession." *Osgoode Hall Law Journal* 24:897–918.

_____. 1987. "Excluded Voices: New Voices in the Legal Profession Making New Voices in the Law." *University of Miami Law Review* 42(7): 29–53.

_____. 1989a. "Feminization of the Legal Profession: The Comparative Sociology of Women Lawyers." In R. L. Abel and P. S. C. Lewis, eds., *Lawyers in Society,* vol. 3, *Comparative Theories.* Berkeley: University of California Press.

_____. 1989b. "Exploring a Research Agenda of the Feminization of the Legal Profession: Theories of Gender and Social Change." *Law and Social Inquiry* 14:289–319.

Mills, C. Wright. 1966. *White Collar: The American Middle Class.* New York: Oxford University Press.

Mincer, Jacob. 1970. "The Distribution of Labor Incomes: A Survey — with Special Reference to the Human Capital Research." *Journal of Economic Literature* 8:1–26.

_____. 1985. "Intercountry Comparisons of Labor Force Trends and of Related Developments: An Overview." *Journal of Labor Economics* 3 (Suppl.): S1–S2.

Monteith, Katherine. 1990. "1989 National Associate Survey." *Canadian Lawyer,* (January) 22–28.

Morello, Karen. 1986. *The Invisible Bar: The Woman Lawyer in America: 1638 to the Present.* New York: Random House.

Mossman, Mary Jane. 1990. "The Past as Prologue." In A. Esau and J. Penner, eds., *Lawyering and Legal Education into the 21st Century.* Winnipeg: Legal Research Institute.

_____. 1992. "Work and Family in the Legal Profession: Re-thinking the Questions." Paper presented at the Canadian Bar Association Gender Equality Conference, Toronto, October.

_____. 1993. "Gender Bias and the Legal Profession: Challenges and Choices." In Joan Brockman and Dorothy E. Chunn, eds., *Investigating Gender Bias: Law, Courts and the Legal Profession.* Toronto: Thompson Educational Publishing.

Mostacci-Calzazera, Liuzana. 1982. Social Networks and Access to Job Opportunities. Ph.D. dissertation, University of Toronto.

Mueller, Charles. 1992. "Work Orientation." *Encyclopedia of Sociology* 4:2260–67.

National Association Law Placement. 1989. *Directory of Legal Employers.*

National Association of Women and the Law. 1993. Brief to the Canadian Bar Association Task Force on Gender Equality, vol. 1.

Nelson, Robert. 1983. "The Changing Structure of Opportunity: Recruitment and Careers in Large Law Firms." *American Bar Foundation Research Journal* 109–42.

———. 1988. *Partners with Power: The Social Transformation of the Large Law Firm.* Berkeley: University of California Press.

Nelson, Robert, and David Trubek. 1988. "Lawyer Professionalism and Its Discontents: From Arenas of Words to Arenas of Work." Paper presented to American Bar Foundation Conference on Professionalism, Ethics and Economic Change in the American Legal Profession, Evanston, Illinois.

New York City Bar Association. 1991. *Report of the Committee to Enhance Professional Opportunities for Minorities.* New York: New York City Bar Association.

Nielson, Sheila. 1990. "The Balancing Act: Practical Suggestions for Part-Time Attorneys." *New York Law School Law Review* 35:369.

Nieva, Veronica F. 1985. "Work and Family Linkages." *Women and Work* 1:162–90.

Niosi, Jorge. 1978. *The Economy of Canada.* Montreal: Black Rose.

O'Connell, Lenahan, Michael Betz, and Suzanne Kurth. 1989. "Plans for Balancing Work and Family Life: Do Women Pursuing Nontraditional and Traditional Occupations Differ?" *Sex Roles* 20 (1): 35–45.

O'Connor, Sandra Day. 1991. "Portia's Progress (Madison Lecture)." *New York University Law Review* 66 (6): 1546–57.

Otvos, Mary. 1992. "Why I'm Leaving Law." *Canadian Lawyer*, February, pp. 12–17.

Pashigian, P. 1978. "The Number and Earnings of Lawyers: Some Recent Findings." *American Bar Foundation Research Journal* 1:51–82.

Penley, Larry, and Brian Hawkins. 1980. "Organizational Communication, Performance and Job Satisfaction as a Function of Ethnicity and Sex." *Journal of Vocational Behavior* 16:368–84.

Podmore, David, and Anne Spencer. 1982. "Women Lawyers in England: The Experience of Inequality." *Work and Occupations* 9:337–61.

Porter, John. 1965. *The Vertical Mosaic.* Toronto: University of Toronto Press.

Prestus, Robert. 1973. *Elite Accommodation in Canadian Politics.* Toronto: Macmillan.

Quinn, Robert, G. Staines, and B. C. McCullough. 1974. *Job Satisfaction: Is There a Trend?* Washington, D.C.: U.S. Government Printing Office.

Rapoport, R. and R. N. Rapoport. 1976. *Dual-Career Families Re-examined: New Integrations of Work and Family.* New York: Harper Colophon Books.

Rebecca, M. 1978. Voluntary Childlessness as a Conflict Reducing Mechanism. Paper presented at the Association of Women in Psychology Annual Meeting, Pittsburgh, Pa.

Repa, Barbara. 1988. "Is There Life After Partnership?" *American Bar Association Journal* 74:70–75.

Reskin, Barbara. 1984. *Sex Segregation in the Workplace — Trends Explanations and Remedies.* Washington, D.C.: National Academy Press.

Rhode, Deborah. 1984. "Moral Character as a Professional Credential." *Yale Law Journal* 94:491–603.

———. 1988. "Perspectives on Professional Women." *Stanford Law Review* 40:1163–207.

Riley, Matilda White, ed. 1988. *Social Structures and Human Lives.* Newbury Park: Sage.

Robertson, Susan. 1992. "A Study of Gender and the Legal Profession in Saskatchewan, 1990–91." A report submitted to the Committee on Gender Discrimination. Saskatoon: Law Society of Saskatchewan.

Robinson, Patricia. 1986. "Women's Occupational Attainment: The Effects of Work Interruptions, Self-Selection, and Unobserved Characteristics." *Social Science Research* 15:323–46.

Robinson, Robert V., and Maurice A. Garnier. 1985. "Class Reproduction among Men and Women in France: Reproduction Theory on Its Home Ground." *American Journal of Sociology* 91:250–80.

Roncek, Dennis. 1991. "Using Logit Coefficients to Obtain the Effects of Independent Variables on Changes in Probabilities." *Social Forces* 70:509–18.

Rosenfeld, Rachel. 1980. "Race and Sex Differences in Career Dynamics." *American Sociological Review* 45:583–609.

Rosenfeld, Rachel A. and Kenneth I. Spenner. 1988. "Women's Work and Women's Careers: A Dynamic Analysis of Work Identity in the Early Life Course." In Matilda White Riley, ed., *Social Structures and Human Lives.* Newbury Park: Sage.

Roos, Patricia A. 1985. *Gender and Work: A Comparative Analysis of Industrial Societies.* New York: New York University Press.

Ross, Catherine. 1985. "Hardship and Depression." *Journal of Health and Social Behavior* 26:312–27.

Rossi, A. 1965. "Women in Science: Why So Few?" *Science* 148:1196–202.

Rueschemeyer, Dietrich. 1973. *Lawyers and Their Society: A Comparative Study of the Legal Profession in Germany and the United States.* Cambridge, Mass.: Harvard University Press.

Sander, Richard, and William Douglas. 1989. "Why are There So Many Lawyers? Perspectives on Turbulent Market." *Law and Social Inquiry* 14:431–79.

Schellenberg, Gaylene. 1993. *Sex Discrimination in Employment*. Appendix 12 to the Report of the Canadian Bar Association Task Force on Gender Equality in the Legal Profession.

Schultz, Vicki. 1988. "Telling Stories about Women and Work: Judicial Interpretations of Sex Segregation in the Workplace in Title VII Cases Raising the Lack of Interest Argument." *Harvard Law Review* 103:1749–843.

Silverstone, Rosalie, and Audrey Ward. 1980. *Careers of Professional Women*. London: Croom Helm.

Simms, Marsha. 1990. "Women in the Lawyering Workplace: A Practical Perspective." *New York Law School Law Review* 35:385–446.

Sheridan, Kathleen. 1980. "Women in Law: Has Anything Changed?" *Barrister* 8:44–48.

Smigel, Erwin. 1969. *The Wall Street Lawyer: Professional Organization Man?* Bloomington, Indiana: Indiana University Press.

Smith, Lynn. 1992. "Gender Equality — A Challenge for the Legal Profession." Paper presented at the Conference on Gender Equality in the Legal Profession, Toronto, October.

Smith, Lynn, Marlyee Stephenson, and Gina Quijano. 1973. "The Legal Profession and Women: Finding Articles in British Columbia." *University of British Columbia Law Review* 8:137–175.

Sorenson, A. B. 1983. "Sociological Research on the Labor Market: Conceptual and Methodological Issues." *Work and Occupations* 10:261–87.

Spangler, Eve. 1986. *Lawyers for Hire: Salaried Professionals at Work*. New Haven, Mass.: Yale University Press.

Stanford Law Project. 1982. "Law Firms and Lawyers with Children: An Empirical Analysis of Family/Work Conflict." *Stanford Law Review* 34:1263–1306.

Spire, Robert M. "Breaking Up the Old Boy Network." *Trial*, February, pp. 57–58.

Stager, David, and Harry Arthurs. 1990. *Lawyers in Canada*. Toronto: University of Toronto Press.

Stager, David, and David Foot. 1988. "Changes in Lawyers' Earnings: The Impact of Differentiation and Growth in the Canadian Legal Profession." *Law & Social Inquiry* 13:71–85.

Stanford Law Project. 1988. "Gender, Legal Education, and the Legal Profession: An Empirical Study of Stanford Law Students and Graduates." *Stanford Law Review* 40:1209–97.

———. 1989. "Law Firms and Lawyers with Children: An Empirical Analysis of Family/Work Conflict." *Stanford Law Review* 34:1263–1306.

Stewart, James B. 1983. *The Partners: Inside America's Most Powerful Law Firms*. New York: Simon & Schuster.

Stinchcombe, Arthur L. 1979. "Social Mobility in Industrial Labor Markets." *Acta Sociologica* 22:217–245.

Strachan, Nell B. 1984. "A Map for Women on the Road to Success." *American Bar Association Journal* 70:94–96.

Swaine, Robert. 1948. *The Cravath Firm and Its Predecessors, 1819–1948.* New York: Privately printed.

Taber, Janet, Marguerite T. Grant, Mart Y. Huser, Rise. B. Norman, James R. Sutton, Clarence C. Wong, Louise E. Parker, and Claire Picard. 1988. "Gender, Legal Education, and the Legal Profession: An Empirical Study of Stanford Law Students and Graduates." *Stanford Law Review* 40:1209–97.

Taylor, Jan Cooper, and Barbara A. Spencer. 1988. "Lifestyle Patterns of University Women: Implications for Family/Career Decision Modeling." In Elizabeth B. Goldsmith, ed., *Work and Family: Theory, Research and Applications.* A Special Issue of the Journal of Social Behavior and Personality 3(4): 265–78.

Tennant, Chris. 1992. "Discrimination in the Legal Profession, Codes of Professional Conduct and the Duty of Non-Discrimination." Unpublished paper, Ottawa.

Thorner, Abbie Willard. 1991. "Gender and the Profession: The Search for Equal Access." *Georgetown Journal of Legal Ethics* 4:81–114.

Tienda, Marta, Shelley Smith, and Vilma Ortiz. 1987. "Industrial Restructuring, Gender Stratification and Sex Differences in Earnings." *American Sociological Review* 52:195–210.

Tucker, M., L. Albright, and P. Busk. 1989. "Whatever Happened to the Class of 1983?" *Georgetown Law Journal* 78:153–95.

Tuma, Nancy, and Michael Hannan. 1984. *Social Dynamics: Models and Methods.* New York: Academic Press.

Veroff, Joseph, Elizabeth Douvan, and Richard Kulka. 1981. *The Inner American.* New York: Basic.

Vogt, Leona M. 1986. *Career Paths Study.* Cambridge: Mass.: Harvard University Law School.

———. 1987. "From Law School to Career: A Highlight Report of the Career Paths Study of Seven Northeastern Area Law Schools." Unpublished report.

Waite, Linda J. 1976. "Working Wives: 1940–1960." *American Sociological Review* 41:65–80.

———. 1980. "Working Wives and the Family Life Cycle." *American Journal of Sociology* 86:272–294.

Waite, Linda J., and Ross M. Stolzenberg. 1976. "Intended Childbearing and Labor Force Participation of Young Women: Insights from Nonrecursive Models." *American Sociological Review* 41:235–52.

Weber, Lorraine H. 1990. "Professionalism and Gender: A Practical Guide." *Michigan Bar Journal* 69:898–902.

White, James. 1967. "Women in Law." *Michigan Law Review* 65:1051–122.

Williams, Joan C. 1990. "Sameness Feminism and the Work/Family Conflict." *New York Law School Law Review* 35:347–60.

Wilson, Hon. Bertha. 1993. "Pressing Ethical Questions Facing the Legal Profession." Paper presented at the Westminster Institute, London, Ontario, March 5.

Wolfram, Charles. 1986. *Modern Legal Ethics.* St. Paul, Minn.: West Publishing.

Wright, Erik O., Cynthia Costello, David Hachen, and Joey Sprague. 1982. "The American Class Structure." *American Sociological Review* 47:709–726.

Wright, Erik O., and Joachim Singelmann. 1982. "Proletarianization in the Changing American Class Structure." *American Journal of Sociology* 88(Supp.): S176–209.

Young, Iris. 1981. "Beyond the Unhappy Marriage: A Critique of the Dual Systems Theory." In L. Sargent, ed., *Women and Revolution: A Discussion of the Unhappy Marriage of Marxism and Feminism.* Boston, Mass.: South End.

Zemans, Frances Kahn, and Victor G. Rosenblum. 1981. *The Making of a Public Profession.* Chicago: American Bar Foundation.

Cases Cited

Bradwell v. Illinois, 83 U.S. 130 (1872)

Brooks v. Canada Safeway Ltd., 1 S.C.R. 1219 (1989)

Ezold v. Wolf, 758 F.Supp. 303 (E.D.Pa. 1991)

Ezold v. Wolf, 56 F.E.P. 580 (1991)

Gillespie v. Board of Education, 528 F.Supp. 433 (E.D.Ark. 1981)

Hishon v. King & Spalding, 467 U.S. 69 (1984)

Hopkins v. Price Waterhouse, 54 F.E.P. 750 (D.C.Cir. 1990)

Index